Violent Radical Movements in the Arab World

Violent Radical Movements in the Arab World

The Ideology and Politics of Non-State Actors

Edited by Peter Sluglett and Victor Kattan

I.B. TAURIS
LONDON • NEW YORK • OXFORD • NEW DELHI • SYDNEY

I.B. TAURIS
Bloomsbury Publishing Plc
50 Bedford Square, London, WC1B 3DP, UK
1385 Broadway, New York, NY 10018, USA

BLOOMSBURY, I.B. TAURIS and the Diana logo are trademarks of
Bloomsbury Publishing Plc

First published in Great Britain 2019

Copyright © Peter Sluglett, Victor Kattan and contributors 2019

Peter Sluglett and Victor Kattan have asserted their right under the Copyright, Designs and Patents Act, 1988, to be identified as the Editors of this work.

Cover design: Adriana Brioso
Cover image © Jose A. Bernat Bacete/Getty Images

All rights reserved. No part of this publication may be reproduced or transmitted in any form or by any means, electronic or mechanical, including photocopying, recording, or any information storage or retrieval system, without prior permission in writing from the publishers.

Bloomsbury Publishing Plc does not have any control over, or responsibility for, any third-party websites referred to or in this book. All internet addresses given in this book were correct at the time of going to press. The author and publisher regret any inconvenience caused if addresses have changed or sites have ceased to exist, but can accept no responsibility for any such changes.

A catalogue record for this book is available from the British Library.

A catalogue record for this book is available from the Library of Congress.

ISBN HB: 978-1-7883-1431-2
      PB: 978-1-7883-1976-8
      eISBN: 978-1-7867-2630-8
      ePDF: 978-1-7867-3636-9

Series: Library of Modern Middle East Studies

Typeset by RefineCatch Limited, Bungay, Suffolk
Printed and bound in Great Britain

To find out more about our authors and books visit www.bloomsbury.com and sign up for our newsletters.

This book is dedicated to the memory of Peter Sluglett (1943–2017).

Contents

Acknowledgements	viii
List of Contributors	ix
Preface *Victor Kattan*	xii
Foreword: Peter Sluglett and the Study of the Modern Middle East *Toby Dodge*	xiv
Introduction: Violent Non-State Actors in the Arab World – Some General Considerations *Peter Sluglett*	1
1 The Muslim Brotherhood and Violence: Porous Boundaries and Context *Khaled Hroub*	25
2 Understanding ISIS: The Interplay between Ideology and Context *Hassan A. Barari*	47
3 Between Religion, Warfare and Politics: The Case of Jabhat al-Nusra in Syria *Mohamed-Ali Adraoui*	65
4 The 2007 Hamas–Fatah Conflict in Gaza and the Israeli–American Demands *Victor Kattan*	93
5 Hezbollah and the Lebanese State: Indispensable, Unpredictable – Destabilizing? *Peter Sluglett*	121
6 When the State Becomes a Non-State: Yemen between the Huthis, Hirak and Al-Qaeda *Daniel Martin Varisco*	137
7 Violent Non-State Actors in Somalia: Al-Shabab and the Pirates *Afyare A. Elmi and Ruqaya A. Mohamed*	161
8 'Being in Time': Kurdish Movement and Quests of Universal *Hamit Bozarslan*	177
Afterword *Abdullah Baabood*	195
Notes	197
Bibliography	215
Index	237

Acknowledgements

I would like to thank Professor Engseng Ho, Director of the Middle East Institute, and Michelle Teo, Deputy Director of the Institute, for their generosity and support which was crucial to seeing this project through to fruition. Special thanks are also due to Sophie Rudland and Sorcha Thomson of I.B. Tauris for their help with putting the book together.

Victor Kattan

Contributors

Mohamed-Ali Adraoui is a political scientist working on contemporary international relations. He is currently a Marie Sklodowska Curie Fellow at the Georgetown University School of Foreign Service and a Visiting Scholar at the Harvard Weatherhead Center for International Affairs. Prior to this, he was a Max Weber Fellow at the European University Institute and a Senior Fellow at the National University of Singapore. He is the author of *Du golfe aux banlieues, le salafisme mondialisé* (2013) and editor of *The Foreign Policy of Islamist Political Parties: Ideology in Practice* (2018).

Abdullah Baabood is an Omani academic and researcher and the former director of the Centre for Gulf Studies at Qatar University and Gulf Research Centre at the University of Cambridge. He holds a PhD in political economy from the University of Cambridge, a master's degree in business administration from Strayer College and a master's degree in International Relations from the University of Kent. Baabood has taught and conducted research at several universities and institutions in Europe, and has published numerous books, articles and conference papers.

Hassan A. Barari is Professor of International Relations and Middle East Politics at the University of Jordan. Prior to that, he was Professor of International Affairs at Qatar University and Visiting Professor at Yale University. He was also a professor of Middle East Politics at the University of Nebraska at Omaha. He served as Senior Fellow at the United States Institute of Peace (USIP) based in Washington, DC for the academic year 2006–7. From 2001 to 2006, he was a senior researcher at the Center for Strategic Studies at the University of Jordan.

Hamit Bozarslan (PhD in history, 1992, and in political sciences, 1994) teaches at the Ecole des hautes études en sciences sociales (EHESS) in Paris. He has published extensively on the Kurdish issue, Turkey and the Middle East. His research is focused on the formation of modern anti-democratic systems in Iran, Russia and Turkey, as well as violence in the Middle East.

Toby Dodge is Professor in the International Relations Department at the London School of Economics (LSE), and was formerly Director of the LSE

Middle East Centre. He is the author of *Inventing Iraq: The Failure of Nation Building and a History Denied* (2003), and *Iraq – From War to a New Authoritarianism* (2012).

Afyare A. Elmi is Associate Professor of Security Studies at Qatar University's Gulf Studies Program. He received his PhD in Political Science from the University of Alberta, Canada. Dr Elmi has been the Lead Principal Investigator of the 'Piracy in the Horn of Africa Research Project'. He is also the author of *Understanding the Somalia Conflagration: Identity, Political Islam and Peacebuilding* (2010).

Khaled Hroub is Professor of Middle Eastern Studies at Northwestern University in Qatar and Research Fellow at the Centre of Islamic Studies of the Faculty of Asian and Middle Eastern Studies, University of Cambridge. He is the author of *Hamas: A Beginner's Guide* (2006) and *Hamas: Political Thought and Practice* (2000), and editor of *Political Islam: Context versus Ideology* (2011) and *Religious Broadcasting in the Middle East* (2012). His latest book (in Arabic) is *The Anxious Intellectual* (2018).

Victor Kattan is Senior Research Fellow of the Middle East Institute at the National University of Singapore (NUS). Before he moved to Singapore, he was an advisor to the Palestinian Negotiations Affairs Department in Ramallah. Victor has published widely in his field and is the author of two books: *From Coexistence to Conquest: International Law and the Origins of the Arab–Israeli Conflict* (2009) and *The Palestine Question in International Law* (2008). Kattan has taught courses at Yale-NUS College, NUS Law and the Centre for International Studies and Diplomacy at the University of London's School of Oriental and African Studies (SOAS). In 2017, he became the inaugural winner of the Asian Society of International Law Younger Scholar Prize.

Ruqaya A. Mohamed has an MA and a BA in International Studies from the United States International University in Kenya and Qatar University respectively. After completing her graduate degree, she worked as a researcher with the Counter-Piracy Research Project at Qatar University under the lead investigator, Dr Afyare Elmi. Mohamed has also worked with international organizations in Kenya on issues relating to Somalia. Currently, she is pursuing her research interests in armed conflict in East Africa.

Peter Sluglett was Director of the Middle East Institute of the National University of Singapore. He taught Middle Eastern history at the University of

Durham (1974–94) and at the University of Utah, Salt Lake City (1994–2011), where he was Director of the University's Middle East Center. He published widely on the modern history of Iraq, including *Iraq since 1958: From Revolution to Dictatorship* (2001, 3rd edn, with Marion Farouk-Sluglett) and *Britain in Iraq: Contriving King and Country* (2007). He also edited and contributed to *The Urban Social History of the Middle East 1750–1950* (2008), *Syria and Bilad al-Sham under Ottoman Rule: Essays in Honour of Abdul-Karim Rafeq* (2010, with Stefan Weber), *Writing the Modern History of Iraq: Historiographical and Political Challenges* (2012) and *Atlas of Islamic History* (2014, with Andrew Currie).

Daniel Martin Varisco is President of the American Institute for Yemeni Studies. He first conducted anthropological fieldwork in Yemen in 1978–9 and has returned to Yemen more than a dozen times as a development consultant and historian. In 2017–18 he was a senior fellow at the Institute for Social Anthropology of the Austrian Academy of Sciences. Varisco is currently a senior fellow at the Mamluk Studies Seminar of the Annemarie Schimmel Kolleg of Bonn University.

Preface

Victor Kattan

The collection of chapters in this book is the product of a workshop on 'Violent Nonstate Actors in the Middle East', held at the Gulf Studies Centre in Doha, Qatar from 14 to 15 October 2015. The workshop was co-organized by the Middle East Institute (MEI) of the National University of Singapore and the Gulf Studies Centre of Qatar University. This was the second workshop organized pursuant to a memorandum of understanding signed between Qatar University and the MEI to stage further joint academic conferences, symposiums and workshops.

Publication of the book was delayed due to the ill health of Professor Peter Sluglett, who was then director of the Middle East Institute, having taken over from Michael Hudson in 2014. Peter passed away on 10 August 2017. Although Peter was not well, his sudden death was still a shock to many of his colleagues in Singapore. Before Peter's passing, he sent the manuscript to I.B. Tauris in London to consider for publication. Following negotiations, I.B. Tauris agreed to publish the collection in his memory.

Peter's introduction was subject to a light edit to take into account recent developments. He also contributed the chapter 'Hizbullah and the Lebanese State: Indispensable, Unpredictable – Destabilizing?', which has been left untouched. The chapter appears to have been completed in early 2017 and therefore reflects political developments in Lebanon up until that time. All of the other articles were updated at the request of the publisher.

I have been asked to explain the goal of the workshop. Unfortunately, I never put this question to Peter. But I do know that he was inspired by the book *Violent Non-State Actors in World Politics* by Kledja Mulaj (2009), which he circulated to us before the workshop. One of the goals of the workshop was to write a book that would make a valuable contribution to the literature on violent non-state actors in the Arab world, which is surprisingly slim. Admittedly, the authors are an eclectic bunch, comprising historians, anthropologists, political scientists, and lawyers. For some readers, the authors' interdisciplinary backgrounds may give the book an uneven quality, but this is arguably compensated by the originality of the contributions, the light shed on some of the lesser known groups, and the particular angles and topics the authors chose to write on. It is to Peter's credit that the authors were given complete discretion to write as they saw fit.

The movements described in this book as violent *non-state* actors can be justified as they do not hold a monopoly on the legitimate use of armed force, nor have they ever been in a position to exercise sovereignty to the exclusion of any other state. None of the groups addressed in this book, from internationally recognized national liberation movements to proscribed terrorist organizations, have been recognized as states. Nor was the 'Islamic State' a state, despite its name: its sovereignty over parts of Iraq and Syria was never recognized as legitimate by any other state, and it has since lost control of its 'Caliphate' as the armed forces of Syria, Iraq, Russia, Iran and the US regained control of territory that was lost in the early years of the 'Arab Spring'.

Hurst has kindly agreed to let us republish the chapter by Professor Hamit Bozarslan, a friend of Peter's, on the Kurdish groups that originally appeared in Gareth Stanfield and Mohamed Shareef (eds), *The Kurdish Question Revisited* (London: Hurst, 2017), 65–71. We felt that we could not exclude the Kurdish groups from a study of violent non-state actors in the Middle East given the vital role they play in the region.

I am delighted that Peter's friend and colleague Toby Dodge, formerly director of the Middle East Centre and professor of International Relations at the LSE, agreed to write the foreword. I could not think of a better person for that task. Toby was a Visiting Research Professor at MEI in 2017, and spent much of that summer with Peter and his wife Shohreh. An expression of gratitude is also due to Abdullah Baabood for co-organizing the conference with Peter and for writing the Afterword.

Foreword: Peter Sluglett and the Study of the Modern Middle East

Toby Dodge

When Peter Sluglett died on 10 August 2017, he and his wife Shohreh were in the process of leaving Singapore to return to the United States and, for Peter, a much-postponed retirement from academia. Against this background, I think the last two projects he was working to finish before he left Singapore stand as a fitting tribute to Peter's long career as a historian of the modern Middle East and a world-renowned scholar of Iraq and Syria. Peter delivered the manuscript of *A History of Syria*, a book he had been writing with Mary Wilson for many years, to Cambridge University Press three days before he was taken ill. This edited volume, *Violent Radical Movements in the Arab World*, is the other work he was bringing to publication as he died.

As Victor Kattan, a friend and mentee of Peter's, says in his preface, Peter's aim for this book was to assemble a multi-disciplinary approach to the study of violent non-state actors in the Middle East. He did this by gathering together a number of scholars from history, anthropology, political science and law. His intellectual aspiration was certainly to develop a Middle East case study for a global phenomenon in order to add powerful examples from the region to the wider debate. However, he also wanted to capture and do justice to the complex empirical realities of the Middle East itself. This aim personifies his working method and intellectual goals over the fifty years of his career as a historian.

Peter was born in the West Country of England in 1943. He was an undergraduate at Cambridge University from 1963 to 1966 and wrote his DPhil thesis at St Antony's College, Oxford, under the supervision of the legendary historian of the Arab world, Albert Hourani, finishing in 1972. His thesis was a study of the creation of Iraq under the British Mandate. This was published as a book, *Britain in Iraq, 1914–1932*, in 1976. It was then rewritten and updated as *Britain in Iraq, Contriving King and Country*, published by Columbia University Press in 2007.

I remember well, on the first day of my own PhD, reading *Britain in Iraq* and being filled with a deep respect for the almost forensic archival research, the groundbreaking scholarship and powerful analytical insights it contained. The book is meticulously researched, beautifully written and clearly the unchallengeable definitive work on this period of Iraqi history.

Peter's next book, *Iraq Since 1958: From Revolution to Dictatorship*, written with his first wife, the German academic Marion Farouk Sluglett, was first published in 1987, updated and republished by Peter, after Marion's death, in 1990. It is hard to overstate the intellectual and political impact of this book. Intellectually it details the tumultuous post-independence history of Iraq, the optimism engendered by the revolution of 1958, led by the charismatic young brigadier, Abdul Karim Qasim, but also the central role that Iraq's Communist Party took in the period from 1958 to 1963, driving forward a political but also cultural movement that aimed to transform Iraq into an economically prosperous, egalitarian but thoroughly modern role model for the wider Middle East. However, the book then examines the coups of 1963 and then 1968 that brought the Ba'ath Party to power. It documents the torture and mass murder that accompanied the Ba'ath's seizure of the state. The brutality of Ba'athist rule in Iraq during this period of Peter's life saw him become a political activist, joining fellow academics to campaign against the thirty-five years of repression and violence that became the hallmark of Ba'athist authoritarianism.

Peter's academic career developed in parallel to his research and writing. He taught Middle East history at Durham University in the UK from 1974 to 1994. He then moved to the University of Utah, Salt Lake City, in the US, from 1994 to 2011, where he was director of the university's Middle East Center. From there he and Shohreh moved to Singapore, to the National University of Singapore and its Middle East Institute, where Peter became the director.

Academically, although Peter continued to work on Iraq until he died, publishing articles and edited volumes, he became increasingly aware that he would not be able to return to the country to carry out sustained research. It was then that he turned to work on Syria. Again deploying his exacting craft as an archival historian, he worked extensively in the archives of Aleppo, explaining Syria's evolution under the Ottoman Empire into the modern day. This research resulted in three books, two edited volumes, *The Urban Social History of the Middle East 1750–1950*, published in 2008, and *Syria and Bilad al-Sham under Ottoman Rule: Essays in Honour of Abdul-Karim Rafeq*, published in 2010, and finally the third book, written with Mary Wilson, *A History of Syria*, finished just before his death.

Peter was certainly a renowned historian of the modern Middle East. However, he was also a great mentor of young academics, a builder of academic institutions and a creator of teams of researchers working and publishing on various aspects of the region. I think it is indicative of this that the present edited volume, along with all the others he edited, contains a number of relatively young but very talented scholars who Peter identified, intellectually nurtured and who will, like many before them, go on to develop groundbreaking academic research, teaching and publishing on the Middle East.

To conclude, Peter was certainly a brilliant historian of the modern Middle East, whose work on Iraq and Syria will remain definitive, read by future generations of academics, students and the wider public who seek to understand Iraq and Syria's place in the wider region and the world beyond. However, he was also deeply committed to the communities that he lived in, whether they were academic, personal or political. He was incredibly generous with his time, his knowledge and his expertise. This commitment to others and the love and respect that we all had for him was shown by Peter's election to the presidency of Middle East Studies Association of North America. The association has over 3,000 members, ranging from graduate students to the professors that dominate the field. Their vote for Peter as their president showed the high esteem, affection and respect he was held in across Middle East studies. This was certainly a result of his wonderful work on the histories of Iraq and Syria but also because of his warmth, his generosity of spirit and his openness to one and all.

London, 30 August 2018

Introduction: Violent Non-State Actors in the Arab World – Some General Considerations

Peter Sluglett

Why do violent non-state actors play such a key role in the political field in the Middle East? This volume represents an attempt to understand and document political movements involving violent non-state actors, a phenomenon that has by now (2017) become almost endemic to the Middle East and the Horn of Africa.[1] Some of these movements have also spread their tentacles from the region to other parts of the world, with apparently random attacks carried out by their surrogates. In general, in the context of the history of the region, such movements are partly an entirely new phenomenon, partly related to the 'unfinished business' of the colonial and post-colonial eras, partly to what seems to be the characteristically unstable nature of most Middle Eastern states, and partly to the tacit encouragement of the Wahhabi/Salafi/*jihadi da'wa* by some regional powers.

These movements elude any simple classification, and any attempt to do so must be approached with the caveat that any 'categories' must be regarded as extremely fluid, seeping into one another. Some movements are 'national', operating only within the boundaries of national states (the PLO and Hamas in Palestine, Jabhat al-Nusra in Syria, Hezbollah in Lebanon/Syria, the Huthis in Yemen, al-Shabab in Somalia), others transnational (Islamic State, the Muslim Brotherhood). As this collection shows, many of those currently active in the Middle East are based, sometimes distantly, sometimes closely, on some form of religious ideology (Hezbollah, Islamic State, Jabhat al-Nusra, the Muslim Brotherhood, Hamas, al-Shabab). Some seek to overthrow the state (Islamic State, Jabhat al-Nusra), others seek to shore up the foundations of the state more efficiently than those who have currently arrogated the task to themselves (Hezbollah, the Huthis). Still others seek some form of secession from the state;[2] some have substantial forces at their command; others have far fewer, but have maintained their militancy and goals over many decades.

In the Middle East, violent radical Islamic movements are a relatively new but very salient phenomenon. The origins of most of them can be traced back to individuals influenced in some way in the late 1960s and early 1970s by the discourse of the Egyptian Sayyid Qutb (1906–66), and their intellectual heirs.[3] Despite frequent disclaimers, almost all are at least partially reliant on outside support, either or both financial and military, from powerful financial and/or political interests beyond their own ranks; many fight as proxies of others in confrontations that appear to be (internal) civil wars but which are actually expressions of regional power rivalry.[4] A unifying feature is a general disdain for democracy and the rule of law, two institutions that are also notable for their absence in contemporary Middle Eastern state structures. This topic will be discussed more fully below.

The colonial context

After the defeat and collapse of the Ottoman Empire at the end of the First World War, in 1918, all its former provinces in what is now generally known as the Middle East came under British or French rule in the form of hastily created 'Westphalian' nation states, under the nominal supervision of the Permanent Mandates Commission of the League of Nations. These, the 'Middle East mandates', were added to the roster of states in North Africa over which Britain, France, Italy and Spain had come to exercise control at various times in the nineteenth and early twentieth centuries.

An important by-product of European colonial intervention was that the social and political trajectory charted by the Ottoman state during its last few decades came to an abrupt end. This trajectory had been in the general direction of what James Gelvin has described as 'defensive developmentalism' – a modernized army and educational system, revamped legal codes, a constitution, the beginnings of parliamentary government, improved law and order, and so on.[5] In consequence, a whole generation, many of whose leaders had been educated in Ottoman civil and military schools, had to adjust its sights and expectations to new geo-political realities, and to become colonial subjects rather than Ottoman citizens. While an earlier generation of historians considered the European-sponsored changes to have had a largely positive impact in the interwar period, the various rebellions against colonial rule, its military underpinnings and the selective promotion or creation of a fairly small and largely unrepresentative ruling class and its protégés by the colonial powers have now been subjected to more critical review.[6]

More importantly, many of the more politically conscious inhabitants of Egypt, Iraq and Greater Syria came to believe that various 'universal' political and human rights were being taken away from them rather than being bestowed upon them, and that the all-encompassing attentions of the colonial state were less welcome than the more laissez-faire attitudes of its predecessor. For most of the interwar period, some two-thirds of all government expenditure in Egypt and the newly created states was '(internal) security related', leaving a relatively small amount for health, education, irrigation and infrastructure, let alone nation building.[7] Of course, given the major developments taking place in the rest of the world at the time, it would not take very long for the inhabitants of the states of the Middle East and North Africa (along with the rest of the colonized world) to learn how to organize politically, and to seek, and eventually gain, their independence, however limited. In fact the achievement of decolonization often had as much to do with the exhaustion of the European powers as with the coherence, integrity or successfully applied pressures of the various national movements.

Thus, as exemplified in Nelida Fuccaro's edited collection *Violence and the City in the Modern Middle East*,[8] the colonial state was characterized by military occupation, with violence as an ever-present ultimate sanction, rather than by some sort of notional 'consent of the governed', as defenders of the mandate system would have it. On a different but related note, the authoritarian nature of many contemporary Middle Eastern states cannot be characterized as being deeply rooted in some primordial past, either 'Arab' or 'Islamic', since most of them, as *entities*,[9] were the product of a fairly recent, and decidedly 'secular', past. This varied from place to place; most parts of Iraq after 1920, and Transjordan, were generally less violent than Egypt, Palestine or Syria between the two world wars, but the general picture is unmistakeable. While representative institutions were introduced in all the states except Palestine, these functioned quite haphazardly, and could be (and were) interfered with and/or shut down at the behest of the colonial rulers.[10] Since the construction of a genuinely representative parliamentary system would have worked to the advantage of liberal and democratic forces, it made perfect sense for the colonial powers and their local allies to deny such aspirations, and to block local attempts to establish a more fully democratic and liberal polity. In this way, as Makdisi says, 'geopolitics ... [have shaped] the limits of the political horizon'.[11]

In addition to representative institutions, Britain and France endowed their new creations with armed forces whose effectiveness varied from state to state. Given the aim of British policy in Palestine, creating an indigenous Arab security force was not practicable, but the *Troupes Spéciales du Levant* in Lebanon and Syria became the nucleus of the armies of the two states after independence, although, like the Egyptian army, the *Troupes Spéciales* had little combat experience before the Palestine War in 1948. The Iraqi army was a rather more serious matter; founded in January 1920, it was deployed extensively against Kurdish and Arab tribal rebellions in the 1920s and 1930s, and its nationalist, partly pro-Axis leaders actually took control of the country for five years (1936–41) after the first military coup in the Arab world in late October 1936. Initially, internal defence was at least partly vested in the hands of non-Muslims and/or non-Sunnis: Christians and Alawites were disproportionately employed in the *Troupes Spéciales* in Lebanon/Syria, while the Iraqi Levies consisted entirely of Assyrians between 1928 and 1955, when the force was disbanded.[12]

Independence movements and the post-colonial state in the Middle East

Between the wars, political parties and movements were founded in all the states under review, with the general but not exclusive aim of freeing each state from foreign rule – Palestine, as always, being a special and more complex case.[13] In spite of many polemical claims to the contrary, 'Arab nationalism' (in the sense of striving for freedom from Ottoman rule) had never amounted to a major political force before 1914, although Ottoman brutality in Lebanon and Syria, as well as the broader ramifications of the 'Arab Revolt', had done much to encourage it during the First World War. The various movements generally survived beyond the more or less artificial grants of national independence to Iraq in 1932, Egypt in 1936, Lebanon in 1945 and Syria in 1946, even beyond the revolutions in Egypt in 1952, Iraq in 1958 and the comparable watershed in Syrian politics in 1961. The nationalist movements were generally uncoordinated and fragmented, and were only united in the reasonably clear knowledge of what they did *not* want, which was the continuation of the indirect rule of the former colonial power and its local agents or collaborators.

Looking at the period between the struggle for national independence and the revolutions of the 1950s, the various components of the national movements in the region between Egypt and Iraq (and, to some extent, including the opposition to the Pahlavis in Iran) can be divided into five principal, though not watertight, types. Going from right-wing to left-wing, there were quasi-fascist groupings like *Misr al-Fatat* in Egypt, *al-Qumsan al-Hadidiyya* in Syria, *al-Futuwwa* in Iraq; various manifestations of the Arab nationalist movement in Iraq and Syria (*Hizb al-Istiqlal* in Iraq, the emergent Ba'th Party in Syria); more or less 'tolerated' national independence movements led by groups of notables like the Egyptian *Wafd* and the Syrian *al-Kutla al-Wataniyya*; social democratic groups like *Jama'at al-Ahali* and its successor the National Democratic Party in Iraq, and the Liberation Movement of Iran, and finally the various communist parties in the region. To this should be added the Muslim Brethren in Egypt and its offshoots elsewhere, which introduced religion as an activist ideology into the political arena after the 1920s. Needless to say, some of these groupings were far larger and/or more influential than others, and in addition, size, in the sense of numbers of members, was not always correlated with influence.

By the end of the 1950s Britain and France had largely ceased to play a significant role in the Middle East and North Africa, although France would long be haunted by the repercussions of the Algerian civil war/war of independence, which lasted until 1962. For those born in the Arab world in, say, the 1930s, the late 1950s was a time of great hope, when anything seemed possible. The British and French had been stopped at Suez; Egypt seemed to have a charismatic young leader, and for the politically active, the 'old political classes' seemed to be getting some sort of come-uppance in Iraq and Syria, as evidenced by the lively debates in the Iraqi and Syrian Chamber of Deputies and the famously 'free' Syrian elections of 1954. Hence the newly decolonized 'public' might be cautiously optimistic about the possibility of the emergence of a plural political system.[14]

In time, Britain and France were replaced in the region by the United States, and in a less ultimately significant but far from negligible way by its competitor, the Soviet Union. The downside was that the post-colonial states that had emerged after the Second World War out of the mandate system, or roughly similar forms of colonial rule, were generally weak and unstable, rarely able to resist either the blandishments of the two great powers or of powerful domestic forces, generally the military. The weak state structures that emerged were characterized by their relative autonomy, as evidenced by the numerous military coups in Syria before Hafiz al-Asad and in Iraq before Saddam Hussein. In a relatively short time, this led to the creation either of one-party states or dictatorships, in which most 'opposition' would be forced underground, and became even more courageous, dangerous and foolhardy than it had been before.

Challenges to absolute state power

For most of the past few decades, much of the political opposition in the Arab and Muslim worlds has been directed by Islamic or Islamist parties, to such an extent that any serious opposition from secular liberal or secular leftist groupings has almost ceased to exist, or at least does not pose a threat to contemporary regimes. Clearly, the fall of the Soviet Union had much to do with the Arab left's drift towards marginality in the 1990s, but before then, particularly on the part of regimes which proclaimed fidelity to Arab nationalism and Arab socialism, secular leftist or communist thinking was a dangerous tendency which had to be reckoned with, and individual leftists and their organizations were feared, hated and/or persecuted by those in power.

The main consequence of the persecution of the left during the Cold War, which no one seemed to have anticipated, was that by, say, the 1970s, it became increasingly difficult for opposition to any regime to express itself at all other than through religious organizations centred on the mosques, which, in Muslim countries, could not easily be shut down. Furthermore, any 'secular' criticisms of (for instance) the Shah's regime in Iran were vilified as communist and hence not permissible. US intelligence agencies supported the Ba'th regime in Iraq throughout the 1970s and 1980s on the grounds that its evident anti-communism (and subsequently its stand against the Islamic Republic of Iran) made it first harmless, and then useful, to US interests. As we know very well, various kinds of fundamentalism eventually became a far greater threat to 'stability' than 'communism' in any of its Middle Eastern manifestations had ever been,[15] a political miscalculation which must count as one of the great foreign policy errors of the US in the twentieth century. By, say, 2000, the Arab world was divided into republics, all of which except Lebanon had become dictatorships, and more or less unreconstructed absolute monarchies. In some of the monarchies (notably Bahrain, Jordan, Kuwait and Morocco), authentic opposition voices could occasionally be heard in parliaments or national assemblies.

To a considerable extent, opposition to the status quo in the Arab world in the second half of the twentieth century was kept in check by social pacts or social compacts. That is, particularly in Algeria, Egypt, Iraq and Syria in the 1950s and 1960s, peasants, workers, women and elements of the urban middle class were incorporated into the political arena by unspoken agreements to the effect that the ideals of human rights, democracy and political pluralism could be sacrificed (or traded) in exchange for full (i.e. guaranteed government) employment, the distribution of land, subsidies on essential items of consumption such as food and fuel and the provision of cradle-to-grave social welfare and educational benefits. It is more or less impossible to sustain 'complete autocracy'; some carrots have to accompany the sticks.

'Buying off' dissent has been a major tactic for the Gulf monarchies, but in some sense it has also been the basis of what Steven Heydemann has called the 'national-populist social pact' in all the states of the Middle East since the 1950s and 1960s.[16] Heydemann was writing in 2007, but by that time the social compact had surely been broken more or less beyond repair in the republics, at least in Egypt and Syria (Iraq was more or less out of the equation by then), not least by the devastating collapse in the price of oil in 1986 and an explosion in the birth rate. It was also broken by the state's deliberate efforts to force the contraction of the public sector and the concomitant increase in the scope and scale of the activities of the private sector, and the creation of a body of crony capitalists close to the various regimes.[17] In general, the privatization or reprivatization of state assets in the 1980s and 1990s in such states as Egypt, Iraq, Syria and Tunisia greatly reduced these regimes' capacity to provide both government employment and a social safety net.[18] In a recent interview with a journalist, Ashraf El-Sherif, a political scientist at the American University in Cairo is quoted as saying, 'I can understand a social contract that is authoritarianism in exchange for development. But in Egypt you have authoritarianism in exchange for non-development.'[19]

In Syria, there were obvious limits, by the 2000s, to how far any 'reform' could go in the face of deeply entrenched vested interests. Bashar al-Asad seems to have found himself confronted with a version of Huntington's 'king's dilemma'[20] if, as may or may not have been the case, it was his intention to liberalize. Since he did not have the means to buy his subjects' acquiescence, the cost of effective modernization would have to have been political participation, and any significant public accountability would not permit his regime, and the complex network of nepotism and corruption that sustained it, to survive. On the other hand, the economic stagnation and dead end that had been reached well before 2011 was equally unsustainable in any version of the long term. The only alternative was increased despotism and state terror, the unhappy but almost inevitable course that has been charted since 2011.

In the Middle East, non-violent mass movements succeeded in overthrowing, first, the Iranian regime in 1979, and, in a different era, but equally unexpectedly, the regimes in Tunisia and Egypt in 2011. Later in 2011, insurrections removed the governments of Libya and Yemen, and initiated a period of civil strife in

Syria that has not come to an end (and caused ongoing chaos in Libya and Yemen). In all five Arab states, slogans called for the 'fall of the regime', and for 'bread and dignity'. As is well known, Islamist movements seem to have been caught off guard in the early weeks and months of 2011 in both Tunisia and Egypt, although their members certainly joined the huge demonstrations as individuals. In both Tunisia and Egypt, the regime leadership fell relatively quickly; as in Iran in 1979, the institutions of both countries proved strong enough to prevent them falling into anarchy, which is what would happen in Libya and Yemen. After a brief 'democratic interlude' in Egypt, power was seized again in June–July 2013 by the Egyptian army, which had stood aside in the early months of 2011. In the Arab monarchies there were crackdowns on dissidents, but the regimes (even Bahrain's) survived because of 'a set of overlapping factors: cross-cutting coalitions, hydrocarbon rents and foreign patronage'.[21] When the poorer monarchies (without oil) seemed to wobble, they were given cash injections by the wealthier ones. Egypt under General Sisi has benefitted from similar cash injections from Saudi Arabia and the UAE since 2013. Of course, whether this formula of 'have-oil-will-pay-up' can survive an apparently unending period of low oil prices is anyone's guess.[22]

Violent challenges to the state

This, then, is the context in which most of the actors and movements described in the different chapters in this volume came to political maturity, and in which they have attacked the status quo in a variety of different ways. With the possible exception of Jordan, Kuwait and Morocco, the rule of law, and what might be described as 'evolutionary politics', the peaceful transfer of power from 'the government' to 'the opposition' (or even signs of a gradual liberalization of politics) is almost totally absent from the region. While the 'Arab Spring' seemed to have held out this possibility early in 2011, the protests eventually proved no match for the repressive powers of the state in Egypt and Syria, and led to civil war in Libya, Syria and Yemen. Only Tunisia seems to be struggling gamely on.

Almost all the movements described in the book came into existence before the events of 2011, however much they may have been galvanized by them. Some (including the Muslim Brotherhood, the PLO, Hamas, Hezbollah in Lebanon) have both 'armed' and 'civilian' wings, and can and do engage in non-violent contact with other entities (and each other). Islamic State in Iraq and Syria, Jabhat al-Nusra in Syria, al-Shabab in Somalia, the more militant manifestations of the Muslim Brotherhood in Sinai and the Huthis in Yemen, seek either to overthrow or replace the existing order. The Muslim Brotherhood, Islamic State, Jabhat al-Nusra and al-Qaeda are all engaged in fighting or in committing acts of violence, mostly against civilians, in Egypt, Iraq, Libya, Syria and Yemen. Some of them have branches or 'franchises' operating all over the Islamic world and beyond, while some of those responsible for recent atrocities in Europe and North America have claimed membership in Islamic State to give their activities greater credibility.[23]

There is another major cause of the rise in religiously inspired violence and opposition to the status quo throughout the Sunni Muslim world: the indirect effects, or the success, of the Wahhabi *da'wa* over the past few decades, with funding from Saudi Arabia and some of the Gulf states, often referred to as the projection of 'soft power'. Thus, in patterns which have long been visible in Afghanistan and elsewhere, the project of turning thieves into policemen has largely backfired on those who promoted it.[24] Once the Taliban had defeated the Soviet army, its members did not hesitate to turn their US-acquired weapons against their new American 'friends'. The spread of the Wahhabi *da'wa* has been extremely visible, perhaps most obviously in Pakistan,[25] but its indirect effects could be seen in Syria, at least since the late 1980s, where outward signs of personal piety became visible in the streets: there was a considerable increase in the number of men with beards, of women with veils, and many hitherto secular individuals became observant Muslims.[26] Mosque attendance rose, especially in Ramadan; many Syrian students went to study at the Islamic University of Medina; many mosques were built with Saudi money, and a small but solid conservative/Salafist/Wahhabi base began to appear within the Syrian religious establishment, disparaging Sufism and discouraging any blurring of interfaith boundaries (that is, any advocacy of religious pluralism).

For clarity, an important caveat needs to be made in the context of the growth and spread of Salafism in recent decades. The most common manifestations of Salafism as they have come into being in say, Lebanon and the Gulf, are generally informal/peaceful movements that reject any kind of hierarchical organization. Their 'members' call on other individuals to embrace forms of personal piety based on a return to the pristine Islam of the Qur'an and Sunna. Although, given the lack of organization, it is often difficult to disentangle the history and activities of members of such quietist groups from those of their more activist or politically organized brothers, it is a distinction which is very real to those involved.[27]

In the overall atmosphere of repression and the absence of the rule of law, violent non-state actors have thrived, coming into existence at different times but largely since the mid-1970s, when major funding became available from the rapid rise in the price of oil. The Wahhabi *da'wa* was not primarily intended to galvanize radical movements, but this was its almost inevitable effect over the years, given the perceived illegitimacy of most Middle Eastern regimes – including Saudi Arabia itself, as illustrated by the occupation of the Great Mosque in Mecca by Juhayman al-'Utaybi in 1979–80, a demonstration of rage against the impiety of the Saudi royal house.

In general, the phenomenon of violent non-state actors, and their ubiquity in the region, is largely a feature of the fact that the so-called third (or even fourth) wave of democracy has passed the region by. It could be argued that the strategic and economic interests of 'the West' made it vital that this should not happen, but however convenient a cover-all, this argument leaves the people of the region without agency. Recent books by Charles Tripp and John Chalcraft have chronicled the struggle of brave souls in the Middle East for justice and liberalism. The sad truth is that even such major instances of mass mobilization as the Egyptian uprising of January 1977[28] did not 'succeed' – and neither, eventually, did the 'revolution' of January 2011. Sisi's Egypt is as, if not more, repressive than Mubarak's.

The order of the chapters follows the date of the individual movement's appearance on the world stage: the oldest, the Muslim Brotherhood, dates back to the late 1920s, Islamic State to 2006 (or even 1999), and the most recent, Jabhat al-Nusra, in 2012. On the more 'political' side, the PLO was founded in 1964, Hezbollah in 1982, Hamas (an offshoot of the Muslim Brotherhood but presently forming the government of Gaza) in 1987, the Huthis in the 1990s/early 2000s, and al-Shabab in approximately 2008.[29]

In 'The Muslim Brotherhood and Violence: Porous Boundaries and Context', Khaled Hroub suggests a new way of looking at the Brotherhood, which, throughout its long history, has vacillated between espousing, and not espousing, violence. It is clear that, given the Brotherhood's roots in the anti-colonial struggle in Egypt between the wars, and its 'honourable' record in the first Arab–Israeli war in 1948, this ambiguity has been there since the beginning. In a famous declaration in 1938, the group's founder, Hasan al-Banna, stated that it was not, and did not aspire to be, a political party, and during its long history it has only resorted to force when force was directed against it. (There is an additional problem of definition, that is, of tracking groups subsequently resorting to violence or jihadism that came from, but are no longer a part of, the Brotherhood.)

There have been intense debates over the propriety or wisdom of resorting to violence. Hroub's main contention is that what he calls 'porous boundaries' have defined the connections and tensions between violence and non-violence, both within the group and between the group and its more extremist contemporaries. Movement backwards and forwards between these boundaries has been governed by 'context'. Borrowing the notions of 'incubator' and 'firewall' from Marc Lynch, Hroub acknowledges that the main crossover is from the Brotherhood to more violent groups, largely on the part of those exasperated by what they regard as the Brotherhood's timidity. Another view is that the Brotherhood can act as a 'firewall', by offering activists the space for non-violent activism while keeping them from the kind of isolation that might make them more radical. 'Context' is what pushes individuals in one direction or another across the porous boundaries (and there was a fair amount of returning to a more conventional fold in the 1990s and 2000s). In general, as can be expected, repressive policies push individuals towards great radicalization, but conversely, as the experience of Jordan, Kuwait and Morocco shows, greater inclusion may create more 'moderate Islamists'. The history of the Brotherhood, particularly in Egypt, offers examples of pressures in both directions, although it is undeniable that the constant repetition by the faithful of sentences like 'Jihad is our way; dying in the way of Allah is our most fervent hope' conjures up images of force, and the invocation of Sura 8, verse 60, which enjoins the faithful always to be ready to attack the enemies of Allah, is difficult to explain away. Generally al-Banna (d. 1949) thought that resorting to force should only take place when all other avenues had been exhausted (in Palestine, for example), although he did oversee the creation of a secret military wing within the Brotherhood to attack the British in Egypt and the Zionists in Palestine. However, the high moral ground became shakier when the military wing was used against the Brotherhood's local opponents and other supporters of the colonial regime.

During the later 1950s, having first welcomed the support of the Brotherhood, the Nasser regime began to distance itself from it, and eventually began to persecute its members. The ill treatment members received in the 1950s and 1960s (imprisonment, torture, execution) was exemplified in the career and writing of Sayyid Qutb (executed in August 1966), to whose intellectual and spiritual legacy most subsequent violent Islamic ideologies can be traced. These years ushered in a period of radicalization and violence, during which Qutb began the theorization of violence that has fascinated some members of the Brotherhood ever since. Qutb's core belief was that humanity can only be saved if Islam prevails throughout the world, and this must be a purified and revivified Islam, since the states of the contemporary Muslim world are *jahili* (meaning comparable to the time of ignorance before Islam). A pure vanguard needs to restore or impose Islam upon the world, by force if necessary (or, in some cases, communities of Muslims should retreat from the world and lead a pure Muslim life). This repudiated the entire legitimacy of contemporary Muslim societies, whose irreligiousness must be fought (i.e. through jihad) by true believers.

Such ideas were warmly embraced by the lower ranks of the organization in the 1970s and 1980s, while the leadership, evidently floundering, tried to cling to the advocacy of non-violence, asserting that it was not the movement's task to set itself up as judges over individuals, nor to engage in the *takfiri* (excommunicatory) activities of Qutb and some of his followers. This was the line advocated by both Hasan al-Hudaybi (d. 1973), al-Banna's successor as Supreme Guide, and the tele-theologian Yusuf al-Qaradawi (b. 1926). Nevertheless, as Hroub says, 'Qutb's ideas have never been entirely effaced from the grand scheme of thought embraced by the Muslim Brethren.' Hence it is easy to see how the movement is at the same time both an incubator of violence and a firewall against more violent extremism. The notion of 'porous boundaries' is helpful in explaining a situation where members cross backwards and forwards largely according to 'context' (repression or inclusion). The chapter concludes with a survey of the movement's behaviour through various periods of modern Egyptian history, leading up to its current marginalization. In July 2013, a few days after Muhammad Mursi's 'freely elected' Brotherhood government was overthrown in a military coup led by General Sisi, the present Supreme Guide, Muhammad Badi' (b. 1943), declared his commitment to peaceful resistance to the new regime.

One of Hassan Barari's main arguments in 'Understanding ISIS: The Interplay between Ideology and Context' is that the ideology of the Islamic State is more political than religious. This assertion is difficult to contradict, except insofar as Islamic State is only attractive to Sunni Muslims, and engages in the kind of extreme *takfiri*/ excommunicatory activities carried out by the followers of Sayyid Qutb.[30] ISIS, currently perhaps the most prominent of many jihadi groups fighting in Syria, was originally an offshoot of al-Qaeda in Iraq (AQI), and was formed in about 2006. It has profited from the highly unstable security situation in Iraq, and the readiness of the Syrian regime to turn a blind eye to their own and other countries' jihadis crossing the border with Iraq to assist in the Iraqi insurgency.[31] ISIS is a product of the socio-economic and geopolitical realities of its time: by 2011, both Syria and Iraq were fertile fields for sectarian violence. The takeover of large parts of eastern Syria and north-western Iraq by ISIS appealed to many Sunnis, especially those who considered themselves marginalized in both Iraq and Syria, as well as the large numbers of 'foreign fighters' who flocked to join the cause. As stressed earlier in this Introduction, dictatorial violence is one of the main drivers of radicalization.

Barari also comments on the idea of the 'neo-Mamluks' or Arab security mafias prominent in Jean-Pierre Filiu's recent book, *From Deep State to Islamic State*.[32] Filiu considers the emergence of ISIS and the 'prevention' of the emergence of democracy as part of a problem of structural violence, carried out by internal security services, that has long characterized most Arab countries and societies. It has also fanned the flames of sectarianism, as the various communities have found themselves having to take up arms to fight for their existence. In other words, radicalization is at least partly a consequence of the chaos in which much of the region has found itself since the US invasion of Afghanistan in 2001 and of Iraq in 2003. Given the virtual collapse of so many states, other more primordial loyalties (tribal, familial, sectarian) have come to the fore. In the summer of 2014, ISIS stunned the world by its audacious capture of Mosul and its rout of the Iraqi army. The US response has been inadequate largely due to the Obama administration's insistence on 'no boots on the ground'. While the US has perforce to enlist the aid of the government in Baghdad, Iraqi Sunnis are profoundly suspicious of what they regard as its pro-Iranian Shia sectarianism.

Barari describes the ill-fated invasion of Iraq in 2003, and the subsequent foundation of al-Qaeda in Iraq by the Jordanian Abu Mus'ab al-Zarqawi. One of the guiding principles of US policy in Iraq was to privilege Shias over Sunnis in a dangerously mechanical way, with the result that the regime became both sectarian and autocratic, and that, ironically, Iran came to wield substantial influence over Iraqi affairs. Hence it was relatively easy for al-Zarqawi to recruit a jihadi movement from the Sunni community, aided by adherents who came flocking across the Syrian border to join the cause. One of the central features of al-Zarqawi's credo was to fight the Shias of Iraq, through the ethnic cleansing of Baghdad and other large cities. This caused a rift with al-Qaeda 'central', which felt it was more important and relevant to target US forces rather than other Iraqis.

ISIS in its various iterations had risen from the ashes of the anarchy after the fall of Saddam Hussein, and was one of the fruits of the US's wrongheaded attempts to impose new and irrelevant political structures on Iraq. The lack of Sunni empowerment, added to Nuri al-Maliki's increasingly pro-Shia sectarianism, simply added fuel to the flames. The situation deteriorated further after the withdrawal of all US forces from Iraq at the end of 2011, while al-Maliki's mismanagement still had to run its course, and while events in Syria were running out of control. Al-Maliki's and Asad's seemingly deliberate casting of the conflict in Iraq and Syria in sectarian terms contributed to making ISIS more attractive to Sunnis.

Overcoming and defeating ISIS cannot be achieved by military force alone, as the last two and a half years have shown; the elimination of radicalization requires the implementation of realistic positive alternatives. The region is faced with a series of radical models, which suggests that a strategy must be developed to address the root causes of radicalization in the Muslim world. Fighting terrorism is one thing: eliminating the causes of radicalization is another. As has been shown in the context of the Muslim Brotherhood, straightforward repression is rarely effective, and Western countries should reconsider the wisdom of giving their unconditional support to undemocratic totalitarian regimes such as those in Egypt or Saudi Arabia. There is no reason to think that the perpetuation of such regimes in power makes the world safer; in the long run, the opposite is more than likely to be true.

In 'Between Religion, Warfare and Politics: The Case of Jabhat al-Nusra in Syria', Mohamed-Ali Adraoui gives an account of the activities of Jabhat al-Nusra (now Jabhat Fatah al-Sham), founded in the heat of the conflict in Syria in January 2012. In July 2016 it declared its independence from its 'parent organization', al-Qaeda, but it is not clear how this has affected its activities on the ground. Like al-Qaeda and Islamic State, and many other less well-known bodies of fighters in Syria, it is a radical, armed, Salafi–Jihadi movement, but one that exists only within the Syrian context, where it has managed to put down deep roots since its foundation. It situates itself in opposition both to the Syrian regime and to other Islamist or Jihadi contenders for support.

Adraoui sketches out the movement's ideology and organization; it distinguishes itself by being a nationalist/jihadi movement, appealing to Syrians in the Syrian conflict. Like many of its contemporaries, it seeks to overthrow the Asad regime and establish a Sunni Islamic state in Syria; it believes that it is legitimate to use violence to overthrow an 'unIslamic' regime. Like some of the other movements discussed in this book, it believes in the righteousness of the practice of *takfir*/excommunication (or *al-wara' w'al-bara'*, loyalty and disavowal) against an unjust and/or heterodox regime. Most members of al-Nusra are Syrians, which of course adds to its legitimacy within Syria, and its core is composed of some of those released from Saydnaya military prison in May–June 2011. However, it also contains a substantial body of Iraqi fighters, who have broken away from Islamic State, and some foreign fighters from further afield. Its main inspirational figure is Abu Muhammad al-Jawlani (b. 1974), and many of its fighters gained experience during the insurgency in Iraq after 2004. It has on occasion inflicted serious damage on the forces of the regime and its proxies, including Hezbollah. It has less universalist aims than al-Qaeda, and does not seek to set up an Islamic caliphate; its enemies are the regime and its allies, and al-Jawlani has specifically cautioned his followers from attacking Western countries (including Israel). Like the Muslim Brotherhood, al-Nusra has a strong service element, trying to provide social and welfare services in the areas it controls, rather than intimidating and punishing them, as has often been the practice of Islamic State. It is based in Idlib and north-western Syria; relations with Islamic State are not especially cordial, largely because of Abu Bakr al-Baghdad's proclamation of a merger between the two groups in April 2012, which al-Jawlani categorically rejected.

Al-Nusra is evidently one of the most effective armed Islamic groups involved in the Syrian conflict; it is very well trained, and receives weapons and other support mostly from Qatar, but also from Kuwait, Saudi Arabia and Turkey. It has also fought Kurdish forces fighting against al-Qaeda and for their own independence along the frontier between Syria and Turkey. Its localized goals are attractive to some of its sponsors, especially Qatar, which distrusts the 'pan-Islamic' aspirations of al-Qaeda and Islamic State. Its local roots and local activities have led it to associate itself with the Free Syrian Army, which has been supplied with sophisticated weapons (ultimately from the United States). It has well-developed media and propaganda outlets, largely in order to offer a counter-narrative to Islamic State, which has also been very active in this field. Adraoui describes al-Nusra's administrative and organizational structure, which seems highly sophisticated, and gives some useful notes on the senior leadership. Although al-Nusra receives support from pro-Western countries, it is fiercely critical of the 'official' Syrian National Coalition, which enjoys Western support. Adraoui also quotes an interesting poll conducted in July 2015 soliciting opinions about al-Nusra from those who did, and those who did not, live in the territories it rules. An important feature of al-Nusra's strategy is not to alienate the populations it controls (as opposed to al-Qaeda): although it insists on the application of Sharia law, it also provides water, electricity, food and medicines in the areas it controls. Its being labelled a terrorist organization by the United States in December 2012 occasioned complaints from many of those it rules, who praised the security and the services it has provided for them.

Al-Nusra also makes a fair amount of money by selling the oil from Dayr al-Zawr (which it controls) to many buyers, including the Syrian government. Some of its success as a movement is undoubtedly due to the brutality of the Asad regime (and its Russian sponsors, particularly since 2016). Like all jihadi groups fighting in Syria, it has gone through a series of different alliances over time, although it has rarely departed from the goal of overthrowing the Asad regime and creating an 'Islamic society' in the Sunni-majority areas it controls. Its 'Syrianness' and national goals have earned it commendations from other participants in the struggle, most notably the Free Syrian Army and local people. As noted earlier, its relations with IS have long been problematic, especially since IS' declaration of a caliphate in June 2014. Nevertheless, outside observers of the conflict in Syria find it difficult to imagine how, given the generally positive way it is viewed by many Syrians, al-Nusra will be uprooted from a post-conflict Syria.

Victor Kattan's 'The 2007 Hamas–Fatah Conflict in Gaza and the Israeli–American Demands' is a carefully documented account of Hamas' seizure of power in Gaza in 2007, based on a thorough assessment of contemporary memoirs, Wikileaks and other publications. Kattan charts the background to these two violent Palestinian non-state actors: The Palestine Liberation Organization (PLO), formed under Egyptian auspices in 1964; and Hamas, essentially the Muslim Brotherhood in Gaza, which broke away from the 'Palestinian mainstream' in 1987. Hamas (and its more violent partner, Islamic Jihad), which had always had a strong base in Gaza, had become exasperated at what it regarded as the inadequacy, hesitancy and lack of progress on the part of Yasser Arafat, Fatah and the PLO in resolving the Palestine–Israel conflict. Both had quite powerful militias, and had grown further and further apart over the years, especially after the PLO was expelled from Lebanon in 1982. Essentially, Hamas was bitterly opposed to any formal recognition of Israel, and had gained increasing clout in the West Bank and Gaza during the first Palestinian Intifada (1987–93). Hamas and Fatah were driven further apart by the 'peace talks' in Madrid (1992) and Washington (1993), and especially by the Gaza–Jericho Agreement in 1994. The latter was a product of the Oslo Accords, a series of secret meetings between members of the PLO and 'second-tier' Israeli officials in the Norwegian countryside.

Kattan skilfully sketches out the gradual sidelining of the PLO in the years after the fall of the Berlin Wall, when it lost is major allies in Moscow and Beijing and when the US drew ever closer to Israel, and became more and more belligerent towards Israel's enemies. By 1993 the PLO had decided to bite the bullet and recognize Israel unilaterally; in fact, it had long abandoned armed struggle, leaving that field to Hamas. Unfortunately, the assassination of Yitzhak Rabin in 1995 effectively marked the end of any serious progress on the resolution of the conflict from that time onwards. Well before Yasser Arafat's death in 2004, the Oslo Accords had become a dead letter, and the PLO's isolation had been further intensified by the major changes in the international political landscape that followed the events of 11 September 2001 in the United States.

Mahmud 'Abbas, Arafat's successor as head of Fatah, was elected president of the Palestinian Authority (PA) in January 2005, in elections in which Hamas did not participate, but a year later, Hamas convincingly defeated Fatah in the elections to the Palestine Legislative Council (74–45). There was no doubt that these were free and fair elections, whose results Israel and the international community had not anticipated. Crippling sanctions soon followed – more crippling for Fatah – whose money came from Western aid and from taxes collected on its behalf by Israel – than for Hamas, most of whose money came from Iran and Qatar. Of course Hamas was not going to comply with the conditions of recognition, renunciation of terrorism and disarmament set by Israel for any negotiations, since differences over these terms had caused the split between Hamas and Fatah in the first place.

In brief, Israel and its allies spent the next eighteen months trying to overturn the effects of the election results, with sanctions of various kinds and the secret build-up of Fatah forces (the 'Presidential Guard'). In March the US State Department drew up an 'Action Plan for the Palestinian Presidency' which was leaked to the Jordanian press; it seems clear from Wikileaks and other documents that neither Israel nor the US would be prepared to tolerate a Hamas presence in Gaza, and was ready to support a Fatah-led coup against Hamas. Other leaks show that there were secret meetings between officials from Egypt, Fatah, Israel and the United States in the spring of 2007 to discuss the most effective ways of minimizing Hamas' influence. Constant clashes broke out in Gaza between Fatah and Hamas; Hamas generally got the upper hand in these incidents, but Israel still vacillated about whether to deliver arms to Fatah, which was calling out for Israeli assistance. Eventually, Hamas took over Gaza and expelled Fatah; on 15 June, 'Mahmud Abbas declared a state of emergency and dismissed the prime minister (Isma'il Haniya, from Hamas), replacing him with Salim Fayyad, whose government soon received international recognition. The balance of probability is that there *was* a plan to oust Hamas from Gaza, although many questions remain unanswered. Clearly, Egypt, Israel and the US and their allies were unhappy about Hamas' resounding electoral victory. On the other hand, it may not be a coincidence that Israel has not had any stake in Gaza since the dismantling of its settlements there in 2005. The expulsion of Fatah has not only divided the Palestinians, but has enabled Israel to isolate, blockade and attack Gaza ever since.

In 'Hezbollah and the Lebanese State: Indispensable, Unpredictable – Destabilizing?', Peter Sluglett describes the phenomenon of Hezbollah as a consequence of Lebanon's status as an institutionally weak state, where militias, often funded from external sources, have long been a feature of political life. The various confessional militias, mostly the product of the civil war in the 1970s and 1980s, have generally been too powerful for the state's own forces to contain them. Hezbollah, founded in 1982 as a militia in the wake of the Iranian Revolution, was a movement of 'Shia Islamists', profoundly anti-imperialist and anti-Zionist, supported financially and militarily by Iran and Syria. It did not and does not seek to capture the state: it seeks to defend it, both from Israel and (more recently) from extremist Sunni groups.

As the chapter shows in some detail, Hezbollah also embodies the rise of the Shias as a significant force in Lebanon, both politically and demographically. In the 1980s, and in 1996 and 2006, Hezbollah emerged as a force strong enough to limit the effect of Israeli operations in Lebanon. In some ways it has also challenged the settlement reached at the end of the Lebanese Civil War, although its inevitably close association with Syria has hardly facilitated that task. It also entered Lebanese politics, participating regularly in elections like a 'conventional' Lebanese political party. By 1990 the Soviet Union and the Eastern European states were no longer a force to be reckoned with in Arab politics, or in the various Arab economies, with the result that the need for 'Syrian protection' for Lebanon remained an important constant for many Lebanese and Palestinians, who were opposed to the activities of Israel, Saudi Arabia and the United States.

The forced evacuation of Syrian forces from Lebanon in the aftermath of the assassination of Rafiq Hariri in 2005 left a vacuum for a while, which was eventually filled by a surprise reconciliation between the Maronite ex-general Michel 'Awn, Hezbollah and, by extension, Syria in February 2006. One of the novelties of this alignment was the splitting of Maronite support between the two broad alliances[33] that now characterize Lebanese politics (8 March, 14 March) and the consequent marginalization of the Maronites as a political force. Furthermore, the assassination of Hariri left the Sunni community without a strong leader, a role that it is not clear that his son Sa'd can easily fulfil.

The political landscape of the Middle East changed irrevocably with the US-led invasion of Iraq in 2003, and its ill-conceived and clumsy encouragement of a regime based on sectarian quotas. This caused a revival of sectarianism not only in Iraq but also in Syria, where Bashar al-Asad's regime was seeking to delegitimize any opposition to it either in anti-imperialist or Salafi/jihadi terms.

For a variety of reasons, Hezbollah had managed to evade calls to give up its weapons since the end of the civil war, on the not always credible grounds that Lebanon was still at war with Israel. The departure of Israeli forces in 2000, largely at Hezbollah's behest, quietened these calls for a while, and a tense if predictable tit-for-tat situation prevailed on the Lebanese–Israeli borderlands which did not extend substantially to the rest of Lebanon. However, in June–July 2006, the simmering conflict exploded into a violent invasion by Israel which lasted thirty-five days, cost over a thousand civilian lives and billions of dollars' worth of structural damage.

The 'war of 2006' effectively restored Hezbollah's reputation and standing not only in Lebanon but also on the 'Arab street'. In addition, Hezbollah acted swiftly to rehouse people displaced by the bombing, and to mount an effective relief effort. However, since then its image has become somewhat tarnished because of its unwavering support for the regime in Damascus, encouraged, obviously, by Tehran. At least initially, it was clear that the 'liberal' opposition in Syria was fighting the excesses of a dictatorship which was every bit as bad as (if not even worse than) the Ben 'Ali regime in Tunisia and the Mubarak regime in Egypt, and indeed it has emerged that both Hezbollah and Tehran had tried to nudge Asad into making some concessions in late 2011 and 2012. The rather tired anti-imperialist and anti-Zionist card was pulled out to justify Hezbollah's support; perhaps fortunately for Hezbollah's credibility, the extent of takfiri/jihadi involvement on the anti-government side has provided somewhat stronger grounds for Hezbollah's stance.

Nevertheless, and in spite of the fact that Michel 'Awn was elected president of Lebanon in October 2016, the country remains beset by major crises which Hezbollah can do little to solve: blatant corruption; the dysfunctionality of government and public services due to inadequate funding; and above all the presence of over a million Syrian refugees, amounting to more than a quarter of the population. Parts of the country have become breeding grounds for jihadis, especially since the boost to jihadi morale everywhere by the takeover of Mosul by Islamic State in June 2014. Although Hezbollah's activities in support of the present Syrian regime may be judged questionable, its widely admired capacity to check Israel's activities in Lebanon, as well as its efforts to combat takfiri/jihadi groups in alliance with non-Shia groups (less radical Sunnis, Christians) suggest a shrewd appreciation of the value of a pluralistic outlook that transcends sectarian boundaries. This kind of pragmatism, Sluglett concludes, is a welcome change from the narrow perspectives of some of the other violent non-state actors studied in this book.

In 'When the State becomes a Non-State: Yemen in the Huthi–'Ali 'Abdullah Salih Alliance', Daniel Varisco describes the intricate politics of Yemen, and the ways in which (and here I am simplifying a much more complex reality) the Huthis gradually emerged as the standard bearers of an 'authentic' Yemeni/Zaydi voice against the inroads of Saudi/Wahhabi propaganda in the 1980s and 1990s. Yemen has constantly been subject to outside invasion, from the Sasanians in the sixth century CE through to the two Ottoman 'conquests', the Egyptian invasion after the fall of the Zaydi imamate in 1962 and the Saudi bombing campaign of recent years. None of these invasions succeeded or are likely to succeed in controlling Yemen completely, largely because of its mountainous terrain.

'Ali 'Abdullah Salih, a (Zaydi) military officer who had seized control of what was then North Yemen in 1978, became president of (United) Yemen after unification in 1990. After a surge of popular opposition to his corrupt and dictatorial rule in 2011 (in the wake of the risings in Tunisia and Egypt), he agreed to resign in return for immunity from prosecution, promising to hand over power to his vice-president, 'Abd Rabbuh Mansur Hadi. However, in spite of an assassination attempt that left him severely wounded, he was still in the country in 2013. (Salih was assassinated on 4 December 2017.)

After the Iranian Revolution, Badr al-Din Huthi and his sons Husayn and 'Abd al-Malik studied in Iran, where they were exposed to Twelver Shia ideology. On their return, Husayn became a member of the Yemeni parliament; he had become extremely anti-American, and gradually became the charismatic leader of the opposition to Salih. In September 2004, Salih sent forces to Sa'dah to have Husayn killed, and this signalled the beginning of a series of wars between 'the government' and 'the Huthis' that lasted until 2010. However, at some point after the events of 2011–13, during which he was officially unseated, 'Ali 'Abdullah Salih reconciled with the Huthis, who had grown quite powerful during the rebellion against him. The Huthis took control of Sanaa in September 2014 from the national army, and in July 2016 the two announced a united front against the Saudis, who are backing the government of 'Abd Rabbuh Mansur Hadi. At the beginning of 2017, in spite of the bombing and other Saudi offensives, 'the Huthis still controlled areas containing the majority of Yemen's population'.

The main constant in this tale of many twists and turns has been Salih's astute management of the tribes, as well as his creation of a fairly large national army, without whose support the Huthis would not have been able to enter Sanaa. For their part, the tribes and their militias have regularly challenged an overmighty state, in patterns of defiance and reconciliation that have been a feature of the history of Yemen during and after the Zaydi imamate. Varisco emphasizes the resilience of tribal organization in Yemen, the survival of tribal customary law, with its focus on mediation, and the tribes' general tendency to engage in armed conflict with each other and the central state only as a last resort. This resilience partly explains why al-Qaeda, with no strong tribal roots, has made relatively little headway in Yemen: of course the Huthis, as Zaydis, are fundamentally opposed to it and to other Salafi movements, often funded by Saudi Arabia.[34]

The Huthis (and Salih with them) are equally opposed to Saudi attempts to control Yemen, which have been a constant leitmotif of Saudi politics since the foundation of the Saudi kingdom in 1932. Current Saudi interference in Yemen seems to have been the brainchild of the current Crown Prince, reflecting what now seem to be perennially exaggerated Saudi fears of Iranian involvement. As Varisco points out, there is no evidence of any major Iranian involvement in Yemen (comparable, for instance, to Iranian involvement in Syria), although pretending it exists and exaggerating its extent is an easy way of attracting US military and diplomatic support. The Saudi bombing campaign has caused the greatest humanitarian crisis in modern Yemeni history, with huge numbers of civilians displaced or cut off from access to adequate food, water and healthcare, and infrastructure (such as roads, schools and hospitals) and world heritage sites severely damaged. Saudi bombing has also allowed *Ansar al-Shari'a*, the local al-Qaeda franchise, to make inroads, especially in the south of the country, where its activities used to be contained by the national army. Until this relatively recent Salafi/jihadi involvement, there was very little in the way of open sectarian (Zaydi/Sunni Shafi'i) rivalry, although, almost inevitably, this is changing.

It will be clear that the role of the Huthis is rather different from that of other violent non-state actors described in this volume, except possibly Hezbollah, since both in their different ways are trying to support an existing 'weak state' rather than aiming to overthrow it. Also like Hezbollah, the Huthis understand that they find themselves in a pluralistic sectarian environment and do not seek to 'convert' beyond the ranks of their own sect. In current circumstances the road to recovery will be long and arduous, since even massively superior firepower is unlikely to permit the Saudis to 'win' in Yemen and reinstate 'Abd Rabbuh Mansur Hadi and his government. Varisco emphasizes that reconciliation and compromise, which have always guided Yemeni politics in the past, are the only likely pathways to stability, although more 'traditional' forms of civil society have broken down in many parts of the country. In addition, non-interference by Saudi Arabia and other GCC countries would also be an important condition for peaceful development in the future. Varisco concludes that the resilience of the Yemenis and their long history of compromise and conciliation form the main hope for a peaceful future.

In 'Violent Non-State Actors in Somalia: Al-Shabab and the Pirates', Afyare Elmi and Ruqaya Mohamed discuss two groups that have come to prominence in the failed state of Somalia. They are both emanations of the disorder that has engulfed the country since 1991, the last point at which it could be said to have had some semblance of a centralized government. There have been times over the past decades when an administration of sorts has exercised control over parts of the country, but this has largely been connected to the ebb and flow of warlords and their militias in the different regions. The chaos and anarchy has permitted the growth of armed Islamist groups and of other armed groups, particularly the pirates, who have become notorious for their activities on the high seas.

So far, all externally and internally driven attempts to create an effective national government have failed. The authors review the literature on violent non-state actors and its relevance to the Somali case. Some commentators have divided the groups into those that are 'cause-driven' (al-Shabab and others) and 'opportunity-driven' (the pirates). Al-Shabab began as a sub-group of a larger organization called *al-Ittihad al-Islami*, the Islamic federation, which sent some of its members to train in Afghanistan with the Taliban in the early 2000s; it was the youth wing of the Islamic Courts Union (ICU), which, at the height of its influence in 2006, controlled Mogadishu and the south of the country until it was thrown out of the capital by Ethiopian forces at the end of that year. Al-Shabab split from the ICU and was designated a terrorist organization by the United States in 2008, when it pledged allegiance to al-Qaeda.

Al-Shabab has continued to control much of southern Somalia, raising money from *zakat* and taxes on sugar and charcoal. It was also prominent in defending its part of the country during the Ethiopian occupation between 2006 and 2009, using explosives, suicide bombings and guerrilla attacks, and has also fought with the forces of AMISOM, the African Union (peace-keeping) mission to Somalia, whom it considers invaders. However, after an initial period of popularity, its local approval declined because of a series of reprehensible suicide bomb attacks on unarmed civilians. Notwithstanding what seemed to be its solid Islamic credentials, it is now simply one of many Islamic movements in the country.

Much the same can be said of the pirates, obviously a more anarchic body who have been 'around' since the collapse of the state in 1991. While they lack an ideological base, their main and ancillary activities have generated employment in areas where little or no other work exists. Some claim to be taking the law into their own hands to fight against illegal fishing and toxic waste dumping, but it is more likely that opportunism, born out of poverty, is the main trigger. Evidently this is a costly business for the international community, but also for Somalia, since the World Food Program has stopped food deliveries after some of their vessels were attacked and impounded.

The authors note that it has been suggested that there may be some connection between al-Shabab and the pirates, given that the pirates have occasionally handed over some of their ransom payments to al-Shabab. However, such practices as ransom-taking are widely disapproved of by devout Muslims, and if true would only contribute to al-Shabab's declining popularity. The two groups continue to function in the absence of a functioning state in Somalia, and also because of a long history of interference in the country's affairs by its immediate neighbours Kenya and Ethiopia. There is also the adverse effect of the activities of the Somali political class, particularly its involvement in, for instance, the corrupt sales of fishing licences to foreigners. In short, both groups are simply two of the armed non-state actors that combine to worsen an already intractable situation in Somalia, and which have become increasingly impervious over time to any attempts to control them either by any centralizing state-building forces or by not always constructive activities on the part of the international community.

Editorial Note: The chapter by Hamit Bozarslan was added after Peter Sluglett passed away, but would have met with his full approval, as it was always Peter's intention to include a chapter on the Kurdish movements in the book. In 'Being in Time: Kurdish Movement and Quests of Universal', Hamit Bozarslan explains how global events, ideologies, and regional political alignments have influenced the 'Kurdish movement' (which, for Bozarslan, describes the plurality of political and military movements in Iran, Iraq, Syria and Turkey) at different moments in time.

Written in 2015, with a brief update to reflect developments since then, Bozarslan breaks down his article into different historical stages to explain the ideological evolution of what he calls the 'Kurdish space' since the fall of the Ottoman Empire. Beginning with post-1918 Kurdish nationalism, Bozarslan mentions Barzandji's 'short-lived kingdom' which constituted a major landmark in the history of the Kurdish movement, followed by the Sheikh Said uprising in republican Turkey. In this period, Kurdish nationalism was not easy to define because of its plurality.

The end of the Second World War saw the formation of the Republic of Mahabad and the Democratic Party of Kurdistan (KDP). In the 1960s, the younger cadres of the Kurdish movement were influenced by left-wing ideas, which were also influential in other parts of the globe, with the KDP espousing socialist ideas, even though its traditional leaders were conservative. This shift towards the left was partly explained by the fact that Syria and Iraq were under the umbrella of the Soviet Union where left-wing ideas occupied almost the entire political terrain. Socialism or communism were viewed as presenting a horizon of emancipation for the oppressed classes and nations – including the quest for independence or autonomy that very much appealed to Kurdish nationalists.

The 1971 military coup in Turkey constituted a serious blow to any hope of change through constitutional reform and democratization. The failure of these reforms destabilized the Kurdish intelligentsia which was seen as too pacifist by the younger generation. Thus the 1970s was marked by a further radicalization of the Kurdish movement that reached its peak between 1975 and 1978. In these years, Abdullah Öcalan founded the Kurdish Workers Party, and urged Kurdish youth (and Kurds generally) to use violence, not only as an instrumental or rational means for liberating Kurdistan, but also for 'liberating the Kurdish being from his interiorized enslavement'. 'In a sense', writes Bozarslan, 'the Kurds had to take the place of the Palestinians in the vanguard of the revolution across the Middle East'.

Following the Iranian Revolution, the occupation of Afghanistan by the Soviet Union, and Egypt's recognition of Israel in 1979, left-wing ideas lost their hegemonic position in many parts of the Middle East, and were replaced by the domination of Islamism – although not completely, as left-wing ideas still remained attractive to Palestinians and Kurds. In Bozarslan's view, Islamism was unable to present a universalist perspective to the Kurds or advance any promise of national emancipation that left-wing ideas were able to. This is why Islamism remained only of marginal influence amongst the Kurds, whereas in Palestine, because of its history and location, Islamism gained more traction amongst some segments of society.

The vacuum of the 2000s–2010s has since given way to the militarization of Kurdish society, after the 'Arab winter' of 2011. In contrast to previous episodes of violence, however, the remilitarization of Kurdish society in Syria and Iraq has sought to defend a 'national territory' rather than fight against the apparatus of an existing state. Although Iraqi Shia militias and Iran's revolutionary guards attacked and occupied the city of Kirkuk with the full support of Turkey following the Kurdish independence referendum on 25 September 2017, the Kurdish movement survived and continues to thrive – albeit in something less than an independent state.

1

The Muslim Brotherhood and Violence: Porous Boundaries and Context

Khaled Hroub

Introduction

Founded in Egypt in 1928, the Muslim Brotherhood (MB or *al-Ikhwan al-Muslimin*) continues to offer an intriguing case of a multifaceted organization, advocating and led by different and sometimes contradictory ideas and strategies. The Brotherhood has famously kept projecting itself in sets of complementary as well as competing binaries, summed up by their mantra in conceiving Islam as *Din wa Dawla* (religion and state). The duality and proclaimed comprehensiveness of the *Ikhwan* has been captured by many of the statements made by Hasan al-Banna (1906–49), the founder of the MB:

> We are not a political party, though politics based on the true principles of Islam lies at the heart of our idea; and we are not a charitable reformist organization, though charity and reform [are] among the greatest of our aims, we are not a sports team, though body and spiritual sport is one of our most important means. We are not any of these formations because each is justified by a specific end and for a limited time frame, and could only be inspired by the mere desire of forming organizations and enjoying their titles.
>
> al-Banna, 1938[1]

In another and similar binary-based statement, al-Banna describes the comprehensive nature of his organization: 'it is a Salafi call, a Sunni way, a Sufi reality, a political institution, a sports group, a scientific and cultural league, a commercial company and a social idea', all connected to an understanding of Islam as a complete system: 'Islam is a creed and ritual, homeland and nationality, religion and state, spirituality and work, Qur'an and sword' (al-Banna, 1938). Out of all these binaries, the most controversial has always been the approach and theorization of the use of force/jihad vs peaceful means to achieve the declared ends.

The question of using force/jihad has haunted the organization since its early years. Should the *Ikhwan* use force if needed, and how and when could it be justified? Over time and diverse experiences, the ambiguities surrounding the MB's violent or non-violent approaches have created foes and enemies for the MB. The defensive views of the MB assert that the organization is historically and fundamentally non-violent, whereas opposing views accuse the Brotherhood of being inherently violent – or at least incubating violence.

The histories of the MB branches in the Middle East and beyond support the argument that non-violence has been the most frequent modus operandi of the organization in most times and places: Egypt, Jordan, Iraq, Kuwait, Morocco, Tunisia, Yemen, among other cases. Depending on the context and the overall circumstances, the various national branches of the MB have opted for religious, social and political activism so long as some space was given for them to operate. However, the tendency to use force has emerged when violence was directed against the organization. Several well-known cases and occasions are often pointed to as strong evidence of the violent side of the MB: the Egyptian MB's Secret Apparatus in the 1950s and 1960s and its violent action and assassinations, which will be discussed below; the Syrian MB's armed uprising against the regime in the late 1970s and early 1980s (Lefèvre, 2013); the Sudanese Islamists' military coup that brought Omar Bashir to power in the late 1980s (El-Affendi, 1991); and a similar military coup attempt secretly organized by *Ikhwan*-influenced Tunisian Islamists but foiled at an early phase before the 'palace coup' that brought Zayn al-'Abidin Ben 'Ali to power in 1987.[2] But the debate on the MB and violence is typically stretched to include violent Islamist groups and individuals that are not officially MB affiliates, where it has been widely argued that the MB's embedded teachings and praise of the use of force have been manifested in the breakaway of violence-oriented elements from the MB, in various cases, phases and countries, in order to form or join jihadist groups. Thus, the debate on the MB and violence is in fact multilayered, and grey areas (and confusion) keep evolving between and around ideas, methods, groups and ultimate ends.

What further adds to such confusion is the ambiguity of the MB's own literature over the idea of the use of force/jihad, marred by contradictory notions and opaque interpretations that would arm advocates of violence and non-violence alike with religious exegeses and justifications. In fact, based on the MB's literature it would be easy to build a strong case for a violent/jihadist approach and an equally strong case for a non-violent/political approach.

Porous boundaries vs context

Given the ambiguity of the ideas, practices and ideology of the MB, this chapter sets out to examine a number of issues relating to the debate on and around the MB and the use and perception of force. It starts with a discussion of some of the foundational arguments within the MB, which have continued to impact the shaping of its position as a group and the mindset of its members regarding violence. Here, the intense internal debates between advocates of violence and non-violence will be highlighted, along with their enduring influences. The chapter then moves to examine the salient episode of the Special Apparatus, a paramilitary sub-group founded within the Brotherhood in the late 1930s that remained in existence in various forms until the 1960s. The analysis will focus on the intellectual debate rather than on a straightforward chronology of events, specifically, on how the resort to violence was justified, internally debated or rejected, then integrated within the broader project of the MB. The aim of this examination of MB intellectual concepts and the theorization of violence is to demonstrate the deep-rooted nature of the notion of *porous boundaries*, as will be introduced in this discussion. The *porous boundaries* notion denotes the intimate connection and tensions between the ideas of violence and non-violence within the MB itself on the one hand, and between the MB as a group and the other more extreme Islamist groups surrounding it on the other hand. The porous boundaries between violence and non-violence, ideas and actions, have continued to remain porous within the broader phenomenon of Islamism, within and beyond the MB.[3]

For further clarification and in order to set the stage for the following analysis, the argument presented in this discussion states that the *Ikhwani* ambiguity over the question of violence has generated porous boundaries on two levels in relation to the use of violence: the level of ideas and perceptions with rival cases for and against the use of force inside the MB, and the level of action and regrouping where porous boundaries kept open channels between the MB and other groups that embraced straightforwardly violent approaches. Thus, internal and external porous boundaries allowed for continuous active traffic across grey borderlines, between ideas and groups. What governs this traffic is in fact the given *context*, which is the other crucial side of the porous boundaries understanding offered here, as explained later in this chapter.

For the time being, we should examine two dominant approaches in the literature that indirectly relate to the notion of porous boundaries as proposed here, and which frequently appear in the discussions about the position occupied and role played by the MB within contemporary violent and non-violent Islamism. These are the 'incubator' and 'firewall' perspectives (Lynch, 2016). From the perspective of the 'incubator' proponents, the crossover movement between the MB and extreme groups takes place principally in one direction: from the MB to extreme groups. Angry and dissatisfied members of the 'timid' and gradual approach of the MB towards changing/Islamizing their society have left the mother organization for the other side of the blurred divide. Because of the continuous flow of individuals and ideas from the MB to violent groups, the MB has been accused of being the 'incubator' of Islamist violence and Islamist radicals. According to this view, the MB nurtures Islamists for a long period of time, indoctrinates them with Islamism and jihadi ideas at the theoretical level and then hands them over well prepared intellectually to violent and extremist groups. In most of the cases, but not all, the incubator view is held by the anti-Islamists, whether governments, political rivals, staunch secularists or others (Shmid, 2014; Esposito, 2002).

Against the incubator idea there is the view that the MB (and other non-violent Islamist parties) do in fact function as a 'firewall' against the otherwise unstoppable mushrooming of violent groups using religion to justify their action. The *Ikhwan* and its likes effectively control thousands of angry young men (and women) and keep them under the thumb of religious instructions that forbid them from using unjustified force against others. Had this 'firewall' ceased to exist, a massive influx would have taken place to the extreme and violent side. Continuing to be part of the political/social scene, the MB offers politically and socially motivated religious segments of society the space for non-violent activism. In most cases, but not all, the 'firewall' view is the one held by the Islamists themselves and their supporters. It is worth noting here that many people, in academic as well as policymaking circles, subscribe to this view without necessarily being pro-Islamist. It has been frequently argued that the engagement of Islamists in politics and legal systems dries up radicalism and limits its spaces, whereas isolating moderate Islamists can push them towards extremism and plays into the hands of radical and violent elements (Wickham, 2015; Masoud, 2014). This point will be further discussed in the final section of this chapter.

The porous boundaries/context argument presented in this chapter about the *Ikhwan* and violence is linked to, but at the same time different from, the juxtaposition offered by the 'incubator'/'firewall' polarity. In the first place, and while neutralizing any hidden slandering or venerating of the Islamists, each of these two depictions entertains undeniable power in capturing the flow of traffic, or lack of it, from non-violence to violence within the Islamists' world. However, this is merely a depiction of what is happening on the surface, with little explanation of what lies behind such dynamics. The other shortcoming of both views stems from the overexaggeration of the porous boundaries in the 'incubator' view – that is, seeing the influx taking place in one direction only – and from the underestimation of the same porous boundaries in the case of the 'firewall' view – not sufficiently acknowledging the porousness of the 'wall'. Both depictions focus on what seems to be a unidirectional move, or stoppage, of the traffic from 'moderate' to violent Islamism.

The 'incubator' vs 'firewall' debate reduces the diversity of explanations to two polarized positions, eliminating the nuances attached to any discussion marked by excessive grey areas and overlapping territories. Further, this debate has become politically charged and partisan, especially after the violent intervention of the Egyptian army that ended the rule of the MB's president, Muhammad Mursi, in July 2013. Because of its partisan nature, this binary argument has evolved selectively and subjectively, where advocates of each side of the argument highlight certain cases while ignoring others, in order to validate their own view. Last but not least, the 'incubator'/'firewall' binary draws more attention to the finality of positions than to the deeper explanation and understanding of the underlying dynamics. What does remains attractive in this simplifying approach is the power of its metaphorical reductionism. But as happens with any metaphor, the embedded penetrating authority of its impactful message is compromised by the capacity to eliminate the crucial significance of the context. And in fact, it is in the context, with its compounded dynamics and underlying factors, that the crux and narrative of the Islamists' story, violent or peaceful, can be found; a story that is almost impossible to sum up in short statements or metaphors.

In light of the above, and instead of a rigid juxtaposed 'incubator'/'firewall' debate, the position that I am arguing from in this chapter is the *porous boundaries vs context perspective*, which can be summed up in the following way. The intellectual and religious affinity and the mutual influence between 'moderate' and 'extremist' Islamist groups is maintained through porous boundaries, through which a continuous flow of ideas and individuals takes place in both directions (from the moderate side to the extreme and vice versa). The volume and direction of traffic across these porous boundaries is controlled by the given context. A radicalizing and oppressive context will encourage moderate elements to travel to the extreme side, and extreme ideas to travel to the moderate side, while a moderate context will encourage moderate ideas to travel to the extreme side, and attract extreme elements to move to the moderate side.

While a porous boundaries/context perspective frees the debate over Islamism and violence from any hijacking and bold statements, it nevertheless acknowledges their temporal and occasional validity. For instance, several case studies of the history of the MB would certainly support the 'incubator' analysis; and several other cases would by contrast support the 'firewall' analysis. In order to understand when, why and under what circumstances the MB functioned, and would function, as an incubator in one case and as a firewall in another, the best and only way is to examine the given context of each case. The context is almost the only plausible explanation for the political, social or militant behaviour of the MB or any other Islamist group. A porous boundaries/context perspective, therefore, contains rather than negates the incubator/firewall binary, but without accepting each designation as the universal portrayal of the dynamics between 'moderate' and 'violent' Islamist groups.

The *Ikhwan*'s foundational ambiguities

A major source of the sheer ambivalence engulfing debates over the MB and the use of force is the ambiguity embedded in its foundational principles since the time of its inception. An elevation of the concept of *jihad* along with call for 'dying for the sake of God' occupied a central place in the group's discourse from the beginning, in tandem with an overwhelming focus on non-violent and charitable activities. Although it adopted social, proselytizing and brotherly religious ways to attract members and spread its ideas, the MB continued to nurture a strong jihadi spirit in its teachings and indoctrination. Over decades, this jihadi spirit, open to many (mis)interpretations and (mis)understandings, has shifted in several cases from the sphere of rhetoric to the sphere of 'action', depending on different contexts. In this part of the discussion there will be a closer examination of some of the *Ikhwan*'s foundational ideas and literature, scrutinizing the prevalence of rival views and schools of thought vis-à-vis the use of force, particularly the influence of the radical, and radicalizing, ideas of Sayyid Qutb.

A convenient starting point here is the never-waning religious and foundational motto of the *Ikhwan*: 'God is our objective. The prophet is our leader. The Qur'an is our constitution. Jihad is our way. Dying in the way of Allah is our highest hope.' Articulated by al-Banna in the early days of the group, this powerful mantra has continued to occupy the hearts and minds of millions of its followers and supporters until the present. Every single MB member regularly repeats this five-sentence proclamation with reverent conviction akin to reciting Qur'anic verses. Rooted profoundly in the *Ikhwani* culture, these words supposedly summarize the group's raison d'être, its approach, strategy and the ultimate objective of the organization as a whole and of its members as individuals.

Delivered in simple yet powerful language, the mantra opens with a crystal clear declaration of the ultimate aspiration for Muslims that 'God is our objective'. It easily links up with ordinary Muslims; many of them would touchingly conform to the religious appeal of such a message. Then, a no less powerful affirmation is conveyed in uttering that the 'Prophet is our leader'; an utterance that despite its abstract form casts deep doubts over the legitimacy of all other forms of leadership. This is followed by a third and equally hard-to-contest statement that '[t]he Qur'an is our constitution', where the contrast is constructed in even sharper fashion against man-made leaderships or constitutions. In three short syllables the *Ikhwan*'s motto combines an unchallenged ulterior objective with an uncontested form of leadership and an uncontested divine source of authority. Subsequent to the bold announcement of utopian objective, intangible leadership and unrivalled legitimacy, all effectively not deployable in the realm of ordinary politics, the declaration goes on to introduce yet another two layers of vagueness; this time underlying the method of implementation, jihad, and the sacrificing cost, martyrdom, that comes with it: 'Jihad is our way. Dying in the way of Allah is our highest hope'. The Arabic phraseology of these short yet imposing sentences produces flowing rhymes, creating enchanting religious music to the ears and hearts of MB members. More dangerously and more relevant to our discussion, these pronouncements offer followers an open and fervent invitation to be prepared at all times to die for the sake of God, a preparation that could only be fulfilled by adopting jihad as 'our way'. For zealous young adherents of the MB there would be no need for any other teaching to ignite the desire for martyrdom within them. From whatever angle one may scrutinize this maxim, the conclusion would be the same: that the ultimate and highest aspiration for a Brother is to die for the sake of God. When this slogan is chanted loudly by tens of thousands in gatherings or street demonstrations organized by the group, it fills the air with triumphant ecstasy for MB members and with simultaneous fear and intimidation for its rivals.

Bringing this early *Ikhwani* motto and declaration from the folds of the past into close focus is far from irrelevant. A careful examination of this foundational message within the context of any MB branch, in different times and countries, makes clear its enduring effect on (re)shaping the MB's political thinking and practice. The effects of the motto could be traced particularly in the creation and maintenance of porous boundaries between violent and non-violent perceptions and practices. The impact and centrality of this declaration has never waned over decades, and it continues to be referred to and embraced by all MB branches and members until the present time. The reason behind this lies in its generic and unifying tones, its vagueness and exegetical nature. Although presented in a simple and direct fashion, it delivers a multilayered message that embodies the entirety of the MB project. Articles, views and extensive analyses are regularly produced by MB leaders and writers focused on this motto, as are attempts to extract ideas and strategies from it.[4]

Another early and still impactful message of the MB that created enormous ambiguity about the real position of the *Ikhwan* vis-à-vis the use of force is the insignia of the organization. The famous symbol of the Brotherhood delivers a message that leaves no doubt about the fondness of the MB for the idea of the use of force. The three main elements visibly occupying the green-background sign of the MB are the two large crossed swords, encompassing a Qur'an in the middle, with the Qur'anic word *wa'iddu*, 'Make ready [your strength]', prominent. The word is perhaps the most problematic part of the MB's emblem. It is the key component of a verse of the Qur'an sura *al-Anfal* (The Spoils of War, 60), sometimes called the *Sura* of War/Jihad. The full verse reads as follows:

> Against them make ready your strength to the utmost of your power, including steeds of war, to strike terror into (the hearts of) the enemies, of Allah and your enemies, and others besides, whom ye may not know, but whom Allah doth know. Whatever ye shall spend in the cause of Allah, shall be repaid unto you, and ye shall not be treated unjustly.[5]

This verse provides all the ambiguity required by any Islamist movement, violent or non-violent, to link its efforts to the broadest of causes and struggles against what it perceives as the enemies of Islam. Translating the Qur'anic word *wa'iddu* to one single word in English that would capture its embedded spirit and connotation is indeed difficult. Literally, *wa'iddu* means 'prepare'; but the Arabic word is in the imperative *plural*, addressing *the* Muslim group or the Muslim community as a whole. Also, the use of this single and yet commanding word leaves the door open for various interpretations, not all directly linked to the use of force. The emphasis here is on the necessity of becoming and staying prepared, without spelling out clearly why such preparedness is necessary. But all this creates a sense of what could be seen as 'positive ambiguity'. Under this call for preparation, as the MB used to argue, fall all forms of activity: practising religious rituals, charity, education, sport, daily work, scouting, promoting good and preventing evil, engaging in politics, military training if possible and ultimately fighting. The entire spectrum of MB activism is therefore channelled into this never-ending process of making ready the strength of both the individual and the group, summed up by the word *wa'iddu*. In fact, this is not a plain word that could be read in its short literal sense either by the MB affiliates or others. *Wa'iddu* would always prompt the remainder of the verse in the mind of the reader or listener, calling upon Muslims to adopt a permanent preparedness, part of a coming jihad against the enemy. *Wa'iddu* has thus evolved into a methodology for the group and its affiliates, an action plan, a strategy and even an omnipresent harmonizing paradigm that ties up all functions and walks of life with which the Brothers would be engaged.

Next to the ambiguities around the use of force created by the 'motto' and the 'insignia' of the MB, it is worth pausing to consider some of the early literature. The documents produced by the MB's founder, al-Banna, at the Fifth Conference in 1938 stand out as particularly significant in this respect, both for their centrality in MB literature as a whole and their direct engagement with the idea of the use of force by the group. Over the first decade or so of its political life, the MB convened six 'general conferences' focusing on the internal affairs of the group, consolidation of a hierarchical structure, clarification of its ideological orientation and self-praise for its organizational expansion.[6] The documents and statements delivered and published by each of these conferences amounted to foundational treatises within the intellectual make-up of the group. A well-known document that is frequently referred to by the MB leaders and members is Hasan al-Banna's 'Letter of the Fifth Conference'. In this long document he repositioned the group and its ideology vis-à-vis a number of salient and pressing issues concerning its ultimate objectives, its strategies and politics and its perception regarding the use of force. Against calls by some enthusiastic members to adopt a more 'forceful' approach, al-Banna boldly advocated a gradual strategy of non-violence, where force was relegated to a stratagem of last resort:

> The Muslim Brotherhood will use force only when all other means prove futile; and when the Brothers are confident that they have completed all means of belief and unity. When they [the MB] use force they will be honest and open, and will send out warnings first, then engaging with dignity and pride, bearing the consequences of their action fully content.[7]

Hasan al-Banna insisted on linking the notion of being strong to 'strength in belief' and strength in maintaining a purified life, attempting to free the notions of 'preparedness' and 'strength' from being exclusively associated with force and material means. For al-Banna, the Muslim Brother should be strong in faith, mind, heart, work and body. These forms of strength that al-Banna placed in front of many Brothers effectively erected many obstacles against the use of force, dismaying the more impatient zealous members who were eager to use force to preach the word of the MB. Perhaps this belief was the reason behind al-Banna's blunt argument against the idea of conducting revolution through the use of force:

> As for revolution, members of the Muslim Brotherhood neither think about it, rely on it, nor do they believe in its usefulness or outcomes. [That said, the MB] say frankly to each government in Egypt that if the situation remains as it is and those in charge are not prompted to offer immediate remedies to problems, then a revolution will be provoked – not by the Muslim Brotherhood and its call, but as a result of the pressures of the status quo, and the ignorance of public affairs.[8]

Ambiguities in action: *al-Nizam al-Khass*

The earliest militant manifestation of the *wa'iddu* paradigm was the creation, in 1939, of a secret military wing within the MB, *al-Nizam al-Khass*, or the Special Apparatus (SP). The purpose of this secret organization as declared by its founders, under the supervision of al-Banna himself, was to give military training to carefully selected Brothers and prepare them to undertake operations against the British, and later on to help the Palestinians against the Zionists in Palestine. Accounts of the history of *al-Nizam al-Khass* vary, with the views from within the MB or their supporters divided between giving credit to the SP for its heroic action and operations against the British, and on the other hand acknowledging fatal mistakes particularly in using force against their political rivals.[9] Critics and foes of the MB use the history of the SP as concrete evidence to condemn the MB as a whole for inherent violence and (later) 'terrorism'. Informed by extensive accounts of the SP (e.g. Pargeter, 2010: 179–210), the discussion here is only meant to provide a few observations in line with the porous boundaries/context perspective.

The Egyptian and regional context at the time when the SP was established was extremely volatile, with three major factors feeding into anger and militancy within Egyptian political groups: first, the succession of corrupt governments and their excessive collaboration with the British and their impositions; second, the British themselves as the occupying colonial power; and third, the rising power and presence of militant Zionist organizations in Palestine. Making the British and Zionism their prime targets gave the MB leadership a compelling justification for setting up the SP. The participation of the SP in the 1948 Palestine War is well documented, and frequently commended by later MB generations as one of the brightest chapters in its service to nationalist and Islamist causes (al-Sharif, 1984).

However, SP activities were never limited to Palestine or against the British, but involved domestic politics as well. Despite repeated assurances by al-Banna and other leaders that the MB would never direct its force against Egyptian opponents, the historical evidence to the contrary is fairly clear. With the passage of time, the SP's praxis exposed much of al-Banna's assurances as hollow. Although not necessarily with the approval of al-Banna or the higher leadership of the MB, the SP used force against its Egyptian political rivals, state officials or personnel (Mitchell, 1969: 58–79). Most of these acts were linked to 'big' causes such as the compromising of Egypt's interests by government officials, showing weakness regarding Zionism or Israel, or the arrest of MB volunteers after their return from fighting in the Palestine War. There are a number of incidents where the SP used lethal force against Egyptians, most notably the assassination of Mahmud Fahmi Nuqrashi, Egypt's prime minister, on 28 December 1948; the assassination of Judge Ahmad Khazindar on 22 March 1948; the targeting of some businesses owned by Egyptian Jews after the creation of the state of Israel in 1948 and the immigration of part of the Egyptian Jewish community. The MB officially distanced itself as an organization from these incidents, claiming that although some members of the group may have carried out these actions, the leadership never approved any of them.[10] After these assassinations, the Egyptian government dissolved the group and proscribed it in December 1948, pushing the SP further underground yet never putting it out of action. The dissolution was followed by a number of violent acts that angered al-Banna and prompted him to issue a public letter declaring the perpetrators (who were effectively members of the SP) to be 'neither Brothers ... nor Muslims', and appealing to 'those young ones' to cease from writing threatening letters and committing acts of violence (Mitchell, 1969: 68–9).

The SP had a less active role in the subsequent years leading to the military coup in 1952 that brought Nasser and his Free Officer comrades to power and ended the monarchy in Egypt. After a short period of good relations with the new leaders, the clash between Nasser, with his nationalist/socialist orientation, and the *Ikhwan*, with their rival (Islamic) ideology, was almost inevitable. A failed attempt to assassinate Nasser in 1954 while he was delivering a speech in Alexandria marked the culmination of growing tension and mistrust between the two parties, and opened a bloody and decisive chapter in the MB's practical and theoretical approach to violence.

The heavy-handed measures that Nasser applied to the MB succeeded in eliminating the group from Egypt's public scene, but sowed the seeds for future Islamist violence. Throughout the 1950s and 1960s, thousands of Brothers faced arrest and long prison sentences. Many more were forced to flee the country, and dozens of prominent leaders were executed. The 'prison years', with their brutality and bitterness, left deep scars on the MB's collective consciousness and imagery (Zollner, 2009). Gradually shifting from the 'traditional' approach of preaching Islamization through peaceful and charitable means, many Brothers started to revisit the original ideas, strategies and entire worldview of the MB. Inside the prison a new 'paradigm' was created and enthusiastically advocated by a gifted writer and ideologue who would leave a formidable mark on global violent Islamism that has lasted to this day: Sayyid Qutb.

Qutb: the never fading impact

Between its emergence and its clash with Nasser in 1954 the MB leadership managed to keep reasonable control of the crossover traffic through its porous boundaries to exercise violence or theorize its use. Also, there were no credible 'sister' Islamist organizations at the time to challenge the MB or offer a more radical and jihadist approach attractive to members with strong tendencies to violence. In spite of the various violent episodes and acts of the SP, as discussed above, the mainstream thrust of the organization continued to be peaceful. The 'misuse' and 'misinterpretation' of religious and exegetical ambiguities surrounding the concept of force/jihad were encountered and dismissed mostly because of the authoritative and charismatic leadership of al-Banna, though not always without difficulty. Hence, during the first quarter of its political life, it is fair to argue that the MB pursued mostly non-violent politics, despite some controlled infiltration of violent ideas and acts into its mainstream. The theorization of violence started to expand within the MB in the mid-1950s when Qutb's ideas started to influence *Ikhwani* culture, accentuated by the intellectual vacuum created by al-Banna's death in 1948. Qutb's ideas encountered a range of reactions spanning reverence and approval, ambivalence and uncertainty, suspicion and wariness, as well as outright rejection, by the various segments of the MB's leadership or its prominent figures (Calvert, 2010; Toth, 2013).

The most serious challenge to the leadership's control over the porous boundaries between the MB and violent ideas and practices came with the emergence of the formidable ideologue Sayyid Qutb and his ideas. Qutb joined the Brothers in 1953, seeing in them the 'vanguard' that he previously called for and envisioned in his writings prior to this time.[11] His uncompromisingly pessimistic views on life and the world hinged on a bold good/evil binary where doomed humanity can never be saved unless Islam universally prevails. The seeds of such a radical outlook were sown in his reflections on the two years he had spent in America between 1948 and 1950 (on a government scholarship provided by the Egyptian Ministry of Education). During his stay and travels across the US, and on his return to Egypt, he wrote a series of devastating observations entitled *Amirica Allati Ra'ait* (The America That I Saw), condemning America and the American people as greedily materialistic, immoral, decadent and motivated only by raw primitive instincts.[12]

Qutb's ideas have been widely and extensively examined in the literature on Islamism (Khatab, 2009; Bozek, 2009; Calvert, 2010; and Toth, 2013). It suffices here to highlight a number of his principal concepts which relate to the ambiguities of the MB stance on the use of force, giving them a clear and attractive ideological structure. In so doing, Qutb had somewhat flattened the borderline between the MB and violence, or at least greatly increased the 'porousness' of these borders, leaving the *Ikhwan*'s future leadership struggling with the impossible task of erecting fences between their organization and violence. Two of the main intellectual attempts to refute some of Qutb's ideas were those of Hasan Hudaybi (1891–1973), the MB's second General Guide who succeeded al-Banna in the early 1950s, and Yusuf al-Qaradawi (b. 1926), a prominent Islamist thinker and MB intellectual figurehead, based in Doha since the 1970s and best known for his television programme *al-Shari'a wa'l-Ḥayat* (Sharia and Life), broadcast on Al Jazeera.

In Qutb's world, human societies, including Muslim ones, have long descended into darkness because of their submission to *jahili* (un-Islamic) systems, led by corrupt desires and rulers. The only way to remedy this collective deviancy from the 'nature of things' is to bring back Islam's dominance over and above all other systems, and for people to surrender serenely to its guidance and comprehensive impositions. To achieve such an end there should be a 'vanguard' of strictly committed groups, adhering to the idea of bringing back God's system. This vanguard must be ready to use all means, if needed, including force, in order to destroy all other systems that would come in the way of the rule of God. For Qutb, bringing back the sovereignty of God (or *al-Hakimiyya*) would certainly require force:'[restoring the sovereignty to God] involves the destruction of the kingdom of man so that the kingdom of God is re-established' (Qutb, 1979: 59–60). More boldly and dangerously, Qutb reached the following stark conclusion: 'Today, on the entire face of the earth there is no Muslim state or Muslim society.'[13] Instead, these have become *jahili* societies led by all kinds of systems except Islam. The *jahili* society, or *Jahiliyya*, is one of the most central ideas proposed by Qutb:

> We are today in a *Jahiliyya* [time of ignorance] similar to the [time of ignorance] that preceded Islam. Everything around us is *Jahili* ... people's perceptions and beliefs, their customs and norms, the sources of their culture, their art and literature, legislation and laws. Even much of what we think of as Islamic culture, Islamic references, Islamic philosophy and Islamic thinking is in fact made by this *Jahiliyya* ... We should rid ourselves of the pressures of the *jahili* society [we are living in] ... It is not our concern to reconcile [or engage with] this *jahili* reality. Our first mission is to change the reality of this society from its foundation, since it is a society that clashes fundamentally with the Islamic approach.
>
> Qutb, *Milestones*, 17–18

With such unflinching declarations, Qutb did in fact open the doors wide for many extreme ideas that disparagingly condemned contemporary Muslim and indeed non-Muslim societies. The best way for the 'purified vanguard' to relate to such corrupt realities is to stay away from these tainted societies. Conceiving of Muslim societies as *jahili* contradicts al-Banna's prevailing approach within the MB, where contemporary Muslim societies are seen as Muslim yet in need of religious guidance and purification. The practical implication of Qutb's theorization is to create an unbridgeable gulf between the entirety of Muslim societies, which are collectively excommunicated, and his own 'vanguard' group (the MB in his idealization). Even if its size and power is minute in comparison with that of the majority, the 'vanguard' group exemplifies absolute righteousness, whereas the 'rest' are placed on the 'other and wrong side' of belief and history. This 'wrong side' should be fought against because it controls power and dictates to Muslims and humans at large systems and outlooks on life that are not divine, and which are contrary to the will of God. With this conceptualization Qutb was clearly establishing permanent channels between the MB as an organization and the use of force, even if those channels were loose and vague. Further elaborating on the inevitability of the use of force (the sword), Qutb unequivocally and unapologetically advocated jihad as the unavoidable and most effective means in the fight against *jahili* systems. Although lengthy and rhetorical, the passage below captures the essence of Qutb's radical jihadi paradigm, presented as boldly offensive rather than apologetically defensive:

> ... anyone that knows the nature of this religion ... will understand the inevitable embarking of Islam on *jihad* by the sword, alongside *jihad* by the word. They would also understand that this *jihad* was never deployed as a defensive move in the narrow sense that is derived from the term 'defensive war', promoted by those defeatists that succumb to the pressures of the present moment or the pressures of wicked orientalists. *Jihad* is a movement to liberate 'man' on 'earth' in various stages and it has renewed means. And, if we are obliged to call *jihad* a defensive move then we need to change the word 'defense' so that it denotes 'defense of man himself', against all factors that limit his freedom and hinder his emancipation. These factors that are represented in beliefs and perceptions as well as in political systems, all of which are based on the economic, racial and class barriers that dominated the earth prior to Islam, and yet forms of such systems are still dominant in present day's *Jahiliyya*. Once we expand the meaning of the word 'defense' we can understand the real motives behind the Islamic rise and advancing the banner of *jihad*, and we can understand the nature of Islam itself and its declaration. A declaration that enshrines the liberation of the man from human servitude, and the elevation of the divinity of God alone as the one who deserves to be worshipped and obeyed, and the destruction of the kingdom of human desire on earth, and the foundation of the kingdom of God's Sharia in the human world.... Thus, the attempt to find defensive justifications for Islamic *jihad* using the limited contemporary concept of defensive war, along with the attempt to find evidence to prove that the chronicles of Islamic *jihad* only applied to external aggression on Muslim domains, even only the Arabian Peninsula for some people, are merely reflecting a superficial understanding of the nature of this religion and role that it has assumed in this world. Such attempts also demonstrate the defeat in the face of reality and in the face of the orientalist onslaught on [the concept of] *jihad* in Islam.
>
> Qutb, Milestones, 64–5

A prolific writer, Qutb's books and his eight-volume interpretation of the Qur'an, *Fi Dhilal al-Qur'an* (In the Shadow of the Qur'an) started to fundamentally change the intellectual landscape of MB thought. Qutb's ideas continued to have great influence on the lower ranks of the membership of the *Ikhwan*, while the leadership kept clinging to non-revolutionary methods. Regardless of how accurate this depiction might be, the almost uncontested long-lasting change that occurred was the creation of even more porous boundaries between traditional MB thinking with its focus on non-violent methods and the violent approaches and ideas advocated and justified by Qutb.

The publication of Hasan Hudaybi's famous book *Du'ah la Qudah* (Preachers, Not Judges) in 1977 could be seen as the direct and official MB reaction to Qutb's ideas.[14] The message of the book is in its title: that the MB and its members should focus on spreading the call to God and preaching, instead of issuing judgements against people. Repeatedly in the book, Hudaybi asserts this message in a nuanced, if dry, religious justification '... [the MB] has committed itself to a policy that identifies religious rulings, but it does not declare itself a judge over individuals [to show whether or not those religious rulings apply to specific individual cases]'(Hudaybi, 1977: 233). Hudaybi articulates the difference between the work of the judge and the work of the preachers:

> ... thus we truthfully say that the difference is great and dangerous between the work of the preacher and the work of the judge, in that the latter is busy identifying religious rulings and applying them to individual events. He [the judge] examines and explores the problem, clears out its ambiguities; verifies the hidden details of its aspects and narratives, and listens to the witnesses. He reviews related documents and allows contestants to provide their own arguments, all this according to established systems that determine and assess evidence. After examining and taking all these steps, [the judge] applies God's ruling to the proven facts before him.
>
> Hudaybi, 1977: 114

This subtle difference between acknowledging religious rulings and applying them to specific individuals or communities has been blurred in Qutb's writings. For example, examining whether Ahmad and/or Ahmad's community became non-Muslims because they committed certain 'excommunicating' acts/sins, a follower of Hudaybi (and al-Banna) would refrain from issuing a verdict mentioning Ahmad and/or his community directly. He would instead state the general rules that stipulate the conditions that should be met and the 'excommunicating' acts that should be committed by any individual or community in order to be considered as non-Muslims. In contrast, the Qutb follower would be specific on the case, directly stating that Ahmad and/or his community became non-Muslims because they had committed certain 'excommunicating' acts. Unlike the Qutbis, the Hudaybis would refrain from attaching the 'non-Muslim' label to any particular individual or society, claiming that they can only highlight the general conditions under which an individual or a society becomes non-Muslim, but cannot and should not apply this to specific cases. Although subtle and perhaps even negligible, this difference has in fact offered a crossover bridge from non-violent to violent perception then violent action, yielding a further expansion of the porous boundaries within the MB thinking and membership.

Hudaybi also addresses the contested issue that hovers around allegiance to, and identification of, the 'Muslim Group' and whether leaving this 'Muslim Group' entails leaving Islam. There is intense controversy in jurisprudence and within the circles of Islamist activism about a couple of *hadiths* by the Prophet that spoke in general terms about 'the Muslim Group'. According to the Prophet, the Muslim *umma* will split into seventy-three sects: all will end up in hell except one, and this one is 'the Group'.[15] This Group is the only one that follows the pristine path of Islam while all others go astray. Throughout Muslim history, groups, parties, sects and collectivities would claim that each of them was the 'Muslim Group' indicated by the Prophet and all other groups were either heretics or un-Islamic. In Qutb's writings there were enough references, direct or indirect, signifying that the Muslim Brotherhood was *the* group (the vanguard) that today's Muslims should join. Against this idea, Hudaybi reiterates al-Banna's traditional view, stating that the founder of the MB never considered it as *the* exclusive Muslim Group that was mentioned in the Prophet's *hadith*, rather a group that aspires to become the Muslim Group – or just a group like any other Muslim group.[16]

More recently, and along the same line of thought that Hudaybi advocated, Yusuf Qaradawi, the Egyptian religious scholar and perhaps the most prominent living MB thinker, has publicly denounced Qutb's radical ideas. Qaradawi started revisiting Qutb's ideas in 2001 when he rejected Qutb's verdict that today's Muslim societies are *jahili* and similar to the *jahili* Arabian society before Islam:

> ... the society that we live in is not analogous to one that the Prophet encountered in Mecca at the beginning of Islam ... the society in today's Muslim world is [a] mixture of Islam and *jahiliya* (ignorance) where elements of both do exist ... but the vast majority of the masses are religious and adhere to Islam ... thus it would be outlandish and even dangerous to judge all these as *jahili* people, just like the people of Mecca at the dawn of Islam.[17]

Further, Qaradawi made a bolder criticism of Qutb's main conceptions, on an Egyptian TV talk show. Reiterating Qutb's verdict that all contemporary Muslim societies had become non-Muslim or *jahili*, Qaradawi stated that Qutb had indeed departed from the moderate line of *ahl al-Sunna wa'l-Jama'ah* (the mainstream Sunni line of thinking). According to al-Qaradawi, the issue of excommunication, where a Muslim individual or a Muslim community is declared apostate or non-Muslim, is one of the most sensitive in Islamic tradition. Qaradawi asserted that declaring that a Muslim community has become entirely and collectively non-Muslim, as Qutb did, never belonged to any school of mainstream Islamic thought.[18]

Over time, the majority of *Ikhwan* leaders and influential figures clearly adopted Hudaybi's approach. Yet, reverence and respect for Qutb, even from those who criticized his ideas, remained profound. The arguments of Hudaybi and Qaradawi seemed firmly rooted in religious justification, backed by Qur'anic and *hadith* texts. However, the arguments remained dry and lacked the revolutionary appeal that Qutb's ideals enjoyed, with their inspiring language. In the end, Qutb's ideas have never been completely effaced from the grand scheme of thought embraced by the MB. Qutb and his radical views remained part and parcel of the education and indoctrination of the MB, especially *Milestones* and *In the Shadow of the Quran*. Therefore, a strange and uneasy coexistence survived between sets of contradictory ideas and ideals in the minds and hearts of many members of the Brotherhood. The societies they live in and belong to have been perceived as both *jahili* and Muslim, and the nature of the interaction of these members with their societies is governed by the dominant perception of these two according to the given context. This coexistence has greatly contributed to the maintenance of porous boundaries that have kept internal channels open between violent and non-violent perceptions and actions.

Context controls porous boundaries

With the discussion above in mind, it is now time to conclude by revisiting the idea of violence in the *Ikhwan*'s thought and practice in light of changing circumstances. The key idea here is to assert the overriding role of the *context* in determining the volume and direction of traffic across the MB inside and outside the porous boundaries of violence. So far, it has been argued that perceptions of violence and non-violence have indeed coexisted within the *Ikhwan*'s culture and practice of activism. With the existence of these two polar approaches, along with shades of understanding and action in between, it is safe to say that there is no 'hard core' or timeless belief within the MB school of thought in relation to the use of force. Those MB members who advocate the use of force and those who advocate peaceful means of action or resistance can find enough evidence in the literature, history and practice of the group to support their position. Equally, academics and experts who argue that the MB is more inclined towards the use of force, and practically functions as an incubator for violent Islamism, and those who argue that the MB is more inclined to non-violence and effectively functions as a firewall against violence, could build equally strong cases, each based on historical evidence and intellectual theorization. Both arguments have in fact reasonable credibility and neither can nor should be dismissed entirely. While each view explains certain ideas and sheds some light on specific periods of time and events in the history of the MB, neither can account for all the modes of thought and/or actions and policies deployed by the group all the time.

Therefore, instead of juxtaposing these two views – the incubator and the firewall – against each other, the porous boundaries notion brings them together in a complementary rather than a contradictory manner. The coexistence of violent and non-violent ideas and approaches within the MB school of thought and practice is governed by fragile and porous boundaries, where ideas and members vacillate and cross over from one side to another. This vacillation of ideas and members between embracing violence or non-violence is controlled and determined by the given context in time and space (Hroub, 2010). If a radicalizing context prevails, entailing oppressive measures such as imprisonment, torture and outlawing of the group, more traffic through the internal porous boundaries will take place from the moderate to the radical side. In this case the MB becomes more of an incubator with more angry and extreme members pressing the leadership for the use of force. In contrast, if a moderating context prevails where the group is allowed to function peacefully and legally, more traffic from the radical/violent side to the other side will take place – through the same porous boundaries. In this case the MB functions more as a firewall against radical ideas and elements through the de facto containment processes of politics. Keeping the above dynamics in mind, it is fair to say that the MB is in fact more receptive to the attractions of non-violence than it is susceptible to the allure of violence. In the long history of the group, the latter has proved to be bloody and costly, with little if any 'positive' outcome.

Examining the extensive experiences, events and case studies where the context was the ultimate determinant in shaping the violent or non-violent responses of the MB affirms the intimate link between the existing porous boundaries and the centrality of the context. A detailed examination goes beyond the space of this present discussion, but it suffices to review the overarching trajectory of the history of the MB and the main episodes therein. Such a review even in a very generic sense will indicate the crucial role of context in controlling the porous boundaries existing within the MB's attitudes and actions in relation to violence.

In their first years in Egypt, under the rule of King Farouk, the *Ikhwan* adhered to peaceful means, *da'wah* and charity work. The national context that allowed them to operate within the system was able to suppress intermittent calls for the use of force. This conduct continued until some aspects of that context, the presence of the British military along with the rise of Zionism in neighbouring Palestine, started to increase pressure on the MB to translate its reverence for jihad into action. The internal reaction was the reluctant setting up of the Special Apparatus in the late 1930s. As the political atmosphere in Egypt became more volatile because of the failures of successive governments, on the eve of defeat in the Palestine War in 1948 and the establishment of Israel, the context pressed further on the MB to become more jihadist, training its own military volunteers and sending them to Palestine. More traffic inside the group took place, across its internal porous boundaries, in the direction of violence and the use of force. A few years later, the brutal suppression of the MB by the Nasser regime further activated violent responses in terms of ideas and actions. In the late 1950s and into the 1960s it was Qutb's radical ideology that dominated the thinking and captured the suffering of the MB. Inside the prisons, many MB members became solidly radicalized, embracing Qutb's ideas and methods, believing in violence and leaving the traditional non-violent ideology of the Brotherhood behind (Pargeter, 2010: 180; Gerges 2005, 2006; Lacroix, 2012). It was a move through the porous boundaries of the MB that certainly occurred under the pressure of the imposing context.

In the early 1970s, with the release of many members of the Brotherhood from prison by President Sadat, Nasser's successor, a new chapter opened for the Brotherhood. Operating almost semi-legally, the radicalized ideas and tendencies of the MB began to wane, reversing the previous direction of the traffic to radicalism. Qutb's ideas started to recede with the wide and collective embrace of Hudaybi's ideas that harked back to al-Banna's original ideology. Radical voices and members continued to appear, since the crossover through the porous boundaries in both directions never stopped, but the volume was insignificant to that in the direction of moderation. Those MB radical voices and elements in most cases, if not all, ended up crossing through the porous boundaries that linked the group with outside radical organizations.

The 'Sadat context' was extended to the 'Mubarak context' where the basic contextual aspects remained the same: a blend of policies that tolerated or suppressed MB activities and presence in accordance with the regime's assessment and consideration of temporal matters. The *Ikhwan* grew strong in membership and influence, somewhat hijacking the role of the state itself in certain poor areas and in the provision of social services. Such rising power tempted some MB members and affiliates to ponder adopting a more aggressive posture against the state, yet the dominant paradigm remained gradual and non-violent. The 'Mubarak context', with the partial freedom that it allowed the Brotherhood, succeeded not only in promoting moderation within the movement, and reducing the traffic to more radical spheres, but also in advancing moderation within the MB to the point where some groups defected completely and created a more 'moderate' group, the *al-Wasat* (Centre) Party.[19]

The next testing context was the Arab Spring, the MB participation in the January revolution in Egypt and the subsequent events that led to the MB's electoral victory and assumption of power in Egypt in June 2012. In the two weeks of the popular revolution that led to the fall of Mubarak on 11 February, the Brotherhood participated reluctantly at the beginning, then geared up to full participation in response to the increasing weakness shown by the Mubarak regime. Other forces of the revolution accused the MB of opportunistic policies, keeping one foot in the revolution and the other outside in order to backtrack in case the revolution failed. In fact, the MB's calculated behaviour towards the revolution reflected the deep 'taming' that the organization had gone through during the Sadat and Mubarak years, where tendencies toward violence had almost been torn out by the roots. The new context of the revolution allowed the *Ikhwan* to take part cautiously, at the lowest possible risk, in the confrontation with the security forces. Because the revolution was short, mostly peaceful and quickly succeeded in toppling the regime, it did not pose a fundamental challenge to the *Ikhwan*'s commitment to non-violence. The *Ikhwan* could indeed claim that they participated peacefully and fully in the revolution alongside all other Egyptian forces, and that any violence involved was in fact deployed by the state (Hamid, 2014).

The real test for the Brotherhood, however, came with the aggressive intervention of the Egyptian army in the political process after one year of the *Ikhwan*'s rule, resulting in the dismissal of their president and his replacement by the head of the army, 'Abd al Fattah al-Sisi, in July 2013. Most objective assessments consider that this was a military coup that deprived the MB of the legitimate power it had gained through free and fair elections. Under the new military regime, 'Sisi's context', the MB leaders and thousands of their members were either jailed – including the ousted president himself who was charged with collaboration with Hamas and selling out state secrets – or forced to flee the country. Dozens if not hundreds were killed in clashes or by targeted assassinations. The bitterness, anger and sense of victimhood that had prevailed during the 'Nasser context' and influenced Qutb's production of radical ideas now returned in full force.

On balance, and after the passage of four harsh years for the *Ikhwan* in Egypt, and despite the high costs that they have paid, they still by and large adhere to the commitment that they made: that they will fight back and confront the new military in Egypt through peaceful means only. Before his arrest by the Sisi regime, Muhammad Badi', the current General Guide, addressed angry mass gatherings in Cairo opposing the intervention of Sisi and the army, and declared what seemed to be the ultimate commitment of the *Ikhwan* to peaceful means: 'Our revolution [against the Sisi military coup] is peaceful and it will remain peaceful. Our peacefulness is stronger than bullets.' As of the time of writing, this mantra seems to have been respected despite the swirling context surrounding the MB and its members.[20]

The experience of MB branches outside Egypt attests to the centrality of the context in controlling violent tendencies (see Ayoob, 2008; Masoud, 2013). Most accounts of Islamism would agree that more repression yields more radical and extreme responses and groups, whereas political engagement on the part of Islamist parties helps to moderate and 'pacify' them.[21] This is seen in the moderating effect that has resulted from the involvement of Muslim Brotherhood branches in the political process in the likes of Algeria, Jordan, Kuwait, Morocco, Tunisia and Yemen. In most of these cases the Islamist organizations that take part in politics, mostly through parliamentary elections or power-sharing, become more moderate and immersed in day-to-day realities than stuck in utopian ideals.[22]

Finally, there is a need to emphasize the other layer of the context/porous boundaries dynamics that goes beyond the internal elements of the Brotherhood itself. As indicated in the introduction, porous boundaries also exist between the MB, as an organization led mostly by non-violent leaders, and other violent/jihadist groups that might attract disfranchised members of the Brotherhood. This dynamic becomes more active when internal pressure by the angry and force-oriented members fails to compel the leadership to change strategies. Those members, or some of them at least, leave the organization and seek more radical and jihadist groups. The Brotherhood is still facing the violence/non-violence test imposed on it by the omnipresent 'Sisi context', and the jury is still out. The Badi' statement that 'our peacefulness is stronger than bullets' is still by and large the view of the vast majority of the Brotherhood. However, it is legitimate to ask if this commitment could withstand all the internal and external pressures facing the *Ikhwan* and tempting them to break away and flood the porous boundaries on the side of the bullets.

2

Understanding ISIS:
The Interplay between Ideology and Context

Hassan A. Barari

Introduction

In his introduction to this book, Peter Sluglett raised a key question as to why violent non-state actors play such an important role in the Middle East. A quick glance at the politics of the Middle East reveals that states are not the only actors in this part of the world. To be sure, the emergence of some homegrown non-state actors in the Middle East over the last two decades has given rise to much speculation as to how deep rooted their achievements actually are. This chapter is an attempt to offer an explanation for the endemic phenomenon of violent non-state actors by focusing on the Islamic State (henceforth referred to as ISIS) in Iraq and Syria. Its initial victory over the Iraqi army in 2014 shocked the world, and although ISIS is now in retreat – thanks to the American military efforts in leading a military coalition – many observers are still grappling with its rise and appearance in the first place.

While this chapter examines the rise and almost demise of ISIS, it also attempts to deconstruct the political context that has made radicalism more or less ubiquitous in the Levant. In doing so, I argue that ISIS is, by and large, not an Islamic or religious phenomenon, but a political one. Socio-economic and political realities and pressures have made many people susceptible to the message of radicalism, and these factors, rather than specific religious beliefs, are behind much of the radicalism in the region. That being said, this chapter does not downplay the relative influence of a certain interpretation of the religious texts and how they are manipulated to help recruit militants. Since the main objective of the book is to help understand and document various violent political movements, this chapter is my modest contribution to shedding some light on the root causes for the emergence of ISIS as a violent non-state actor.

With the onset of the 'Second Arab Awakening'[1] in early 2011, both Syria and Iraq became fertile ground for sectarian violence and eventually for the sudden and spectacular rise of ISIS. With the more or less simultaneous eruption of the Arab Spring,[2] sectarian tensions – already aggravated by the external intervention in Iraq eight years earlier – pitted Shias against Sunnis, thus making a radical militant group such as ISIS an appealing choice for many Sunnis, both in Iraq and, eventually, as the civil war continued, in Syria. ISIS' conquest of vast swathes of territory in both Iraq and Syria attracted many disenfranchised Iraqi Sunnis as well as some 30,000 foreign fighters. Much to the chagrin of moderates in the Arab world, ISIS excelled in pursuing a sophisticated social media campaign that has helped to recruit radical Muslims from around the world. Its far-reaching propaganda machine transformed the group into the new magnet of jihadi militants. It goes without saying that both Iraq and Syria have become the number one destinations for a third wave of global jihadists and dedicated Islamic extremists.[3]

Key to understanding the emergence of ISIS is an appreciation of the general political context that has, by and large, shaped intra-state as well as inter-state political interactions in a region that has proved largely impervious to the three waves of democracy that have characterized most of the world outside Europe and North America. Observers and political commentators have already focused on the ideological roots of this phenomenon, centring their argument on one simplistic idea: that militants are driven by a strict and narrow interpretation of an ideology. Statements and apoplectic rants made by key leaders of ISIS tend to reinforce this notion of the ideological dimension of the radical movement. Too much focus on ideology can only give credence to the Islamophobic conviction that as a religion, Islam is inherently dangerous regardless of the context. Hence, if we take this argument at face value we end up blaming the religion rather than the perpetrators themselves.

While this chapter does not downplay the significance of ideology in this part of the world, it argues that there is a different and additional story to tell. In doing so, the chapter highlights and examines the framework of dictatorial or repressive violence as a main driver of radicalism. The French historian Jean-Pierre Filiu offers new insights into the discussion of ISIS when he argues that the neo-*Mamluks*, or the 'Arab Security mafias', are the key reason behind the emergence of the Islamic State.[4] Filiu makes the case that the various internal security services have played a paramount role in shaping the politics of the Middle East. The 'Deep State', he argues, is determined to hold on to power, thus undermining both the Arab uprisings and the transition to a more democratic consensus.

Seen in this way, I argue that rather than considering the ruthless behaviour of ISIS and its viciousness an oddity, it makes more sense to examine it as an integral part of the ever-present climate of 'structural violence' that has been the hallmark of most Arab countries and societies since at least the 1960s. Hence, analysing the rise of ISIS within the framework of the repressive and authoritarian violence pervasive in the region can yield a better understanding both of the root causes of radicalism and how to rein it in. Without unpacking the political context, we run the risk of becoming misled into believing that ideology alone is behind radicalism and terrorism. This sort of wrong focus can only lead to the emphasis on battling terrorism while turning a blind eye to radicalism.

That being said, I argue that the repressive framework is not confined to an autocratic political framework, as in the case of Egypt or Libya, but also a sectarian framework, as has become the case in both Iraq and Syria. ISIS has exhibited an even more violent and more thoroughly sectarian nature than al-Qaeda. It is hard to avoid the conclusion that the failure of political and historical reconciliation in Iraq, as well as the lack of an effective, inclusive, democratically elected government, created a context conducive for ISIS to flourish.

Moreover, ISIS as well as other militant groups can burgeon within the context of the endemic chaos that has come to define much of the region since the fall of Saddam's regime in 2003 and again since the beginning of the Arab Spring in 2011. This has been more obvious in countries such as Libya, which suffers from a substantial political vacuum. With the onset of the Arab Spring, some societies (Libya, Syria, Yemen) have more or less disintegrated and thus the moral authority of the state and its institutions has come under question. As a corollary, older forms of identity – whether tribal, sectarian or ethnic – rather than notions of national identity have come to play a key role in regional political constellations. In these circumstances, ISIS served as an attractive model.

This chapter attempts to offer an in-depth answer to two key, interrelated questions. The first question has to do with the role of sectarian identity in shaping the thinking and modus operandi of ISIS. If anything, ISIS does not operate in a vacuum, and indeed, the politics of identity – aggravated by external intervention – has helped ISIS come to the fore with gusto. A second question is linked to the role played by the political context that has given impetus to the rise of radical Islamism in the Middle East.

Accordingly, this chapter is divided into three sections. The first section sets the historical scene that has helped radical movements, ISIS in particular, emerge and flourish in a tumultuous region. The second examines the sociology of violence and how the autocratic framework, whether sectarian or political, has paved the way for radicalization. A third section addresses radicalism as the root cause of terrorism. In this section, I make the case that allocating resources to fight terrorism is necessary, but by no means sufficient, to uproot radicalism and prevent it from pervading the societies of the Middle East.

The historical context

In the summer of 2014, the world was stunned to see Jihadi fighters belonging to ISIS combining religious fanaticism and some military expertise to inflict spectacular defeats on the seemingly well-equipped Iraqi army. Many observers were in disbelief when the Iraqi army retreated, leaving huge quantities of modern US weaponry behind. Within a short time, ISIS chalked up clear victories against Syrian, Iraqi and Kurdish armed forces.

Jolted by swift ISIS victories and the fear of its expansion in Syria, the United States began its sporadic bombing campaign on 23 September 2014. American effectiveness in battling ISIS was initially compromised by objective political realities. First, President Obama was adamant not to have 'boots on the ground'. Instead, the American strategy centred on a very simple idea: to have an Iraqi partner in the fight against ISIS and thereby to entice the Sunni community away from it. It was hoped that Iraqi Sunnis would be mobilized and turn against ISIS, thus helping defeat the organization. Unfortunately for the US plan to defeat ISIS, there were obvious disadvantages in choosing the Iraqi *government* as a potential ally in this fight, since it became largely sectarian in nature and proved largely unwilling to share power, money and jobs with the Sunnis. By and large, Sunnis see the Iraqi government as nothing but a sectarian one, only representing a Shia community intent on the exclusion of Sunnis. Not surprisingly, many Sunnis in the region were less afraid of ISIS than of the Iranian-backed and Iraqi Shia-controlled government. Hence, the US failed to eradicate ISIS in both Iraq and Syria using this strategy; the only partners it could rely on were elements among the Kurds, whose activities are generally opposed by the US' 'partner', Turkey.

Many pondered how long ISIS could hold out against the might of a broad coalition that included great powers with unmatched military capabilities. Yet in spite of the international coalition's bombardment of ISIS throughout Syria and Iraq, the coalition's military success was relatively modest. To answer the question of how ISIS resisted this powerful enemy, it is worth examining the historical context that allowed ISIS to emerge and prosper.

Interestingly, although the media seems profoundly obsessed with ISIS, it seems that ISIS is still fenced in by walls of ambiguity. This is especially true among some Arab intellectuals who are enamoured of the idea that ISIS was created by the United States,[5] an example of the kind of obsessive conspiratorial thinking that is pervasive throughout much of the Middle East. Many refer to Hillary Clinton's view that American hesitancy in the first stage of the Syrian revolution helped ISIS emerge.[6] Of course, there are others who insist that ISIS is nothing but an *Iranian* invention, and that the embattled Syrian president released hundreds of ISIS members from Saydnaya prison in September 2011 in order to infuse the revolution with Islamist terrorism. Indeed, many of ISIS' militants were former inmates of the prison who were radicalized by their experience in jail. Needless to say, some even accuse Turkey and other Gulf states of funding and arming ISIS, and it is of course true that apart from its setting up an Islamic caliphate, most of ISIS' ideology is almost indistinguishable from the Wahhabi doctrine that functions as the 'official ideology' of Saudi Arabia. What mars most of these analyses is the fact that authors often seek relevance at the expense of rigour. Furthermore, apocalyptic rants from members of ISIS and some Western elected officials or media commentators have in a sense destroyed any type of grey zone, thus creating a kind of hate speech on both sides of the divide. Few, if any, examine the conditions that allowed such radicalism to take root.

Influenced by dogmatic and untested ideas of the neo-cons about regime change, President George W. Bush ordered his army to invade Iraq in 2003, thus unleashing a series of events whose impact would be felt far across the region. Explicit in the American official discourse was the desire to 'democratize' Iraq and empower the Iraqi opposition, who had until then lived mostly in the diaspora. The Iraqi opposition parties, long fragmented, coalesced around two straightforward ideas: removing Saddam Hussein and bringing 'democracy' to Iraq, which involved a programme of de-Ba'thification and Shia empowerment, which involved positive discrimination in favour of the Shia majority.

The conventional wisdom on authoritarian stability was shattered in one stroke. It seems to have been believed that change in Iraq in 2003 would pave the way to set up a model of democracy for the region. Fourteen years after regime change in Iraq, that country is far from being either stable or democratic. While the Americans were celebrating 'mission accomplished', a Jordanian jihadi – Abu Mus'ab al-Zarqawi – had a different opinion. Having experienced the shock of the new American project of empowering the Shia majority at the expense of Sunnis, he started planning an insurgency campaign that would, in less than a decade, reach a pinnacle of violence. He formed an organization called 'al-Qaeda in Iraq', which was at first recognized but later disavowed by 'al-Qaeda central'.

Casting aside the role of ideology, one can cite two factors that helped al-Zarqawi build what later became ISIS. The first is the thoroughly ill-advised American policies in remaking Iraq. The US policies, of dissolving the Iraqi army, de-Ba'thification and courting all parts of Iraqi society except the Sunnis, contributed to the Sunnis' belief that they were going to be politically excluded from the new Iraq. The new regime in Iraq was fast becoming sectarian in nature and autocratic in essence. Secondly, Iran took advantage of the new situation and began to dominate Iraq by expanding its influence over Shia political forces. By propping up the Shias and simultaneously excluding the Sunnis, Iran helped make the Sunnis feel even more apprehensive about the unfolding situation. Amid this emerging reality, al-Zarqawi capitalized on Sunni grievances and managed to create a safe haven for his Salafi jihadi group among the Sunni community. He became a wild card in Iraq and his eventual death in 2006 did not weaken the rationale of the organization he had created.

Al-Zarqawi's ability to recruit fighters was also enhanced by regional developments. Syria, for instance, feared the discourse of the neo-conservatives about regime change through the spread of democracy in the Middle East. It is therefore not unnatural in this case that Syria would have preferred to see the Americans fail in Iraq. As a corollary, turning Iraq into a quagmire for American troops proved handy. Like-minded states colluded with the fighters who were seeking to get to Iraq to fight American troops. At least until late 2004, President Asad of Syria turned a blind eye while hundreds, if not thousands, of foreign (and Syrian) fighters crossed from Syria into Iraq to join the battle against the American occupation. In a few years, Iraq turned into a hub for al-Qaeda, with al-Zarqawi as its undisputed point man.[7] Given al-Zarqawi's aggressive mindset, the organization would take a more bloody turn.

Although al-Zarqawi's oath of allegiance was made to Osama bin Laden of al-Qaeda, he was by no means subservient to al-Qaeda in terms of vision or even strategy. Differences between al-Zarqawi and al-Qaeda, albeit hidden from public view, were of paramount significance and would account for the eventual divorce between al-Zarqawi's successors – particularly Abu Bakr al-Baghdadi – and al-Qaeda. Equally important, the character of al-Zarqawi and his stubbornness may help us understand his quasi-independence from al-Qaeda. While he did not part ways with Osama bin Laden on the need to fight the Americans, he established a defiant mindset among his followers in Iraq, who began to see the priorities of jihad in a diametrically different manner.

If anything, the politics of identity played a key role in shaping al-Zarqawi's worldview. America's ill-advised policies in the immediate aftermath of the occupation of Iraq contributed in no small way to the disintegration of Iraqi society. Soon, the societal fault-lines began to take a sectarian tone. It was in the context of Shia control of the political process –made possible by the complicit and unforeseen consequences of the American position and the growing influence of Iran in Iraq – that sectarian identities manifested themselves in ways that damaged the prospects for political reconciliation. Sunnis in Iraq felt that they were alone and unprotected, and that the emerging new order in Iraq would not only be at their expense, but also would exclude them from public life.

Al-Zarqawi was quick to capitalize on the Sunni sense of exclusion. When he set up *al-Tawhid w'al-Hijrah* (the forerunner of AQI) in 2003, he played up the identity issue. In a meticulous way, he began to incite a sectarian war against the Shias. His calculation was straightforward: Sunnis would join his organization against the infidels. In his many statements and speeches, he referred to the Shias as lurking snakes and a creeping enemy.[8] Thus, fighting the Shias occupied a central pillar in al-Zarqawi's worldview, and would continue to do so until his death in 2006. When he died, he left behind some coherent guidelines to allow his followers to pick up where he left off. When the 'Islamic State of Iraq' was declared in October 2006, the fixation with this identity-based approach continued unchecked. This trajectory would manifest itself more clearly when the Syrian crisis erupted. Against this backdrop, ISIS came into being.

While this organization is evidently rooted in Salafi jihadi ideology, one should not be oblivious to the emerging context that made such an ideology relevant, and equally important, the final divorce between al-Qaeda and ISIS. The key bone of contention between the two organizations centres on their different sets of priorities, a struggle in which al-Qaeda had to submit, out of necessity.[9] Indeed, the establishment of al-Qaeda and later ISIS in Iraq passed through four stages. In the period between 2004 and 2006, al-Zarqawi established 'al-Qaeda in Mesopotamia'. During this stage, the organization targeted both American and Shia forces. This period came to an end with the death of al-Zarqawi in 2006. Soon, the radicals established the Islamic State in Iraq (ISI), only to find themselves under attack toward the end of the American occupation of Iraq. America's clear strategy with the awakening (*sahwa*) helped defeat ISI. But with the onset of the Arab uprisings in 2011, ISI took advantage of the emerging chaos and declared the establishment of ISIS. At this point, President

Obama withdrew the last US forces from Iraq, and hence created a vacuum in which ISI became much stronger. The new emerging rift between al-Qaeda and its al-Nusra branch in Syria on the one hand and ISI on the other hand led to the establishment of ISIS, and paved the way for the fourth stage after June 2014, when ISIS chalked up major victories, now controlling a huge chunk of Syria and Iraq and also many of the oil wells of the region. Emboldened by its victories, ISIS established an 'Islamic State' or 'Islamic Caliphate' headed by Abu Bakr al-Baghdadi.

During the early stages of the attack on Saddam's regime, jihadists had begun to change much of the old rhetoric of al-Qaeda. Now in line with the jurisprudential principle of *al-Wala' wal-Bara'* (loyalty towards Muslims and disavowal of infidels), al-Zarqawi declared his new doctrine that stated that there was no distinction between a foreign enemy (= the far enemy) and those Muslims who collaborated with the infidels (Shias included). The final split between al-Qaeda and ISIS led to polarization. Each one followed a different modus operandi, with ISIS cultivating a reputation of brutally targeting its adversaries, particularly the Shias, and forcing local populations under its control to implement Islamic religious law. It is this point that gave ISIS – as a new and highly effective non-state actor – its hallmark.

In a nutshell, the emergence and development of ISIS is circumstantial. The demise of Saddam's regime led to a security vacuum and a political environment fraught with uncertainty. During the nine-year US occupation of Iraq, the Americans did not succeed in establishing an effective army, nor adequate security forces to fill the vacuum created by the fall of the Ba'thist state. Equally important, given the imbalances that the US invasion created, the political empowerment of the Shias took place at the expense of the Sunnis. The lack of an inclusive democratic government, coupled with the presence of a particularly sectarian prime minister, Nuri al-Maliki (2006–14), turned Iraq into a hostile place for the majority of the Arab Sunni population. Against this backdrop, ISIS slowly but surely came to the fore. The nine years that followed the demise of Saddam were fraught with problematic developments. Nevertheless, the context is more complicated. As Peter Sluglett noted in the introduction of this book, 'in the context of the history of the region, such movements are partly an entirely new phenomenon, partly related to the "unfinished business" of the colonial and postcolonial eras, partly to what seems to be the characteristically unstable nature of most Middle Eastern states, and partly to the tacit encouragement of the Wahhabi/Salafi/jihadi da'wa by some regional powers'.

Structural and cultural violence

The term 'structural violence' is not a new one. It refers to a situation where the social structure may hurt people by denying them the potential to obtain their basic necessities. In his seminal study on this issue, Johan Galtung made a useful distinction between three key concepts that make up what he calls the violence triangle: structural violence, cultural violence and direct violence. Both structural and cultural violence lead to direct violence, whereas the latter reinforces the former.[10]

Structural violence takes place when a certain class, or sect in this case, is seen to have more access to social goods than other classes or sects. It is a situation where an unequal advantage is ingrained in the social, political and economic systems that govern the dynamics of a given society. At this point, personal suffering is linked with social, cultural and political choices. Equally important, cultural violence is linked to dominant beliefs and attitudes ingrained since childhood about the utility and importance of violence.

We have witnessed various forms of direct violence in both Iraq and Syria, where the victims are mainly Sunnis (although it should be emphasized that Sunnis form 70 per cent of the population of Syria). Ethnic cleansing, humiliation and repression are the hallmarks of the approach used by the ruling Shia elite in Iraq and the Asad regime in Syria. The many militias affiliated with the Syrian and Iraqi regimes (and, to be fair, their opponents) have committed many atrocities, including rape and even ethnic and sectarian cleansing. Indeed, the omnipresence of both structural and cultural violence in Iraq and Syria produced two different yet interrelated outcomes: chaos and the emergence of ISIS as a model to balance structural violence. Ever since ISIS gained a foothold in a conflict-torn zone in the Middle East, the regional power dynamic has shifted significantly. It seems that politicians are still engaging in the blame game for the rise of ISIS.

With the onset of the so-called Arab Spring in 2011, some key countries – Syria and Iraq in particular – became in essence 'failed states'. Of course, Iraq was on the slippery path towards becoming a failed state long before the advent of the Arab Spring. Chaos rather than stability characterized the two states, and the Syrian civil war is being fought by proxies on both sides. In Aaron David Miller's words, ISIS

> ... emerged, gained power, and is now operating more effectively because it exists in an environment of failed or failing states. This, in an environment

notable for its lack of a viable order – authoritarian or otherwise – and a coherent state that can offer an alternative to IS by offering good, reliable governance, political inclusion, and economic opportunity to both sides of the Syrian–Iraqi border.[11]

This reality accounts, in part, for the advent of such an organization as ISIS.

Many commentators on Middle Eastern politics are not oblivious to the fact that several countries in the Middle East, not just Syria and Iraq, are not really functioning polities. Aaron David Miller observes that initially

> ... the contagion of bad governance (or no governance at all) could be contained as a 'local' problem. But alas, that is not the case: the Arab world is melting down. Libya and Syria are torn apart by civil war; Iraq is decentralizing; Yemen now faces a determined Houthi insurgency; the Lebanese state has lacked the capacity to control its own territory for years, and the putative state of Palestine is riven with political divides.[12]

Attention should therefore be paid to the endemic anarchy that has befallen the Middle East during the second decade of the twenty-first century. The ascent of ISIS is better understood within the context of the prevalent climate of 'structural violence' that has dominated the scene over the last few years.[13] Even a brief glance at many of the Arab uprisings clearly shows that the anarchy is more or less ubiquitous. At the time of writing, Libya, Syria, Iraq and Yemen are a shambles. Additionally, Egypt's situation is far from benign, with a military dictatorship running the country while the Sinai Peninsula has degenerated into anarchy and has become largely uninhabitable thanks to the presence of radical militants affiliated with ISIS. In Syria, a fusion of arms and money is coming from almost all regional backers of the various sides of the conflict. In a sense, the battle is not only *in* Syria but also *for* Syria.

The best example of the 'failing state' is arguably to be found in Iraq. As mentioned earlier, Iraqi politicians – empowered first by the American occupation of Iraq and then by the growing influence of Iran – failed miserably to build a new nation based on inclusive democratic institutions. To the vast majority of Sunni Iraqis, and indeed the Kurds, the present central government in Baghdad is nothing but an embodiment of Iraqi Shia identity. Worse, successive central governments in Baghdad have been accused of being puppets of Iran. To be sure, the latter played the sectarian card to secure a strong foothold in Iraq. By design or default, Iranian influence in Iraq has had a negative effect on the political process and indeed has blocked what might have been processes of historical and political reconciliation between the various components of Iraqi society.

Not surprisingly, the sectarian nature of the Iraqi government has alienated the Sunnis who see the government as anti-Sunni. Explicit in the attitudes of Sunnis in Iraq, as well as Syria, is that the moral authority of the state has come under question. Nationalism has largely ceased to be an identity that represents all Iraqis or all Syrians. With the failure of the state and with the descent into anarchy and insecurity, people began to identify with sub-national identities, such as tribes and sects, for protection.

This climate of ever-present structural violence has led, in part, to the rise of ISIS, but equally important, to the present relevance of ISIS as an attractive model in other areas such as Libya. Seen from a different perspective, the rise of this model – bad as it may look – can work for people who experience traumatic situations. It is the context, rather than the ideology, that makes ISIS and like-minded groups relevant for some people. It follows that as long as sectarian politics continue unchecked, little can be done to repel or limit ISIS, let alone to prevent the emergence of other militant groups. In other words, these organizations are always bound to surface as long as the Sunni predicament in Iraq and Syria is not solved in an acceptable manner.

Indeed, the situation in Iraq and Syria is by no means exceptional. When the United States toppled the Taliban regime in Afghanistan in the wake of the terrible attacks of September 2001, many observers were quick to hail the occupation as a clear defeat for al-Qaeda and the Taliban. And yet, military victory did not last for long, and did not in the final analysis translate into a political victory for the Afghan people. The lopsided political process led to instability, and Afghanistan is far from being a post-conflict zone. Certainly, various offshoots of al-Qaeda resurfaced, specifically ISIS. All the political and military investment in fighting al-Qaeda did not succeed in wiping out such organizations once and for all, simply because the conditions that have produced these organizations are omnipresent now in Iraq, Syria and Libya.

Important as it may be, defeating ISIS requires much more than the military dimension. Inflicting defeat on ISIS may not generate regional stability nor strengthen Arab societies or make them immune to the radical message. Again, when the Taliban regime fell apart, no one seems to have foreseen the turbulent time ahead, and therefore little attention was paid to the growing conditions of instability. Unfortunately, politicians underestimated the resolve and determination of the radical militants to hold their ground.

It is evident that the region is not heading toward the same old balance of power. Nor is it heading toward a more peaceful future, given the failure of the Arab uprisings to bring about stability and democratic governance, although, with hindsight, that was far too much to have expected. In some places, particularly Tunisia and Egypt, the autocratic past was dismantled painstakingly and with vigour, but future stability is far from certain. Hence the future may be fraught with disorder, chaos and primitive affiliations. In other words, the autocratic stability model is not in competition with a democratic model, but rather with a radical model, which is fixed on setting agonizing conflicts in motion. In short, the emergence and relevance of this model may serve as a good reminder – and herein lies the crux of the matter – of the need to understand and address the conditions that turn 'ordinary people' into radicals, an issue to be considered in the following sections.

Radicalism vs terrorism: a paradigm shift

The wealth of evidence gathered suggests that a better, and more effective, way of pulling the rug out from under the feet of the terrorists, and of winning over their societies, entails rethinking the sequences of terrorism and radicalism, and strategizing accordingly. In this section, I argue that there is a need to devise a strategy not only to fight against terrorism, but also to address the root causes of radicalism, especially in the Islamic world.

In his study on the need to fight radicalism, Omer Taspinar of the Johns Hopkins University sketches out the polarizing debate in the United States about 'the underlying causes of violent extremism in the Islamic world'.[14] On the one hand, there are those who argue that the best way of defeating terrorism is by focusing on the conditions that create terrorism. In other words, it is not enough to dedicate resources to fight terrorism, but instead the focus must be on preventing radicalism, given that prevalent socio-economic and political conditions (poverty, isolation, lack of economic and social opportunity) make many people susceptible to the message of terrorists. Thus, fighting radicalism – they argue – provides the best possible approach for defeating terrorism, for a number of reasons.

In the first place, radicalism is linked to the ideological and political dimension of the threat. For this reason, 'no matter how diverse the causes, motivations, and ideologies behind terrorism, all attempts at premeditated violence against civilians share the traits of violent radicalism'.[15] Second, unlike terrorism – which is deemed a lethal security challenge – radicalism is a *political* challenge. Hence, a political approach, rather than a coercive one, should be considered in dealing with radicalism. It is not clear yet when a radical turns into a terrorist. In fact, not all radicals are terrorists whereas all terrorists are radicals. Hence, one could make the case that focusing on radicalism is the best preventive strategy, not only to weaken terrorists, but also to prevent their message from resonating widely among radicals. It is at this stage that non-coercive measures could pay off. Third, one should pay attention to the radicalized social habitat. It is hard to avoid the conclusion that radicalized societies suffer from structural violence and a deep-seated sense of deprivation, humiliation and frustration. Among these societies, there may be a degree of support for terrorists.

On the other hand, there are those who are not really moved by the arguments advanced by the first school of thought. The correlation between socio-economic and political conditions and terrorism is dismissed by those who make the case that many terrorists are neither poor nor uneducated. They argue that the majority of terrorists come from the middle class and indeed are, or often are, educated. Unlike the first school of thought, in this case, terrorism should be dealt with as a security threat with no socio-economic dimension. The remedy, according to proponents of this line of thinking, is to 'fight against Islamist terrorism with a single-minded focus on state actors, jihadist ideology, counter-intelligence, and coercive action'.[16]

Interestingly enough, extreme Islamist organizations such as ISIS do not speak for 'Islam', nor do they enjoy the backing of ordinary Muslims. Recently, a Doha-based organization released a poll in which 89 per cent of respondents in twelve Arab countries said that they were opposed to ISIS.[17] Even in non-Arab Muslim countries, the view of ISIS is almost entirely negative. In the aftermath of the Paris attack (November 2015), Pew Research Center conducted a poll in eleven Arab and Muslim countries. The overwhelming majority of people from Nigeria to Jordan to Indonesia expressed negative views of ISIS.[18]

Indeed, personal piety does not correlate with radical views. As clearly illustrated by John Esposito, terrorists do appeal to religious or political convictions to recruit fighters or suicide bombers, as do others such as the Marxist Tamil Tigers in Sri Lanka when they appealed to Hindu identity to attract fighters and suicide bombers for their cause. Even many of those who condoned the terrible attacks of 11 September 2001 defended their position in secular and worldly terms rather than by citing the Qur'an. One respondent in Indonesia said that the American government was too controlling and colonizing.[19] Hence, fears of occupation or political domination can serve as a driver of radicalism.

To sum up, the most successful way of handling terrorism is by addressing its root causes. In other words, radicalism is the key element behind terrorism. If this stage is defined, then there is a clear need to devise a strategy to deal with the socio-economic and political conditions that breed radicalism. Having established that a military approach in dealing with ISIS is far from enough, perhaps education and economic empowerment of the societies involved can serve as the best antidote to radicalization. As Robert Satloff argues, ISIS may be defeated, but it will appear again in a different form. This cycle, in his words, 'will be repeated until Sunni governments, societies and communities effectively snuff out the mindset and circumstances that allow such extremism to take root'.[20]

Apocalyptic rants from some radical Islamists should not distract us from the root causes of radicalism in this part of the world. The autocrats in the Arab world long played up the danger of radical Islam only to perpetuate their hold on power and maintain their relevance in the region. Many autocrats exploited the West's panic in the wake of the events of 11 September 2001 to secure more Western support for their regimes. In other words, some Arab leaders have used Islamism as a demon to frighten the West,[21] and to a considerable extent this tactic has paid off. Many Western countries continue to support undemocratic regimes such as in Egypt and Saudi Arabia and later provided what is called security rent (money provided by outside governments to maintain stability and security).

In *From Deep State to Islamic State*, Jean-Pierre Filiu argues that the various deep states have staged counter-revolutions in the wake of the failure of the Arab Spring, which has led, in part, to the emergence of ISIS:

> The Arab revolutions have been foiled – Tunisia apart – by successful counter-revolutions organized by the 'deep state'. In Syria – as in Egypt and Yemen – the deep state is the hard core of a regime that strongly resembles those of the Mamluks in Egypt and the Levant long ago.[22]

The ebb and flow of the conduct of the autocrats has, in part, created the dynamic for the emergence of Islamic State. According to Filiu, the Syrian neo-Mamluks are behind the rise of the Islamic state, not to mention the destruction of Syria.[23] The neo-Mamluk regimes have played with jihadi fire in their bid to defeat the Arab Spring, and in doing so they have contributed to the emergence of ISIS. One cannot help but argue that authoritarian regimes and their readiness to tolerate, or indeed foster, jihadi groups have been a key cause for the advent of ISIS.

If anything, the deep state acts outside the law. It is as if those in charge of the deep state deem themselves to be the custodians of the wellbeing of the nation or guardians of a higher interest that justifies them in doing what it takes to keep the state intact and immune to change. Whether by design or accident, the elite of the deep state believe that they should do what it takes. And this do-what-it-takes attitude is rooted in a patrimonial view of the state itself, and a paternalistic view of the citizen. In fact, both views reflect the deep state actors' view of collective self-interest. The term 'deep state' refers to a series of opaque and indeed secretive actors or institutions within the state who control key policy decisions hidden from public scrutiny.

In both Egypt and Syria, for instance, the deep state approach has been quite pervasive. The Egyptian counter-revolution was organized by the deep state partly to prevent the transformation of Egypt into a transparent democracy and partly to get rid of the Muslim Brotherhood once and for all. On the other hand, the history of the Syrian regime is characterized by the manipulation of politics by the deep state. Thus it should not be surprising that the number of those who hold distaste for these regimes is on the increase because of their undemocratic, repressive and kleptocratic character. Once a radical movement steps in to capitalize on this state of despair, there is a chance that the disgruntled population will not oppose it.

Conclusion

Emerging seemingly from nowhere, ISIS captured the attention of scholars, commentators and policymakers. Over the course of 2013–14, the appearance of this new movement led many long-time observers of Middle Eastern affairs to ponder whether we were witnessing a fundamental changes to the geographical contours of the Sykes–Picot Agreement of 1916.

This chapter has discussed the emergence of ISIS as a non-state actor and its notorious savagery by examining the context rather than the ideology that has bred the radicalism of non-state actors, with particular emphasis on ISIS. It has also placed ISIS within the broader global jihadist movement. The mantra that Salafi ideology generates terrorism became a convenient argument for many autocratic Arab leaders who sought to use Islamism as a bogeyman. Evidently, autocratic leaders have linked Islamists and terrorism to scare the West, and created the impression that the alternative to their undemocratic regimes is not democracy but Islamist terror. When Western leaders accept this reasoning they make a cardinal error because it is inaccurate to view ISIS as a purely terrorist organization.

While ISIS is an extension of the broader global jihadist movement in terms of ideology and perspective, its political and social genesis is rooted in the heart of the Levant, particularly in Iraq and Syria. With the blend of Iraq-based al-Qaeda and many former members of the all too hastily disbanded Iraqi army, one can talk about the Iraqization of the movement, which also accounts for its viciousness and lethal methods in addition to its various priorities.

As well as being an Islamic problem, ISIS is a political one. The US-led occupation of Iraq brought about a rupture in Iraqi society, although sectarianism in the form of anti-Shiism had been a feature of Iraqi policies since the war with Iran. Subsequent American policies – such as disbanding the army and de-Ba'thification –profoundly altered an increasingly fragile status quo. These ill-advised policies created a vacuum that triggered an unprecedented Sunni–Shia rift, allowing radical militants to gain a foothold.

The greater empowerment of Shias and the failure to bring about a political reconciliation among the warring factions in Iraq caused a rupture in the country's social fabric. Worse, the ascendance of Shias, coupled with the rise of Iran as the most influential actor in Iraq, led to the disempowerment of the Sunnis. All the Sunnis' legitimate complaints fell on deaf ears as al-Maliki's government began harassing Iraq's Sunni communities and leaders. Not surprisingly, the Sunni feeling of abandonment and discrimination created an important opening for radical Islamists to step in and champion their claims. ISIS managed to instrumentalize Sunni grievances, and hence was perceived as an actor capable of defending Sunnis in the face of the Iran-backed Shias, especially given the powerlessness of the state to protect them.

As observed in this chapter, ideology cannot be dismissed. However, there is a great deal of structural violence in both Iraq and Syria. The presence of unequal advantage in both Iraq and Syria is rooted in the political, economic and social systems. Given the lack of democracy or respect for diversity and pluralism, there has been a degree of cultural violence that is linked to the prevalent conviction that violence can pay off. This stance had an opening when chaos descended on Iraq and Syria.

Of course, a full appreciation of ISIS and its relevance has to be linked to the long history of the existence of autocratic regimes in the conflict-torn zone in the Middle East. Therefore, one should focus more on political and social contexts rather than ideology. For this reason, ISIS' outreach campaign targets disgruntled Sunni youth while also focusing on the 'near enemy' (Shias, other non-Sunni Muslim groups and 'heretical' non-Muslim minorities such as the Yazidis and *Ahl-i Haqq*).

There is no quick fix for this situation, but two points should be clear. First, ISIS is symptomatic of the dysfunctional political situation at the heart of the Levant and the spread of outsider-backed civil war in restive societies. Second, any solution to the Syrian conflict must put an end to the disintegration of the country and the continuation of the rivalry among warlords and militias. The continuation of the crisis – never mind the regional and global proxy wars in Syria – can and will always provide ISIS and like-minded groups with further support. Seen in this way, one can argue that emasculating ISIS entails approaching the Sunnis with a different bottom-up approach to degrade ISIS. Thus the Iraqi government needs to work with ordinary Sunni citizens to convince them that the government is inclusive and for all Iraqis regardless of their ethnic or sectarian backgrounds. For this to materialize, Sunnis need to be assured that they have a stake in the central government in Baghdad. As long as Sunnis view the Iraqi government as the epitome of Iranian-backed Shia hegemony, radical groups can exploit the rift not only in Iraq but also across the region. Indeed, ISIS is the product of both socio-economic and geopolitical realities dominant during the Arab Spring.

3

Between Religion, Warfare and Politics: The Case of Jabhat al-Nusra in Syria

Mohamed-Ali Adraoui

In the West, the threat posed by IS has become an understandable, but convenient obsession. However, Jabhat al-Nusra has embedded itself so successfully within the Syrian opposition – within the revolution for a long time – that in my view it has become an actor that will be much more difficult to uproot from Syria than IS. Islamic State is all about imposing its will on people, whereas al-Nusra has for the last five years been embedding itself in popular movements, sharing power in villages and cities, and giving to people rather than forcing them to do things.[1]

Like many other countries located in the increasingly unstable Arab region, Syria is no longer a sovereign state. It has ceased to be a single unified territory ruled by a specific entity claiming to exert a monopoly over the legitimate use of force. More damagingly, the common narrative that was supposedly shared by the whole national community has been fractured and fissured. New boundaries have appeared in the last five years, as well as new hierarchies of authority and identification. Increasingly, Syria seems to reflect a new mode of conflict, a form of experimentation in some sort of warfare which is completely new to the region in terms of figures (Iraq in the aftermath of the US invasion in 2003 had experienced this but not at the level of the transnational jihadi engagement which has been occurring for several years now in the Syrian context), one which could recur in the future, should the same sort of actors and dynamics present themselves. Despite its collapse in 2011, the regime has been able to mobilize certain political and military resources, both internal and external, thereby contributing to the present political flux in Syria. This flux has facilitated the entry of newcomers into the Syrian battlefield and largely contributed towards transforming the initial wave of protests into sectarian struggles.

Among the various dynamics, the appearance and rise of jihadi Salafi movements is undoubtedly one of the principal features dominating the Syrian conflict. The struggles, conflicts and interferences within the overall conflict are caused by the plurality of players whose agendas, strategies and ideologies often differ, with the result that players frequently find themselves unable to avoid interacting in some capacity on the battlefield.

Being both a cause and a consequence of the denominational and ethnic divides observed in Syria, the jihadi Salafis have been successful in capturing some parts of the territory and now represent a threat to what is left of the Assad regime as well as to major regional and world powers (Russia, France, United States, Turkey ...). However, these jihadi Salafis are also, at least symbolically, an easy target for other players, since their ideology, consisting primarily of radical violence against those whom they consider their enemies, provides a convenient justification for the offensives against them.

All jihadi Salafi groups take advantage of the increasing sectarian reflexes that have risen after the regime deliberately sought to weaken its opponents by framing the conflict as a religious confrontation, but they have nonetheless differed when dealing with local specificities. It seems that the main feature consistent across these groups is the aim to establish a global, transnational and unitarian Muslim state, with jihadis ruling the entire *umma*, through political radical reformation and violent militancy as mandated by their version of the legal-religious corpus (Sharia). However, certain jihadi actors have distinguished themselves by sinking their roots into Syrian realities and validating their presence and legitimacy in the language of nationalistic-motivated purposes. This is particularly the case of Jabhat al-Nusra li'l-Ahl al-Sham, whose ideology, strategy, evolution and sociology is the focus of this chapter. This 'Front of Support for the People of the Levant' (hereafter al-Nusra) proves to be a novel case of interest in analysing how a violent non-state actor can adapt its transnational, insurrectional and revolutionary purpose to accommodate the demands of an increasingly complex and externally supported civil war that has evolved from an attempt to initiate substantial domestic reform to calls for the overthrow of a regime that has enjoyed a ruling hegemony for more than forty-five years.

Where does al-Nusra come from, both ideologically and geographically? How has this religious, political, social and military movement been able to play a significant role in the struggle against the Syrian regime? What can explain how this group has morphed from a relatively marginal player into one of the most dominant actors within the strategic field? Indeed, the story of al-Nusra shows how a single jihadi network, with origins outside the area of immediate conflict, has successfully established itself in territory under siege and gained popular support from both international communities and locals by offering a strong counter-narrative designed not only to defeat the regime, but also to deter locals from supporting other Islamist or jihadi contenders on the ground.

This chapter will illuminate al-Nusra's ideological sources, modes of organization, strategies, integration processes and relations to other players of the rebellion, within Syrian territory over the last five years. Born in the realm of transnational jihadism, al-Nusra has nonetheless evolved into a nationalist-jihadist movement, in order to fit in with local demands and appeal to rebellious Syrians. In other words, al-Nusra has shifted from an imported phenomenon into a bicephalous movement capable of converting and translating national anti-regime feeling into a religious and radical agenda with local support. Having achieved over recent years a truly 'shifting web of affiliations and fluid structures' (Comerford, 2015), al-Nusra offers a meaningful illustration of how certain jihadi players might react and formulate their strategy when confronted with a conflict from which they were initially distanced, but in which they have been successful in validating their interference and solidifying their presence to modify both conflict narratives and power structures.

The origins of al-Nusra as an imported phenomenon: its ideological and regional roots

From the beginning of what has turned into a major civil and regional war (with huge international repercussions), the central aim of al-Nusra has been to topple the Assad regime in order to establish a 'Sunni Islamic State in Syria' (Comerford, 2015). As a Salafi and jihadi movement, al-Nusra leaders and fighters share a revolutionary and insurrectional orientation dedicated to the service of a fundamentalist and transnational project. Seeking the restoration of the Caliphate consistent with their understanding of Sharia law as the only permissible source of political and religious authority ruling all of the Muslims throughout the world (al-Umma), 'jihadis' argue that all modern territorial, political and intellectual concepts pertaining to how a society may be organized are irrelevant as long as they do not stem from their own understanding of Islam. In this view, religion goes beyond echoing a faith to informing political power, legislation and the modes of organizing the public sphere. This vision originates from an intransigent understanding of the creed that seeks to challenge the numerous evolutions impacting the Islamic societies that have arisen since the supposedly first and best generation of Muslims, knows as the 'Pious Ancestors' (al-Salaf al-Salih).

In this respect, as 'Salafis' (believers following the same path as al-Salaf al-Salih), jihadis consider that it is legitimate to use violence, for instance in the political field, to overthrow a regime that is apparently violating Islamic norms. Unlike 'quietist' or 'activist' Salafis who believe either in individual reformation through preaching, far from the path of political militancy or classical politicization (creating parties, running for elections, etc.), jihadis emphasize that to become better Muslims (al-Jihad) may require radical and vehement action, thereby justifying military violence against any actor appearing to be an enemy.

The construction of the Assad regime as truly 'unIslamic' is justified on the basis that it is secular, nationalist and ruled by heterodox Shias. In fact, for several years (since the rule of Hafiz al-Assad, 1970–2000), the regime has been accused of betraying 'authentic Islam', justifying the decree calling for it to be overthrown. Premised on the structuring concept of 'loyalty and disavowal' (al-Wala' wal-Bara') (Wagemakers, 2012), which is at the heart of jihadi thought, any collectivity that becomes religiously discredited is liable to be excommunicated and challenged forcibly, in order to replace it with a new and 'truly Islamic' religious and political order. The ending of any loyalty to the Assad regime makes way for the transfer of loyalty to an Islamic vanguard, offering to lead the fight against all sorts of enemies, before establishing the Caliphate. Principally made up of Syrian fighters, al-Nusra's story in Syria illustrates the successful integration within the national realm after military groups moved from Syria to Iraq with the aim of being part of the rebellion against the Ba'th government. Since the outbreak of the Syrian Revolution in 2011, the various jihadi groups present in Iraq, such as the Islamic State of Iraq, led by Abu Bakr al-Baghdadi, as well as the proliferation of al-Qaeda's leadership in some parts of Iraq after the ousting of Saddam Hussein's regime in 2003, have played a dominant role in reinforcing the jihadi bloc in Syria.

As it became clear that the Assad regime would not countenance a peaceful settlement, there arose a self-conscious radicalization of the opposition, pioneered by members of al-Qaeda and the Islamic State in Iraq, as well as the future head of al-Nusra, Abu Muhammad al-Jawlani. This resulted in the desire to establish a jihadi hub in Syria, particularly by recruiting fighters released by the Assad regime from the Saidnaya military prison in May–June 2011, notably after Decree 61 of 31 May 2011 (Lister, 2015). This was arguably the embryo that would give birth to the al-Nusra Front. A small band of seven fighters (led by al-Jawlani), known as the 'Khurasan group', came to Syria with the mission of contacting released jihadis and creating sleeper cells of what was intended to metastasize into a larger hub dedicated to a rebellion against the regime.

Between October 2011 and January 2012, high-level meetings chiefly in the area of Homs were organized so that fighters, mainly former members of Abu Musʽab al-Zarqawi's group in Iraq, starting with al-Jawlani, returned home to Syria to give birth to a military movement named 'Jabhat al-Nusra li'l-Ahl al-Sham' on 23 January 2012, which formed its first local jihadi cells in Hasakah Governorate. On this day, in a video posted on YouTube, the group calling itself 'Liberators of the Levant' (Ahrar al-Sham), related to al-Nusra, made the following statement:

> To all the Free People of Syria, we announce the formation of the Liberators of the Levant Brigades . . . we promise Allah, and then we promise you, that we will be a firm shield and a striking hand to repel the attacks of this criminal al-Assad army with all the might we can muster. We promise to protect the lives of civilians and their possessions from security and the Shabiha (pro-government) militia. We are a people who will either gain victory or die.

The endeavour to 'establish a group including many existing jihadists, linking them together into one coherent entity', with a dedication to 'reinforce and strengthen the consciousness of the Islamist nature of the conflict' (Quilliam, 2015), has rapidly made al-Nusra one of the most efficient and dreaded factions within the Syrian rebel forces. Using tried and tested tactics learned in their military struggle in Iraq, al-Nusra fighters and troops consisted of 300–400 soldiers in 2012 (Hurriyet, 2013), and around 6,000 fighters in 2014 (Rand Corporation, 2014), which represents around 9 per cent of the anti-regime forces today. Preliminary efforts by al-Nusra were reminiscent of classical terrorist attacks and fit into typical insurrectional strategies to defeat the regime and exert power over the territories they seized, especially as seen in January 2012 in the al-Midan district of Damascus, where it attacked riot police who were being ferried to an anti-government protest.

Similarly, in early 2012, al-Nusra made use of 'suicide bombings and remotely detonated car bombs' (Sherlock, 2012), leaving twenty-six dead, mainly civilians. In terms of its military achievements, an early success for al-Nusra was to inflict serious damage on the forces of the regime as well as the forces of the regime's proxies, such as Hezbollah. A contrasting duality began to define al-Nusra's identity and policy; it was arguably not a benign presence but the progress it had made in weakening the regime's forces was undeniable. This may explain the disparate perceptions of al-Nusra that exist within Syria. On 12 December 2012, the United States designated al-Nusra as a terrorist organization and an affiliate of al-Qaeda in Iraq. However, several factions of the Syrian rebellion, such as spokesmen of the Free Syrian Army and leaders of the Syrian National Coalition (Quilliam, 2015), have affirmed that al-Nusra is an integral force in leading the fight against the regime.

Al-Nusra's 'moderate' strategy: hitting the 'near enemy', obtaining local support and rooting into the society

Despite al-Nusra's avowed alignment with al-Qaeda's global strategic ambitions, it has clearly struggled to establish an Islamic Emirate ruled by religious legislation in Syria, and the eventual prospect of establishing a transnational Caliphate supposedly echoing the first centuries of Islam remains moot. In fact, al-Nusra's participation in the Syrian civil war has led it to adopt a more collaborative and flexible strategy.

From the beginning, al-Nusra's declared enemy has always been the regime and its allies and proxies. Unlike several other jihadi groups whose agenda has seemed to be more ambitious, such as the Islamic State of Iraq and the Levant (so renamed in 2013 after it was born in Iraq in October 2006 in the aftermath of the US invasion as the Islamic State of Iraq, and today known as Islamic State), al-Nusra has from early on engaged in a sort of nationalization process through which all military and political efforts were directed against the Assad regime and its supporters. Targeting this 'near enemy' as a matter of priority, al-Nusra has found resonance and relevance by matching the cardinal cause shared by all Syrian rebel groups that have mushroomed over the last couple of years. This exclusive focus on toppling the Ba'thist government through the mobilization of the local population has transformed the jihadi movement, to some extent, into a nationalist-jihadi armed force that is directly responding and reacting to the immediate political demands coming from the locals. While, ideologically and officially, some Western states and allies – regarded as 'far enemies'– are still described as iniquitous to Islam (the United States, Israel, etc.), al-Nusra's leaders have claimed since the early months of the Syrian conflict that their central goal is to overthrow Assad and combat his proxies and allies. Al-Jawlani, for instance, continued this line of rhetoric in 2015 by stating that the objective of al-Nusra is 'to accomplish one mission, to fight the regime and its agents on the ground, including Hizbullah and others'.[2]

In pursuit of this objective, some elements of jihadi principles have been downplayed when necessary, following the guidance of al-Qaeda scholars such as Abu Mus'ab al-Suri (Lia, 2008). Instead, emphasis is placed on the importance of responding to the needs of the population in order to appeal to them politically and enjoy a larger constituency from which to recruit soldiers. The same logic has been successively reinforced, and the current leader of al-Qaeda, Ayman al-Zawahiri, reaffirmed at the beginning of 2015 that al-Nusra should continue to rely on some key principles, such as (Lister, 2015):

- Fostering continual integration within the Syrian rebellion and local populations.
- Favouring all sorts of rapprochement with other Islamist and jihadi groups, and promoting closer military cooperation in order to generate more effective military operations.
- Unifying all the legal religious systems in the territories which are under their control.
- Focusing on the most strategic regions in Syria so as to offer a possible haven for al-Qaeda and affiliates in the future.
- Avoiding attacking the Western side to focus on the fight against the regime and its supporters.

In addition, as revealed in early 2014 by one of al-Nusra's top officials, Sami al-'Uraydi, the movement seeks to make its position in Syria more acceptable and legitimate by fostering the perception that it leads through 'people-oriented' policies. The substance of these policies involves services and social welfare; assessing security needs; avoiding being perceived as extremists, unlike the Islamic State, which is known to exert tougher religious control and mete out punishments to the populations it controls; maintaining strong relationships with local communities and other fighting groups (although divergences may exist); and putting the focus on combating the government's forces and allies.

Trying to appear as 'moderate fighters and rulers' according to Syrian standards at a time of bloody civil war, al-Nusra attempts to take advantage of the civilians' troubles and consolidate their position as an alternative to both the regime and other Islamic and rebellious groups. Mainly influential in the Sunni-majority areas in north-western Syria, this movement is based in Idlib Governorate, and was active in eleven of Syria's thirteen provinces, being present in places such Aleppo, al-Raqqah, Dayr el-Zawr and Dar'a, with Idlib its capital city. In January 2014, it was estimated that al-Nusra was in control of a dozen Syrian towns. In August 2015, however, the jihadi group announced that it would be withdrawing from the front line against the Islamic State in northern Syria, as Turkish and US military intervention in the region had greatly intensified.[3]

In 2012, al-Nusra saw a marked increase in its power and influence, owing largely to its success in attracting more foreign fighters, united by the desire to protect the Syrian majority. These foreign fighters saw themselves as sharing a common religious background with the Syrian population, as they were exclusively Sunni, and became invested in the domestic struggle to overthrow the regime, whose bedrock of support is mainly 'Alawi, a fairly localized sect, affiliated, however distantly, to Twelver Shiism. The success in recruitment over 2012 and 2013 was integral to al-Nusra's prestige and military success on the ground. There are differing estimates among experts as to the extent of this increase in recruitment but the consensus remains that the proportion of foreign fighters has unquestionably increased over the last four years. This development is not entirely unsurprising; a significant number of al-Nusra's members come from Iraq, where they had been affiliated to Islamic State, and joined the core of al-Nusra's early membership, namely the former prisoners released in 2011. And yet, al-Nusra cannot be defined simply as an extension of the main Iraqi jihadi movement in neighbouring Syria. Some argue that Syrians are still in the majority among al-Nusra members (more than 80 per cent), while others claim they have become a minority (Quilliam, 2015; Comerford, 2015) and that the 'motivations of foreign fighters in Syria are shifting away from a pure focus on protecting fellow Muslims (from Assad) toward an idealized image of living in a universal "Islamic State"[4] that is seen as already having been established' (Comerford, 2015).

Despite the obvious historical relations between al-Nusra and the Islamic State in Iraq, the civil war has not generated any merger, since al-Nusra's leaders, starting with al-Jawlani, have staunchly refused to cede control and have chosen to remain as an independent movement.

Admittedly, as has already been noted, a large part of al-Nusra's members come from Iraq and used to be part of what would become the Islamic State in 2013, which in turn allowed al-Nusra to gain power and win numerous battles in its first two years of existence. However, tensions between both organizations hit a high in 2012, when Abu Bakr al-Baghdadi unilaterally proclaimed the merger between the two forces on 8 April and al-Jawlani officially rejected it and renewed his pledge of allegiance to al-Qaeda, and more specifically to the Amir Ayman al-Zawahiri. Even as the Syrian affiliate of al-Qaeda, the Nusra Front continues to enjoy some real independence and its strategy of 'Syrianization' (although this is tactical) remains central, but divides and disputes between transnational jihadi groups and the rising influence of foreign fighters present major challenges to its dominance in the rebel coalition (Lister, 2015).

Military tactics, weaponry and political strategies

As the declared enemy, the regime and its proxies unsurprisingly have formed the main target of al-Nusra's military offensives. Since 2011, al-Nusra as a military force has been known for utilizing the tactics employed for years in Iraq against US troops and the regime's facilities, such as conventional assaults on military bases, car bombs, suicide attacks, the targeting of checkpoints and pro-government media stations and personnel and members of the Shabiha (the regime's militias), as well as the assassination of political and military figures. The group is notable for its targeting of government sites including attacks on areas of residence for 'Syrian military's general staff', 'the government's elite Air Force intelligence headquarters', 'state television building and security compounds' and the 'army officers' club' (Sherlock, 2012). Arguably, the suicide bomb attacks (such as those against a military base in the centre of Damascus) have 'shifted the balance of power away from the regime' by inflicting damage on strategic and 'well-guarded strongholds' (Sherlock, 2012), although the killing and maiming of civilian bystanders rather restricts the favourable reception the group receives.

By June 2013, the Front had claimed responsibility for fifty-seven suicide attacks that were targeted against the regime's interests in Syria. One year before, al-Nusra conducted several assaults on the government TV station in Drusha near Damascus. Furthermore, as both a cause and consequence of the rising sectarianism that increasingly colours the Syrian civil war, al-Nusra shares the view held by both Islamic groups and pro-regime forces, namely that the conflict is religious, one in which the 'true' defenders of Islam oppose the 'renegades'. This has further shaped how references to the enemy have evolved to include terms such as 'falsifiers of Islam' and how such terms have caused the spillover of the conflict, even as al-Nusra maintained that it was only anti-regime. In October 2015, for instance, al-Nusra deliberately targeted 'Alawi-majority towns and villages, mainly located in the area of Lattakia, regarding any community related to this religious affiliation as explicitly close to the government. As al-Jawlani declared, 'There is no choice but to escalate the battle and to target Alawite towns and villages in Lattakia.'[5]

At the same time, al-Jawlani officially offered a financial reward to anyone who killed President Assad and the head of Hezbollah, Hasan Nasrullah, both of whom are considered to be responsible for the situation on the ground and for the bloody fate of the Syrian people. Al-Jawlani's promise was to give 'three million euros for anyone who can kill Bashar al-Assad and end his story'.[6]

Today al-Nusra is recognized as one of the most effective Islamic armed groups involved in the Syrian conflict, having garnered a reputation as the 'most effective fighters in resistance to the Assad regime' (Riedel, 2013). This may be due to the training they have received from veterans of al-Qaeda in Iraq as well as from the military advice and materials provided by regional sponsors. In most cases, al-Nusra adopts a pragmatic military strategy through which commanders make 'tactical judgements about alliance and hostility' with the aim of achieving a 'detachment of military power from the ideology and affiliation' (Comerford, 2015). Such a strategy has been divisive: while it has attracted numerous fighters, especially from regions where the regime has conducted brutal military assaults, it has also created among some locals, and especially in the case of foreign fighters, a sense of disillusionment, as it was interpreted as a sign of weakness and reluctance to challenge the adversaries on an equal footing (Comerford, 2015).

The patronage of major regional powers (Turkey, Saudi Arabia, Kuwait, Qatar, etc.), and the funding, support and weapons from several networks related to these countries, has made al-Nusra one of the best-armed movements on the Syrian battlefield. It is estimated that 40 per cent of al-Nusra's needs are met by Saudi Arabia and Qatar,[7] particularly since al-Nusra has become part of the 'Army of Conquest' (see below). Turkey is also frequently evoked as one of the main supporters of the Front, especially since al Nusra, in addition to its fighting against the regime, is able to pressurize the Kurdish forces in north-western Syria that find themselves surrounded both by jihadi organizations and the Turkish army in some areas.[8]

Although it undoubtedly acts within the Syrian strategic landscape as a proxy fighter for the benefit of the anti-Iran objectives and anti-Assad motives of the regional powers, al-Nusra remains an independent actor with a very specific national purpose at the end of the day. As its leaders frequently highlight, the nationalization strategy it has adopted is a matter of expediency demanded by the military and political configuration of the Syrian landscape, which requires pragmatism and flexibility for the organization's survival. This is why certain sponsors like Qatar, aware of how problematic their support for an al-Qaeda affiliate could be, promised to boost funding for the Front Nusra if they change names and 'disengage from al-Qa'ida', in the hope that this would turn al-Nusra into a 'more traditional anti-state proxy force' (Comerford, 2015).

Yet another strategic relationship of interest is the one al-Nusra has with the Free Syrian Army, especially from 2011 to 2013, one that has enabled the jihadi movement to obtain some crucial weaponry, such as TOW missiles (extremely efficient anti-tank weapons), from the non-jihadi side and initially supplied to the FSA by Western actors like the United States.[9] This procurement of weapons has proved to be beneficial, as the first successes achieved by al-Nusra have made it possible to enlarge some of its initial Sunni support to a small area of neighbouring Lebanon, where the Syrian civil war has overflowed. Beyond reinforcing al-Nusra's prestige and popularity, expanding into Lebanon is also a way of 'smuggling ... foreign volunteers and weapons from across the border from' this location (Sherlock, 2012).

When it comes to the pernicious issue of foreign fighters, unlike the eager recruitment as part of the Front's 'Syrianization' policy, the inflow of recruits represents both a strategic advantage and a source of tension. Indeed, the 'extreme violence' that al-Nusra displays is caused by the 'recruitment of radical fighters from abroad to join Syrians', and this evolution has jeopardized al-Nusra's political and symbolical positions in areas like Idlib. This has further augmented the suspicions of local Syrians, who have found that though the Front's official purpose is to act in the framework of a Syrian perspective, actions contrary to the Syrian interest have been undertaken, making the Nusra Front appear increasingly like an occupying power. For instance, it appears that, in 2013, these 'Nusra fighters [including a significant proportion of foreigners] have begun unilaterally asserting control over five towns (Binnish, Harim, Sarmada, Darkoush, Salqin) in northern Idlib', provoking widespread protests from many locals (Lister, 2015). In this respect, the initial strategy, which consisted of al-Nusra 'ingratiating itself within the Syrian population rather than dominating it' (Gartenstein-Ross and Jawad al-Tamimi, 2015), has been fraught with tension and resistance. Part of the explanation for its increasingly contested presence is the fact that al-Nusra has clearly become, in some areas, 'caught up in some sort of ideological and factional struggle' (Lund, 2015). In fact, the notion of martyrdom seems to dominate the mind of many of al-Nusra's foreign fighters, as evidenced by an incident in May 2014, when an American citizen carried out an attack on the ground for the first time. The recruitment of individuals from Chechnya, other Arab countries and some European states (e.g. France, Belgium and the United Kingdom) has gained the Nusra Front the reputation of a jihadi operator appealing to foreigners. According to al-Jawlani himself, around 30 per cent of his fighting force come from abroad.[10]

Finally, in terms of media activism, al-Nusra has launched several initiatives with the objective of communicating with the rest of the population (starting with the people under its rule), other Islamic and rebellious groups, its adversaries and regional and world powers. Part of al-Nusra's public relations and propaganda efforts include the magazine *al-Risalah* (the Message), first issued in July 2015, as well as a media outlet called *al-Manarah al-Bayda* (the White Minaret), which is accessible through the highly influential jihadi forum, *Shumukh al-Islam* (the Greatness of Islam). These are designed to advertise the statements and videos of the leaders, celebrate the heroic actions undertaken by the fighters and send cautionary messages to the Western states, allies and enemies. One of the main reasons why al-Nusra has engaged intensively in the realm of media activism, especially cyber militancy, has to do with the rise of the Islamic State, and the need to offer contrasting jihadi narratives at a time when the proclaimed Caliphate of the Islamic State was gaining prominence and eroding the base of support and the pool of potential recruits to al-Nusra and other jihadi players in the current Syrian context.

Leadership and hierarchy

Al-Nusra's organization in Syria has a highly flexible structure. Although not all features of the movement are well known, it is possible to describe two of its main bodies. First, there is a religious entity called *Majlis al-Shura* (consultative council), headed by 'Umar al-Hadawi, which is in charge of preaching and the decision-making at the top of the group. It deals with all strategic issues and focuses on controlling local religious entities based in the governorates where al-Nusra is in control. The council determines the main actions to be undertaken in terms of social organization, legislation, religious teaching and current affairs. The council is independent, as its leadership is formed by members who settled in Syria at the beginning of the civil war, but interactions do exist with al-Qaeda's affiliates across the Middle East (especially in Iraq) and beyond. On the other hand, al-Nusra also has a military structure interacting regularly with the consultative council. It is principally in charge of the operational dimension, which recruits and trains fighters. As a religious body, the military command is divided among several provinces. The council is said to be the leading body, especially when it comes to setting the political and strategic agenda of the organization. This implies that when key decisions are to be made, the religious authority supposedly has the last word. At the regional level, al-Nusra is led by a cleric (*shaykh*) and a commander. The former role is referred to as the 'religious commissioner' (*zabit al-shar'i*).

In the territories ruled by al-Nusra, these leaders hold official positions of power while militarily al-Nusra's structure consists of conventional units divided into brigades, regiments and platoons. However, when al-Nusra has to fight in areas where it has no predominance and needs to face the regime or other parts of the rebellion, its structures become clandestine and function on the basis of a secret cell system. Recruits have to go through a ten-day training period, after which they are moved to a fifteen- to twenty-day military training programme.

Over the last few years, growing tensions and divisions have arisen within the leadership of al-Nusra, particularly due to divergences of view on how to deal with strategic matters. Relations with the chief competitor, the Islamic State, and with certain regional actors as well as other Islamic and rebellious groups, have brought to the fore disagreements capable of causing divisions within al-Nusra. Internal dissent, for instance, has led to some expulsions, with several former chiefs using these expulsions as a pretext to join (or rejoin) the Islamic State or other jihadi forces such as *Ahrar al-Sham* ('Liberators of the Levant') and *Harakat Sham al-Islami* ('Movement for the Islamic Levant'). As of early 2016, the present leadership is said to be made up as follows:

- Hamid Hamad Hamid al-Ali: As an al-Qaeda member who has served as a leader for al-Nusra, he is best known for having played a major role in raising tens of thousands of dollars for the benefit of the Front, and for organizing the transfer of thousands of foreigners to Syria to join al-Nusra.
- Muhsin al-Fadli: He is said to have been the chief of the Khurasan group (that al-Nusra never explicitly recognized). He may have been killed during a US strike in July 2015.
- Maysar Ali al-Juburi (also known as Abu Maria al-Qatani): Originally a member of al-Qaeda in Iraq, al-Juburi came into conflict with the leadership of that organization and moved to Syria with the aim of assisting in the creation of al-Nusra. He is said to have been replaced by Sami al-'Uraydi and was demoted to a standard member.
- Saleh al-Hamawi (also known as Abu Muhammad): One of the founding members of al-Nusra, al-Hamawi was expelled from the leadership during the summer of 2015 for advocating an even more Syria-centred strategy, whereas some chiefs were much closer to the international leadership of al-Qaeda.
- Abu Muhammad al-Jawlani: The current head of al-Nusra used to be a member of al-Qaeda and Islamic State in Iraq and claims to be the 'Amir' of the Nusra Front. His name, 'al-Jawlani', refers to the Golan Heights, a region

occupied by Israel since the Six-Day War of 1967; he is also nicknamed 'the Conqueror Shaykh' (Shaykh al-Fatih). Al-Jawlani was reported to have been killed in October 2013 near Latakia, but this announcement was withdrawn shortly afterwards. He is famous for being interviewed in late May 2015 by Ahmad Mansur, a well-known al-Jazeera journalist, an interview in which his face was hidden and in which he focused on discrediting the Western-supported Syrian opposition (e.g. the Syrian National Coalition). During that same interview, al-Jawlani spoke of his vision and strategy for Syria during and after the civil war, and affirmed his belief that the people should be consulted before 'establishing an Islamic State'. He also emphasized al-Nusra's refusal to target Western interests and its prioritization of Assad and his proxies, referring to the Islamic State as an adversary: 'Nusra Front has no plans or directives to target the West. We received clear orders from Ayman al-Zawahiri not to use Syria as a launching pad to attack the US or Europe in order not to sabotage the true mission against the regime. Maybe al-Qaeda does that but not here in Syria. Assad's forces are fighting us on one hand, Hezbollah on another, and ISIL on a third front. It is all about their mutual interests.'[11]

- 'Abd al-Muhsin 'Abdullah Ibrahim al-Sharikh: He moved from Iraq to Syria in 2013 and is now one the main leaders of al-Nusra.
- Sami al-'Uraydi (also known as Abu Muhammad al-Shami): After replacing al-Juburi, al-'Uraydi became one of the most influential people at the top of the organization, and he is considered today to be one of the principal spokesmen for al-Nusra.

Territorial control: al-Nusra's policy towards local populations

The success and continued survival of al-Nusra is a result of its ability to move beyond the image of a terrorist movement that only stands for radicalism and violence. As the study below reveals, the Syria-centric approach of al-Nusra has enabled it to gain leverage in the territories it has conquered and with their populations, according to its ideology and interests in the context of a bloody civil war, even though these occupations are not without their problems. Since 2011, the Front's functions have been the subject of increasing complaints as the premise for al-Nusra's seizure of power has shifted from a desire to act as a protecting body to what is argued to be an excessive zeal to exercise religious control, which has resulted in the waning of support from local communities. A further cause of local anxieties is the presence of foreigners claiming to rule this de facto independent emirate. In July 2015, the BBC reported on a poll conducted by ORB which solicited Syrian opinions about al-Nusra.[12] Some 1,365 people were interviewed, of whom 674 were living under the rule of the Assad regime, 430 in an area dominated by rebel groups, 170 under the authority of the Islamic State and 90 located in regions held by the Kurds. Listed below are the responses to the question 'What would you think about the influence of this actor [al-Nusra] in the war in Syria?' The numbers in **bold** are percentages.

On a Syria-wide level

'Completely positive': **16**
'Fairly positive': **19**
'Completely negative': **22**
'Fairly negative': **41**
'Do not know': **2**

In regions dominated by the Assad regime

'Completely positive': **7**
'Fairly positive': **6**
'Completely negative': **25**
'Fairly negative': **60**
'Do not know': **2**

Living under the authority of rebel forces

'Completely positive': **26**
'Fairly positive': **32**
'Completely negative': **17**
'Fairly negative': **23**
'Do not know': **2**

Under IS control:

'Completely positive': **26**
'Fairly positive': **33**
'Completely negative': **21**
'Fairly negative': **18**
'Do not know': **2**

Located in the Kurdish-ruled area:

'Completely positive': **19**
'Fairly positive': **32**
'Completely negative': **16**
'Fairly negative': **32**
'Do not know': **1**

Having earned a reputation as the defenders of oppressed Sunni identity without alienating local populations like Islamic State, al-Nusra's strategy offers al-Qaeda a favourable context in which the jihadi design could expand, through an Emirate, without moving forward to declare a Caliphate.

In matters of governance, al-Nusra hopes to extend its vision to the whole of the Syrian people, once the regime is overthrown, and seeks to do so by espousing the centrality of Sharia law and Islamic identity. However, it has focused primarily on the immediate needs of security and welfare among a population whose main bone of contention is with the negligence and brutality of the regime. Basic provisions such as electricity, water, food and medicines are frequently distributed for the benefit of the civilians, which reinforces al-Nusra's popularity and esteem amongst the local population. It comes as no surprise that when the United States declared al-Nusra a terrorist organization on 11 December 2012, many Syrians living in regions ruled by al-Nusra vehemently protested, arguing that al-Nusra provided much-needed services to the population.

However, this benevolence has been increasingly questioned within the Islamic courts and social systems that the Nusra Front has established since 2011, where the number of executions carried out is comparable to those carried out by Islamic State. Furthermore, the use of kidnapping and the capture and exploitation of oilfields by al-Nusra to supplement its regional funding has also discredited the organization. An example of one such kidnapping featured two Italian humanitarian workers, Greta Martelli and Vanessa Marzullo, who were taken near Aleppo and released on 15 January 2015 in exchange for €12 million, according to some media outlets.[13] However, it is arguable that the oil sector is even more strategic as it guarantees high incomes and significantly shapes al-Nusra's military priorities. As estimated by some experts, every 50,000 barrels sold from the Syrian oilfields generate $1 million in revenue, while 380,000 barrels are said to be produced every day. The extreme profitability of oil may explain the intensely disputed battle for control of the region of Dayr al-Zawr, which lasted from April to July 2014 and pitted the Islamic State on the one hand against a coalition of rebellious forces, including al-Nusra, on the other. As one of the main oil-producing areas in Syria, the battle was extremely hard fought, resulting in hundreds of casualties. Another case similar to that of Dayr al-Zawr is the case of Mayyadin, located near the al-Ward oilfield, which was occupied in 2013. The exploitation of the al-Ward oilfield, with assistance from Turkey, brought about a substantial increase in al-Nusra's wealth and consolidated its ability to attract recruits and ensure popular support. In November 2013, the biggest oilfield in the country (al-'Umar) was seized by the Front, further enhancing its capacity to appeal to recruits and strengthen its campaign in the areas it controlled. Thus, it seems that the political economy of warfare in present day Syria has been a major factor in determining the legitimacy of al-Nusra, as the scale of the resources of which it has gained control is linked to the support it has attracted from parts of the population. By acquiring control of these resources and offering a compelling counter-narrative to the regime, and to some extent, to other contenders, al-Nusra has been successful in acquiring both social and political backing and legitimacy.

International support and al-Nusra's integration in the regional game

Al-Nusra's success is not solely attributable to local support and its continued local integration through its 'Syrianization' strategy. The regional flux surrounding the Syrian civil conflict has also worked to the benefit of the jihadi camp and, in turn, al-Nusra. The unpalatable nature of Assad's policy (supported by Iran and Russia as well as significant armed movements such as Hezbollah, together with Iraqi and Afghan militias, etc.) and the laggard efforts of Western states in addition to their inconsistent and apparently confused approach – for instance, countries like the United States and France accusing al-Nusra of extremism at the same time as providing it with indirectly military and political backing – have made the jihadis much more attractive to many local populations.

Adding to al-Nusra's strategic advantage is its ability to participate in the regional configuration by utilizing its jihadi agenda to serve the interests of certain de facto sponsors. For instance, al-Nusra has benefited from Qatar's intervention and funding, especially in terms of negotiations related to kidnappings, as when Qatar facilitated discussions between the jihadi movement and foreign countries for the release of a group of Greek Orthodox nuns in March 2014. Furthermore, it has been argued, that at least until 2015[14] the Qataris were among the main fundraisers for al-Nusra. This relationship between the

Front and some regional sponsors (Saudi Arabia, Qatar, United Arab Emirates, Kuwait, Turkey, etc.) also reflects the ambiguity and vacillating nature of interests and strategies on the ground. In fact, the sponsorship from Gulf states in terms of military training and their enhancement of al-Nusra's social legitimacy – intended to curb the group's jihadi excesses – has helped to promote anti-Iranian and anti-Assad objectives.

More particularly, by adapting its ambitions and tactics to the pressures from other states, the Front's evolving role as an actor on the ground allows it to preserve its predominance and enables it to remain relatively independent with respect to most of its regional supporters. The de facto partnership with Qatar, a key country in the region, is also a matter of a shared ideology and political agenda. The desire to overthrow the Assad regime has certainly brought different states together, but also explains, for instance, the huge discrepancies between Western countries and regional insiders who turn out to favour religious armed movements such as al-Nusra. Though certain fears may have been raised by a Gulf country like Qatar, it should not be noted that shared Islamic narratives also matter when it comes to assessing the influence, strategy, role and impact of the jihadist movement. For instance, the designation of al-Nusra as a terrorist organization was not a perception shared by the anti-Assad side. The Emir of Qatar thus argued in an interview with CNN correspondent Christiane Amanpour that al-Nusra's religious agenda, and more specifically its claim to lead a military jihad against somebody considered to be 'usurping' Islam, meant that its use of violence was not necessarily illegitimate. On the contrary, according to the Qatari monarch, it would be a mistake to proscribe al-Nusra simply because of its self-claimed ideological justification:

> I know that in America and some countries they look at some movements as terrorist movements ... But there are differences. There are differences that to some countries and some people any group which comes from [an] Islamic background is a terrorist. And we don't accept that. It would be a 'big mistake' to consider every Islamic movement to be 'extremists'.[15]

In addition to the common strategic agenda connecting Qatar and al-Nusra, it should be emphasized that the notion of 'terrorism' as an intellectual and political issue benefits jihadist organizations involved in the Syrian conflict. As an unclassical military struggle, in which certain categories considered 'classical' in international relations ('ally', 'enemy', etc.) are framed in a fuzzy way by the various points of view involved, and given the huge impact of non-State violent actors, movements like al-Nusra, though several aspects put pressure on them (such as being labelled as a terrorist organization, being discredited as a fighting for a religious State, etc.), also benefit from this regional layout. Different agendas may help advance al-Nusra's strategy of Syrianization, by focusing on the defence of the Sunni population on the ground and using this to appear as a 'moderate' force in the eyes of state actors, especially when they also claim to be protecting fellow believers like Qatar. The very complexity of the Syrian conflict (with its global, regional, national and local components) is one of the reasons why non-state actors can flourish. Where different types of division exist – Arabs–Kurds; regime–rebellious groups; pro-regime outsiders–anti-regime outsiders, etc.) and contenders do not always side with the enemy of their enemy, al-Nusra has been capable of finding partners and even allies to lead its fight against the regime (besides Qatar, the likes of Saudi Arabia and Turkey, for instance) and, less often, similar rebel groups competing for control of the same territories as the jihadist movement. In an interview with the Saudi channel *al-Baraka* in the aftermath of the summer 2017 Gulf crisis that started with the blockade of Qatar by a coalition of four Arab countries (Saudi Arabia, Bahrain, the United Arab Emirates and Egypt), the former Qatari Minister of Foreign Affairs, Hamad Bin Jassim, justified support for al-Nusra in the Syrian conflict (contradicting what his Emir had claimed a few years earlier):

> When events began in Syria, I went to ... Saudi Arabia and met with King Abdullah ... upon the instructions of His Royal Highness the Father. I addressed the situation. He said: 'We are with you. You lead the file and we coordinate with you.' We took the responsibility and we have all the evidence on this issue. Any support was going to Turkey and was coordinated with the US forces. The distribution of military support was happening [sic] by the American, Turkish, Qatari and Saudi forces. They were all there, the military personnel were there. Maybe a mistake happened, where a particular faction (al-Nusra) has been supported for a period of time but not Daesh; accusing us of supporting Daesh is an exaggeration. Maybe there was a relationship with al-Nusra. I swear, I do not know about this topic. I say, even if there was a support to al-Nusra, but they told us al-Nusra is unacceptable, the support has stopped. And the focus was on liberating Syria. We were fighting over the prey, meanwhile the prey escaped.[16]

Being less ideological than the Islamic State has allowed al-Nusra, in the complex structure of the Syrian conflict, to appear less radical than other jihadist actors, mainly IS. By using a more pragmatic policy, initiating contact with Israel in the Golan Heights and sending wounded soldiers to receive medical aid on the other side of the border (Silverstein, 2016), al-Nusra has reinforced its position inside Syria's borders. It has also remained primarily focused on the fight with the regime, unlike IS, which is more committed to a military struggle with Kurdish forces in Syria and Iraq, as well as the international coalition since 2015,[17] in addition of other foes.

Relations with other rebel groups: a case of 'coopetition'?

The complex dynamics influencing al-Nusra over the last few years are manifested in its connections, partnerships and rivalries with other rebel and Islamic groups and the ways in which these ties have been negotiated and framed. To a large extent these shifting relations reflect the different stages of the Syrian revolution, which has turned into a major civil and regional war.

As one of the principal actors in this conflict, al-Nusra has realigned itself through several political shifts in response to various strategic changes that have occurred. In this regard, al-Nusra embodies the idea of 'coopetition', where cooperation and competition coexist as the organization negotiates its way through a changing military and political landscape.

At its inception, al-Nusra was initially an imported movement, borrowing military knowledge as well as governance techniques learnt in Iraq after the overthrown of Saddam Hussein's regime and during the fighting and insurrection against the US army and successive governments (mainly headed by Shias after 2004). In order not to be seen as being solely motivated by a transnationalist jihadi agenda, al-Nusra split from the original Islamic State in Iraq, before seizing some areas from the Assad regime and implementing a new form of governance. In achieving these strategic gains, facilitated by cooperating with or combating the other (internal or external) parties involved in the Syrian conflict, the Front has engaged in a series of alliances, reversals of policy, adaptations, temporizations and reinventions that have allowed it to increase its legitimacy and capacity on the ground and cast it as a major stakeholder. To anchor itself in the Sunni-majority towns and villages, al-Nusra has exhibited pragmatism, although it still has to negotiate between conflicting visions when it comes to the global strategic landscape, and more precisely its relations with al-Qaeda (the transnational network), Islamic State, other parts of the rebellion (including other jihadi movements) and various regional sponsors.

The traction gained by al-Nusra has even won it praise from the other members of the insurrectional forces, especially in 2012, where some top officials from the Free Syrian Army (FSA) criticized the United States decision to label the Front as a terrorist organization. Even though the FSA does not agree with all the military operations conducted by al-Nusra (especially those involving the killing of civilians), some FSA spokesmen have thrown their support behind the movement and said 'We are all al-Nusra', suggesting that al-Nusra has earned its stripes as a defender of the Syrians and as an opponent of the regime. Prioritizing military coordination instead of the establishment of ideological supremacy has largely enabled al-Nusra to unite the rebel forces against the regime, despite some periods of tension. For instance, during the successful offensives against the Syrian army between March and May 2015 in Idlib Governorate, al-Nusra cooperated with other jihadi forces, some Islamist military organizations and the Free Syrian Army.

Despite sharing common ideological and organizational roots, the dynamics of the Syrian conflict and the rise of the Islamic State have put al-Nusra on the defensive, especially since the proclamation of the Caliphate in June 2014. In fact, the downward spiral in relations began in April 2013, when Abu Bakr al-Baghdadi released an audio on the web in which he stated that al-Nusra was part of his network and that the movements were about to merge to give birth to an hegemonic jihadi organization across Syria and Iraq. This breach in al-Nusra's strategy of independence led to a declaration by al-Jawlani, who renewed his pledge of allegiance to Ayman al-Zawahiri and refuted any such merger. Between 2013 and 2015 there have been numerous clashes between al-Nusra and Islamic State, particularly as they promote different political agendas (a Caliphate vs an Emirate), different programmes of expansion and diverging strategies to appeal to the local population. Both movements also compete for the control of oilfields, for example in Dayr el-Zawr in 2014, where several al-Nusra commanders and fighters were killed and the rest of its members mostly expelled from the region after offensives against the Islamic State. Clashes between these groups in the previous resulted in a combined casualty figure of about 3,000.

Al-Nusra's main objection to Islamic State is to the latter's proclamation of a Caliphate and subsequent rejection of any other attempt to build a sort of Islamic state in the world. This unilateralism is criticized by al-Zawahiri, the leader of al-Qaeda, who argued that all Muslims should have been consulted about the idea of proclaiming a Caliphate. Echoing these sentiments, al-Jawlani has described the Islamic State project as 'illegitimate' and called on IS members 'to repent and to return to the Sunni people' (Lister, 2015). In September 2015, al-Zawahiri released another recording in which he too characterized the Caliphate as illegitimate, while at the same time advocating closer military cooperation on the ground in the face of far mightier enemies (with several international powers intervening directly in Syria in 2015 and 2016). Al-Jawlani responded to his mentor by stating that he did not envisage the end of the conflict between al-Nusra and Islamic State as long as the latter refused to recognize the Front's leadership.[18] Although the Front's relations with al-Qaeda have remained strained, it has generally followed al-Qaeda's direction, especially when the Islamic State has tried to foster divisions between al-Nusra and its parent organization.

However, the connection with Islamic State is not immutable and is in fact a very complex connection, like al-Nusra's links with the FSA and other jihadi organizations. There have been cases where, in the face of formidable adversaries on the ground, al-Nusra and the Islamic State have found a way to unite their efforts against the regime and its proxies. This was particularly the case against Hezbollah in August 2014. Both movements released a video of an operation in which they jointly targeted the Shia party in the eastern mountains of Lebanon, where they have also cooperated in order to kidnap soldiers belonging to the Lebanese army.

Since the internationalization of the war in 2015, with some European countries such as France as well as the United States and Russia taking the offensive, al-Nusra has been pursuing its military cooperation strategy with other Islamic and jihadi forces even more intensely. On 13 July 2015, al-Nusra with thirteen other peer movements, such as *Ahrar al-Sham* (Liberators of the Levant) and Liwa al-Khilafa ('The Brigade of Defenders of the Caliphate'),[19] announced the birth of Ansar al-Shari'a ('Supporters of Shari'a), a military jihadi coalition fighting in Aleppo Governorate. More importantly, a few months earlier, in March 2015, the Front became part of the new Army of Conquest (Jaysh al-Fath), an alliance of Islamist factions active in a number of governorates (such as Idlib, Hama and Latakia). Believed to be supported principally by Turkey and Saudi Arabia,[20] this army is united by the desire to overthrow the regime and fight Hezbollah. By early 2016, the Army of Conquest had experienced several victories, mainly in the area of Idlib, but had also been compelled to surrender to Hezbollah, for example in the Qalamun mountains.

Inside or outside global armed jihad? Al-Nusra's split from al-Qaeda in summer 2016

Intense debates inside the al-Nusra Front had been visible since 2015 about whether or not to remain affiliated to al-Qaeda. On 29 July 2016, al-Jawlani made an announcement that his movement had changed its name and should now be referred to as Jabhat Fath al-Sham ('Front for Conquest of the Levant'), emphasizing that it had 'no affiliation to any external entity'.[21] Although this may be seen as an attempt to appear more moderate within the Syrian conflict, especially compared to the Islamic State's maximalist strategy of a permanent state of war, this decision was the product of heated debate inside al-Nusra. Seen by James R. Clapper Jr, US Director of National Intelligence, as 'a PR move'[22] designed to ease international pressure on the jihadist movement, this change in fact addressed arguments about strategic within al-Nusra. These arguments were observable since at least 2015, when in May of that year, Abu Maria al-Qahtani, the commander of al-Nusra in Deir Zor, advocated separation from al-Qaeda not only because of the necessity of focusing on the fight against the regime, but also, and maybe primarily, because the appeal to global armed jihad was not the main reason that many of its fighters – except foreigners, who were more willing to fight 'the enemies of Islam' wherever they existed – had joined al-Nusra. Furthermore, two currents within the movement had opposed each other on the issue of remaining an al-Qaeda affiliate. The youngest generations of Syrian fighters distinguish themselves by being 'more inclined towards the new Syria-focused approach' (Lister, 2014d), while for some commanders, remaining affiliated to al-Qaeda is important as it allows the movement to retain its appeal to foreign fighters – those who wish to join a global jihadist. In the context of the growing rivalry between the Islamic State and the jihadist movements whose strategy could be summed up as 'Syria and Syrians first', a commitment to remain part of the al-Qaeda organization was arguably the best way to attract new fighters and challenge any pretention to represent the Sunnis in Syria.

However, the decision, made official in July 2016, turned out to be a milestone in the Syrianization process initiated by al-Nusra as a force aiming at playing a central role in the war against the regime or any contender claiming to exert primacy over the Syrian rebellion. Although connections undoubtedly still exist with al-Qaeda, al-Nusra as a social movement dedicated to the service of jihadist narratives has significantly reinforced its legitimacy with rebel groups and the Syrian people by becoming Jabhat Fath al-Sham. This has enabled al-Nusra to collaborate with most rebel groups while the regime has reinforced its capacity to wage war, especially after the Russians came to its rescue in September 2015. In other words, by adopting a 'long game approach' (Lister, 2015), al-Nusra has been successful in recruiting from within increasingly disenfranchised social groups in the areas of Idlib and Aleppo in 2016. At the same time, some of its leaders did initiate the process of establishing a potential Islamic Emirate in Idlib, highlighting in this respect that a sort of state-building focus could be the next step in al-Nusra's strategy in Syria. Debates about the relevance of establishing an official Emirate (although the area of Idlib has in effect been ruled as such for the last few years) over several months, from late 2015 to July 2016, show the importance of this issue (Lister, 2015), particularly in terms of reaching out to the Syrian Arab and Sunni opposition. Leading figures of al-Qaeda (Saif al-Adel, Abu Muhammad al-Masri and Abu Khayr al-Masri) came to Syria at that time to ensure that al-Zawahiri's agenda for Syria would be respected. Indeed al-Zawahiri considers the Levant to be the main battlefield for the jihadist vanguard, which is why al-Nusra's strategy has been the focus of so much attention.

So far, it is hard to say whether al-Qaeda fully supports the split led by al-Nusra in summer 2016. If some of its main figures promote the idea that the best strategy for diffusing the jihadist global narrative is by embedding it in the Syrian armed revolution, others are fearful that this Syrianization policy could ultimately turn into an all-consuming national struggle wherein the religious discourse would only act as a watchword to mobilize people and reinforce local legitimacy regardless of any deeper agenda on a more global scale. The assessment that prevailed in summer 2016, when al-Nusra became a member of Jabhat Fath al-Sham, can be best described as maintaining ideological loyalty to al-Qaeda, but without any organizational ties or preference given to global narratives. For instance, non-Syrian fighters, although they may remain influential in the military leadership, are encouraged not to make their presence felt in the province of Idlib and are no longer really present in local religious police units or behavioural enforcement forces (Lister, 2015).

Hayat Tahrir al-Sham: towards a definitive rupture with al-Qaeda?

A couple of months after the split, on 20 January 2017, several jihadist leaders, including Jabhat Fath al-Sham/al-Nusra's, announced the merger of their movements with the aim of more effectively challenging the regime and its allies one and a half years after Russia engaged its expeditionary force in Syria against the rebellious armies, targeting al-Nusra[23] in particular. Jabhat Fath al-Sham, the Ansar al-Dine Front, Jaysh al-Sunna and Liwat al-Haqq, as well as the Nur al-Dine al-Zenki Movement, have combined to form the Organization for the Liberation of the Levant (Hayat Tahrir al-Sham or HTS). This new entity has allowed al-Nusra to rebrand itself a second time and to reaffirm that they represent a 'fully independent' movement with no ties to any 'foreign body or organization'.[24] The military leaders come mainly from al-Nusra and Ahrar al-Sham, who deploy the elite units (called Inghimassi), which are active mostly in the city of Idlib, where they are responsible for suicide bombings. In October 2017, al-Jawlani became the Emir of Tahrir al-Sham, illustrating that al-Nusra is today the main component of this new organization. The main body in charge of social, legal and religious affairs is the Majlis al-Shura, which is also dominated by members originating from al-Nusra. However, within this consultative council, all the groups involved in HTS are present and deal with all military and social issues faced by the people living under its rule. From the beginning, it was made clear that the council would have as its principal mission to work towards unification of the different components and to reduce any tensions which may exist, specifically relating to grievances against al-Nusra/Jabhat al-Sham, the main jihadist force inside this new organization.

It turns out that the strategy followed by al-Nusra when joining HTS is clearly to reinforce Syrianization. This has been pushed to such an extent that it has become a very contentious issue between al-Qaeda and al-Nusra since early 2017. The division has now reached the point where al-Qaeda is seriously considering creating a rival movement that would fully pledge allegiance to the global brand to the detriment of HTS. Both political and military factors have generated tensions between the two sides. Though the split that occurred in summer 2016 was to some degree approved of by the al-Qaeda leadership, it is now known that al-Zawahiri had not been consulted about the rebranding and vehemently rejected it when he was informed thereof (Lister, 2017). On 23 April 2017, an audio statement eventually made the ideological split official and the Syrianization policy was clearly identified as a source of major dispute that could lead to a divorce between al-Nusra and al-Qaeda. Calling for an end to this evolution into a nationalized form of jihadism, al-Zawahiri urged that 'mistakes should be corrected' in order to reinforce the transnational and global agenda, considered to be the best strategy to obtain 'victory' (Lister, 2017). More significantly, al-Zawahiri targeted al-Nusra's Syrianization policy:

> [Some] wish to deceive you into buying the myth that only if you were to change your jihad to an exclusively nationalist Syrian struggle, the leading international criminals would be pleased with you ... [C]ritical assessment and correction of mistakes is the first step in the path to victory.

Al-Qaeda's strategy would then be to create a new jihadist force with the support of al-Nusra's leaders who have sided against the July 2016 split, such as

Sami al-'Uraydi and Iyad al-Tubasi (known to have been close to Abu Mus'ab al-Zarkawi). Fearful of losing another affiliate after the loss of its members to the Islamic State a few years before, al-Qaeda's pressure to bring back all al-Nusra leaders and fighters into its orbit could nevertheless reinforce the ongoing tensions within this movement and finally provoke a permanent divide between the two. On the other hand, several years of bloody war and the growing necessity for Syrian jihadist forces to unite against a regime that seems able to recover from defeats thanks to foreign intervention have thrown al-Nusra into a dilemma. Will it be able to rally the rebel groups around its flag if it is also the one recognized by al-Qaeda?

This issue has become more critical since across-the-country support for HTS is more uncertain today than it was for al-Nusra a few years ago. Indeed, a poll conducted between 10 and 28 July 2017 by the ECHO Research Center at Laurentian University on 4,858 people showed that 77 per cent disagreed with HTS ideology and 73 per cent rejected local councils affiliated to HTS in Idlib, while 66 per cent perceived the movement to be part of al-Qaeda in Syria. More interestingly, the same poll revealed that 42 per cent used to consider that HTS was consistent with the role of opposition to the regime, but this is no longer the case, while 7 per cent regarded it as a counter-revolutionary group[25]. These developments help explain why the idea of establishing an Emirate in the northern part of Syria was finally rejected by some of al-Nusra's key leaders in 2016, who will *nolens volens* have to consolidate their Syria-focused strategy or face the penalty of being seen to be opposed to the wishes of the majority of the population. In other words, as long as it is seen as an anti-regime force, al-Nusra's jihadist ideology has been relatively well accepted and even legitimized. Yet, the deep and long-held desire of most people facing the regime is to recover a form of national sovereignty after Assad is toppled. Al-Nusra's undeniable success on the battlefield and its capacity to challenging all other military forces do not mean that its narrative has definitively triumphed over the other ideological options in the current Syrian context.

Therefore, al-Nusra's leadership is increasingly pushed towards huge-impact decisions for the future of their movement. While some of them (Sami al-'Uraydi, etc.) are still attached to the al-Qaeda legacy and affiliation, several others (Abu Maria al-Qahtani, Abdullah al-Sanadi, Saleh al-Hamawi, etc.) wish to avoid both political and ideological isolation. Salej al-Hamawi, for instance, confessed that in mid-July 2016, al-Jawlani was faced with an ultimatum (Lister, 2017): '[E]ither disengage [from al-Qaeda] and merge with Islamic factions, or face isolation socially, politically and militarily.'

Al-Nusra now faces a Hobson's choice scenario regarding its own identity as a sociological movement. Besides debates about the nature of its 'Syrianness', this movement also sees itself as both a military force and a political organization seeking to exert sovereignty over territories within its reach. The more it grows in size and military power, the more likely it is to outshine its jihadists partners/rivals and return to the initial motivation of the global revolution agenda, thus undermining its political capacity to unite Syrians. In other words, expansion may be a double-edged sword for al-Nusras, making a reassessment of the factors that have led to its undeniable success more urgent than ever. Is it because it started as an affiliate to al-Qaeda that the movement has been able to attract so many people and amass considerable resources, or is it because of its pragmatism in the way military operations have been conducted and popular support fostered? Or to put it another way, as a religious, political and military movement that has achieved some degree of success in the context of the Syrian conflict today, how can al-Nusra attain sustainability?

Conclusion

In studying the history and development of al-Nusra, the centrality and benefits of nationalizing an ideology stand out. Although it remains dedicated to a violent transnational struggle in the name of religion, al-Nusra's strategy highlights how local and national circumstances influence the vision of foreign actors (even if the jihadi actors have unquestionably played a role in the rise of sectarianism in Syria). Evolving from the status of a foreign movement to a domestic one, al-Nusra has certainly become a major force to be reckoned with, not only in the present Syrian context but also for many years to come. As Charles Lister points out:

> Jabhat al-Nusra has embedded itself so successfully within the Syrian opposition – within the revolution for a long time – that in my view it has become an actor that will be much more difficult to uproot from Syria than IS ... Islamic State is all about imposing its will on people, whereas al-Nusra has for the last five years been embedding itself in popular movements, sharing power in villages and cities, and giving to people rather than forcing them to do things. That has lent it a power IS just doesn't have.[26]

Might we envisage the emergence of nationalized forms of jihadism in the future? In 2018, al-Qaeda had been in existence for 30 years, most of it as mainly a religious, political and military movement, fearful that territorializing its influence would make it an easy target for its enemies (Gerges, 2014). However, with the successes of al-Nusra in the context of a complete failed regime, combined with the rise of sectarian tensions and the fact that the ongoing conflict has now spawned regional and international rivalry, has this organization found the most efficient model of sustainability for a jihadist group? By putting down roots in Syria while remaining ideologically affiliated to the global jihadist narrative, has al-Nusra found the social basis that al-Qaeda has been lacking for years? Or will the developmental process increasingly generate tension and possibly a rupture between al-Nusra and its founding ideology, leading to a new generation of non-state violent actors who will solidify political legitimacy on the ground while still being capable of embracing the transnational, thereby echoing, to an extent, the path taken by Hezbollah for several decades (Clark, 2017)? In any event, al-Nusra remains a rewarding field of study for anyone interested in analysing how a transnational founding ideology and a strategy of political embeddedness within one given society interact with each other.

4

The 2007 Hamas–Fatah Conflict in Gaza and the Israeli–American Demands

Victor Kattan

In his introduction, Peter Sluglett argued that governmental repression and a lack of democracy are constant themes that drive radicalization and political violence in the Middle East. This is especially true of the violent non-state actors operating in the West Bank and Gaza, although the failure to hold general elections since 2006 is largely due to the ongoing disagreements between Fatah and Hamas that arose during the conflict in Gaza in 2007. An additional caveat is that the situation confronting Hamas and Fatah in the West Bank and Gaza differs to the other organizations described in the contributions to this book in that Israel's 'deep state' exercises a degree of direct and indirect control of the occupied territories, which is unparalleled in its extent and scope compared to other parts of the Middle East. In Syria, Iraq and Yemen, governmental forces are only in sporadic control of large swathes of territory.

The description of Hamas as a violent *non-state* actor could, however, be questioned given that it plays a significant role in the politics of Palestine, which has been recognized as a non-member state of the United Nations since 2012. Indeed, for almost a year in 2006–7, Hamas had a majority of seats in Palestine's legislature and held several key cabinet posts including that of prime minister and foreign minister. The argument here is that Hamas' ability to act as a governmental or 'state' actor was significantly impaired by the events in Gaza in 2007 when Hamas took sole control of the Gaza Strip. This was arguably one of the most significant events in intra-Palestinian politics over the last forty years, whose reverberations continue to be felt today. This is why a detailed account of what happened that fateful year and in the years leading up to the 'great schism' remains important to understating Palestinian politics today.

Nothing is ever what it seems in Palestine

The rout of Fatah from the Gaza Strip in June 2007 remains a controversial, disputed and largely misunderstood moment in the history of the Israeli–Palestinian conflict. Hamas claims that following its victory in the legislative elections in January 2006, and its refusal to adhere to demands that it recognize Israel, abide by past agreements and abandon the armed struggle, there emerged a conspiracy to overthrow it. Had Hamas not acted when it did, Fatah's armed forces in Gaza would have routed Hamas. In effect, Hamas contends that what happened in June 2007 was an act of pre-emptive self-defence that prevented a Fatah coup, rather than a coup by Hamas that was long in the making.

The Hamas version was first articulated by Alastair Crooke, a former MI6 agent and former adviser to EU High Representative Javier Solana, on his website Conflicts Forum in January 2007 (Crooke, Conflicts Forum online, 7 January 2007). Crooke repeated the allegation in an interview with Al-Jazeera two weeks later (Crooke, Al Jazeera, 24 January 2007). Following the routing of Fatah from Gaza in June, when Crooke's allegations appeared to have been vindicated, Crooke referred to American and British efforts to finance, train and arm the security forces led by Gaza strongman Muhammad Dahlan to confront Hamas in a review in the *London Review of Books* (Crooke, 5 July 2007: 3).

The White House and the State Department refused to comment on Crooke's allegations when they first surfaced in 2006. However, after Fatah's rout, US Secretary of State Condoleezza Rice told a press conference in Cairo that Hamas was being armed, in part, by the Iranians, to the detriment of 'the legitimate Palestinian Authority security forces', which she described as not being in 'a very good situation' (Milton-Edwards and Farrell, 2010: 284, quoting Rice). In her memoir, *No Higher Honor*, published three years later, Rice alluded to a training programme for the Palestinian Authority (PA) security forces when she expressed her view that Hamas 'decided to launch a preemptive strike against the rapidly improving security forces of Mahmoud Abbas' (Rice, 2011: 581). Likewise, Elliot Abrams, the Deputy National Security Adviser, accused by Crooke of organizing the coup, dismissed the claim in his memoir, *Tested by Zion*, where he explained that while the US was seeking to enlarge and professionalize the Palestinian Authority security forces, the claim that 'we were arming them was not true because all our aid was nonlethal' (Abrams, 2013: 228).

In order to make sense of these conflicting accounts and shed light on what may have happened in Gaza in June 2007, this chapter makes use of leaked documents from the period just before the election of Hamas in January 2006 to the end of June 2007, following Fatah's rout from Gaza. The documents include references to the UN Special Coordinator Alvaro de Soto's End of Mission Report to the UN Secretary-General in New York (May 2007) that was leaked by an individual within the Secretariat to the *Guardian* newspaper in London in 2007; US diplomatic cables disclosed to the organization WikiLeaks by US soldier Chelsea Manning in November 2010; and documents disclosed by former Palestinian negotiators from the private archives of the Negotiation Affairs Department of the Palestine Liberation Organization (PLO) in Ramallah to the Al-Jazeera network and the *Guardian* newspaper in January 2011. These documents provide a compelling account of what may have transpired when complemented by contemporary newspaper reports, memoirs and scholarly works. The documents also provide an insight into the role of the 'deep state' in intra-Palestinian politics and shed light on some of the challenges facing violent 'non-state' actors opposed to Israel's ongoing occupation.

Before addressing the causes of Fatah's rout from Gaza, it would be helpful to remind ourselves of how these events came to pass. Accordingly, this chapter opens with an overview of the main political actors in Palestine with military wings before exploring Fatah's relationship and political differences with Hamas and Islamic Jihad, which should be understood more in terms of rivalry than of enmity. The challenges that national liberation movements faced in the post-9/11 era are then addressed, followed by Israel's decision to redeploy its troops from Gaza in 2005, the legislative elections that brought Hamas to power in 2006, and finally the events that led to Fatah's expulsion from Gaza in 2007.

Fatah and Hamas: conjoined at birth

In light of the bitter animosity that developed between Fatah and Hamas, it is worth recalling that many of the founding fathers of Fatah were members of the Muslim Brotherhood, the movement that gave birth to Hamas, founded in the Gaza Strip in 1987 (Mishal and Sela, 2000: 34; Hroub, 2002: 35; Tamimi, 2007: 18). Like Siamese twins conjoined at birth but who grow up not always seeing eye to eye, Fatah and Hamas share a common goal in seeking to end the Israeli occupation of Palestinian lands but they do not always agree on the methods of struggle or on the shape that a Palestinian state should take. Islamic Jihad, not Hamas, was the first Palestinian Islamist movement to adopt armed struggle as a tactic in the early 1980s when it was aligned with Fatah, until the outbreak of the First Intifada in 1987. In the 1980s, most of Islamic Jihad's leaders were former activists from Fatah and the Palestine Liberation Army that provided operational experience to Islamic Jihad (Hatina, 2001: 27).

Despite ideological and tactical differences, it is important to emphasize that Fatah, Hamas and other Palestinian resistance movements view themselves primarily as liberation movements. The focus on Palestine is what distinguishes Palestinian Islamist movements from other Islamist movements in the Arab world. Indeed, Islamic Jihad went so far as to call for the unification of Sunni and Shia Islam and the mobilization of all Muslims for the liberation of Palestine through armed struggle (Mishal and Sela, 2000: 32). For many years, the Muslim Brotherhood vacillated between emphasizing the centrality of liberating Palestine before creating the Islamic state that it envisaged encompassing much of the Middle East, or prioritizing the Palestinian cause before any other defensive jihad (Tamimi, 2007: 28–9). In contrast, the PLO has never shown any inclination to establish an Islamic state that would unify the global Muslim community. This was not only for ideological reasons, but because doing so would alienate the PLO's support base among the member states of the Arab League, upon whom it is heavily dependent, especially Egypt (Cobban, 1984: 28–31). The Egyptian Government's influence over the PLO, especially in its early incarnation, provided one explanation as to why the Muslim Brotherhood in Egypt in the 1950s and 1960s (when it was being suppressed by the Nasserist regime) considered the Palestine issue as secondary to creating an Islamic state, preferring instead to establish a strong Islamic society that would consist of conscientious, enlightened and well-trained Muslims (Tamimi, 2007: 28).

Fatah's credentials as a national liberation movement are easier to demonstrate given its leadership role in the PLO that was accorded the status of a liberation movement in the United Nations in 1974 (UN General Assembly Resolution 3237 (XXIX), 22 November 1974). But it could equally be true of Hamas, even though Hamas has eschewed membership of the PLO. Thus Hamas, despite not being a member of the PLO, explicitly defined itself as a liberation movement in a document drafted by its Political Bureau for European diplomats in the mid-1990s: 'The Islamic Resistance Movement (Hamas) is a Palestinian national liberation movement that struggles for the liberation of Palestinian occupied lands and for the recognition of Palestinian legitimate rights' (Tamimi, 2007: 147). The description of Hamas as a national liberation movement found more recent expression in the *Document of General Principles and Policies*, which was published by Hamas on 1 May 2017, where Hamas describes itself as a 'Palestinian Islamic national liberation and resistance movement'.

The causes of the Fatah–Hamas division

The fall of the Berlin Wall in 1989 had dramatic repercussions for the balance of power in international relations, and the Israeli–Palestinian arena was no exception. Yet Islamic Jihad, Hamas and Fatah differed in their assessments of the impact that the end of the Cold War would have on their movements. Whereas Yasser Arafat (1929–2004) and his followers in Fatah argued that it was necessary to forge a more realistic approach to negotiating a peaceful settlement with Israel that necessitated abandoning armed struggle, recognizing Israel and exchanging land for peace, Islamic Jihad and Hamas reached the opposite conclusion. Meir Hatina, based on his readings of articles published in *al-Mujahid* newspaper in Beirut and Gaza between 1989 and 1991, and an interview with Islamic Jihad's founder Fathi al-Shiqaqi (1951–95) in the Iranian paper *Kayhan al-'Arabi* in 1993, explains that Shiqaqi and other leaders in Islamic Jihad thought that the international balance of power would remain unchanged following the end of the Cold War. Accordingly, the great powers would still support Israel despite the upheavals in Eastern Europe and the Soviet Union. In Shiqaqi's view, the United States, having supplanted Britain as the 'policeman' of the Middle East, would seek to mould the region according to its geopolitical interests by strengthening Israel and sidelining the Israel–Palestine dispute. Islamic Jihad believed that any peace agreement concluded in these circumstances would amount to submission, in which the stronger side would impose its will on the weaker (Hatina, 2001: 68–9).

Given that Hamas and many Islamists view Palestine as a *waqf* or sacred religious endowment that can never be alienated or ceded to any foreign power, it is not surprising that Hamas was bitterly opposed to the Oslo peace process (Hroub, 2002: 69–70). (The notion that Palestine enjoys a special status also finds expression in the *Document of General Principles and Policies* that was published by Hamas on 1 May 2017, although this document indicates a greater willingness to find a compromise with Fatah in that it 'considers the establishment of a fully sovereign and independent Palestinian state, with Jerusalem as its capital along the lines of the 4th June 1967, with the return of the refugees and displaced to their homes from which they were expelled, as a formula for national consensus'.) In this connection, we must remember that the Oslo negotiations were conducted in secret in the Norwegian countryside and that knowledge of the talks was deliberately withheld from Hamas and other Palestinian factions, even within the Fatah organization. This was despite the fact that senior Fatah leaders in the know had met with Hamas leaders in the presence of the late Hassan al-Turabi, the leader of the Muslim Brotherhood in Sudan, in Khartoum, as late as January 1993 (Tamimi, 2007: 190). Hamas was very active in the Gaza Strip and the West Bank during the First Palestinian Intifada (1987–93), while Fatah was holed up in Tunis where the PLO leadership had been headquartered after having fled Israel's invasion of Lebanon in 1982.

Following Arafat's public declaration of support for Saddam Hussein during the First Gulf War, the PLO was in bad shape and in financial difficulty. Israel had been learning at first hand about the precarious state of the PLO's affairs from an informant it had in Tunis who had bugged the office of 'Abd al-Hakam Bal'awi, the PLO's Ambassador to Tunisia, who had taken over as chief of intelligence after the assassination of Abu Iyad (Heikal, 1996: 469). And then there were rumours that Israel was talking to Hamas. According to Khaled Hroub, Sheikh Yasin, the founder of Hamas, claimed that the Israeli government had asked Hamas to take over the administration of the Gaza Strip, but that Yasin turned down the request, saying that it would be 'crazy for us to consent to be mere stand-ins for Israeli rule' (Hroub, 2002: 2). But what Hamas would turn down, Fatah would accept when it concluded the Gaza–Jericho agreement (1994) with Israel, fulfilling one of Israel's long-term policy goals known as the 'Gaza First Plan'.[1] One of the reasons why 'Gaza First' had been rejected by the Egyptians at Camp David was that 'Gaza first could mean Gaza last, the only piece of land the Israelis would be willing to concede' (Corbin, 1994: 47).

Compounding matters for Fatah were the talks between prominent West Bank Palestinians and Israel in Madrid (1991) and Washington (1992) that excluded the PLO. The knowledge that Hamas was talking to Israel and that a deal might exclude the PLO worked to Israel's advantage. And then there was the assassination of Arafat's security chief Atef Bseiso in 1992, either by Israel, the Abu Nidal Organization or the Jewish extremist Kach movement (that implausibly claimed responsibility), diminishing Arafat's already small circle of advisers (*New York Times*, 1992: 9 June, A9). The international situation was not propitious either, with China and India, the PLO's greatest allies in the Third World, recognizing Israel in 1992. In the words of Yossi Beilin, one of the architects of the Oslo Accords:

> It was clear that the PLO was feeling pressure, that it couldn't reconcile itself to the fact that it was playing no part in the bilateral or the multilateral talks [in Washington], that it was in danger of losing its primacy over Hamas. A settlement with Israel in which PLO-Tunis had a major role to play, including a foothold in Gaza, could constitute a lifeline.
>
> Beilin, 1999: 67

Indeed, as Hroub explains, in light of the growth of Hamas' influence, 'PLO leaders wanted to curtail the growing influence of Hamas and to gain access to the territory of Palestine as quickly as possible' (Hroub, 2002: 102). Given the increasing popularity of Hamas in Gaza, Israel also had reasons to negotiate with the PLO, since 'it might not be long before a weakened Arafat and his PLO would no longer be there to deal with' (Corbin, 1994: 36). But by recognizing Israel and agreeing to the executive, legislative and security limitations that Israel had imposed on the Palestinian Authority in the Interim Agreement (1995), which prevented the Authority from acting as an independent and sovereign entity, the PLO was thrown into a quandary. Worse still, the PLO agreed to postpone discussion of the settlements, borders, refugees, Jerusalem and water until 'final status negotiations' that came and went past the deadline of 4 May 1999. In the meantime, Israel continued to expand and build new settlements, especially in and around East Jerusalem, and pressured Arafat to crack down on Hamas and other Palestinian resistance movements on the basis of a promise to withdraw from parts of the West Bank and Gaza that was dependent on a degree of Israeli good faith that quickly evaporated. With opinion always divided between the old and new guard in Fatah over the sagaciousness of the Oslo process from its very beginnings, it was inevitable that relations with Hamas and Islamic Jihad would always be frosty.

Fatah, Hamas, and the illegitimacy of armed struggle in a post-9/11 world

Aggravating Fatah's and Hamas' difficulties were changes at the international level in which wars of national liberation were falling into disrepute, as the Soviet Union's alliance with the Third World began unravelling. After the death of Mao Tse-tung in 1976, when China began purchasing arms from Israel, and after Moscow's fateful invasion of Afghanistan in 1979, which alienated the Muslim world, Fatah lost the support of two of its patrons and arms suppliers (Burton, 2018). President Ronald Reagan's assertive foreign policy, which sought to undermine national liberation movements and the causes for which they struggled, appeared to be paying dividends, and the alliance between the PLO, Cuba and Nicaragua was singled out for specific censure in an article by Jeane Kirkpatrick, United States Ambassador to the United Nations (Kirkpatrick, 1981: 29). As UN Ambassador, Kirkpatrick articulated the reversal of Carter's Third World policy at the UN (Gerson, 1991) where the Carter administration's censure of Israel for its settlement policy in Jerusalem had enraged the neoconservatives (Moynihan, 1981: 23-31). Just two years after Israel's 1982 invasion of Lebanon, and the expulsion of the PLO from Beirut, US Secretary of State George Shultz was waxing lyrical about the state of US-Israel relations, telling a conference on international terrorism in Washington, DC, that '[t]he terrorists who assault Israel are also enemies of the United States' (Netanyahu, 1986: 20-1).

Mahmoud Abbas recalls that it was after the three-month-long siege of Beirut in 1982 that the PLO moved to accept UN Security Council resolutions 242 and 338 (Abbas, 1995: 20-1). In contrast to the PLO, the Muslim Brotherhood, still smarting from the Camp David Accords, was planning to wage a defensive jihad and opposed territorial compromise with Israel. The Camp David Accords were perceived by many Arabs to have been too generous to Israel because, in addition to breaking ranks with the other Arab states by recognizing Israel, the Accords excluded the PLO from the autonomy negotiations with Israel and did not explicitly demand statehood for the Palestinians. In 1981, President Sadat paid the ultimate price for signing the Accords when he was assassinated by Egyptian Islamic Jihad.

After the invasion of Lebanon in 1982, a meeting between Islamist leaders sympathetic to the aims of the Muslim Brotherhood was secretly held in Amman in 1983 where 'a unanimous decision was taken to give financial and logistic support to the effort of the Ikhwan in Palestine to wage Jihad' (Tamimi, 2007: 45). In retrospect, the decision by the Brotherhood to wage jihad in 1983 was a turning point. Just as the PLO began to seriously consider abandoning armed struggle, the Palestinian Brotherhood was embracing it. A Hamas pamphlet, translated by Hroub, explains Hamas' thinking at the time:

> In the seventies there were many indications that the PLO may be prepared to accept a lesser settlement than is indicated in the Palestine National Charter. Then, in the eighties, following the outbreak of the Iraq-Iran war, the Palestinian cause was marginalized at both the Arab and international levels ... And the policies of the Zionist entity have become more obdurate and arrogant with the encouragement and support of the United States of America, which signed a strategic cooperation agreement [with Israel] in 1981. In this period, the Golan Heights has been annexed, Israel destroyed Iraq's nuclear reactor, and it then invaded Lebanon and laid siege to Beirut in 1982, which constitutes the greatest insult to the Arab *umma* since the 1967 war.
>
> Hroub, 2002: 37

It was only after much arm twisting and cajoling from the United States that the PLO would finally reach the decision to abandon armed struggle, which would eventually result in Arafat's recognition of Israel in 1993. But because Arafat recognized Israel – without Israel recognizing Palestine – Israel could decide when and how to withdraw from the West Bank and Gaza, let alone Jerusalem, and whether to recognize Palestine at all. On 9 September 1993, Arafat recognized the right of the state of Israel to exist in peace and security and renounced the use of terrorism and other acts of violence. By contrast, Rabin merely agreed to recognize the PLO as the representative of the Palestinian people (Watson, 2000: 315–16).

The assassination of Yitzhak Rabin on 4 November 1995 and the election of Benjamin Netanyahu brought a chill to the peace process, with Hamas and Islamic Jihad playing into Likud's hands by systematically undermining Fatah's efforts to negotiate a final status agreement with Israel by placing bombs on public buses at inauspicious moments.[2] As the violence in Gaza and the West Bank reached fever pitch during the Second Intifada (2000–5), Fatah then got involved in armed struggle once more following the failure of the Camp David negotiations in the summer of 2000 by establishing the Fatah Tanzim and the al-Aqsa Martyrs' Brigades to compete with Hamas and Islamic Jihad.

And then, as if out of nowhere, came the most audacious terrorist attack in the modern history of the United States of America, when on 11 September 2001, two Boeing 767 planes were flown into the Twin Towers in New York City and a third plane, a Boeing 757, took out a wing of the Pentagon. (A fourth plane crashed into a field near Shanksville, Pennsylvania, after its passengers tried to overcome the hijackers.) The attacks were swiftly blamed on Osama Bin Laden's al-Qaeda network. Bin Laden had singled out Americans and Israelis for attack in his 'Declaration of the World Islamic Front for Jihad against the Jews and Crusaders', a statement published three years earlier in *al-Quds al-Arabi*, an Arabic language newspaper in London (*al-Quds al-Arabi*, 1998). It was probably not a coincidence that Palestine was number three on a list of reasons why jihad against America was deemed justified by Bin Laden, after the US military presence in Saudi Arabia and the sanctions against Iraq. Khalid Shaykh Muhammad, the principal architect of the 9/11 attacks, cited American support for Israel as his principal motivation for undertaking the attacks, as did his nephew Ramzi Yusuf for the World Trade Center bombing in February 1993 (Hegghammer and Wagemakers, 2013: 288). The attacks took place almost one year after Ariel Sharon's provocative visit to the Haram al-Sharif, which had sparked the Second Palestinian Intifada (Goldenberg, *Guardian* online).

Three days after 9/11, Ariel Sharon, now Israel's prime minister, brazenly compared Arafat to Bin Laden. During a conversation with the US Secretary of State Colin Powell, Sharon told Israel Public Radio, 'Everyone has his own Bin Laden. Arafat is our Bin Laden' (*Guardian* online, 2001). Not to be outdone, Benjamin Netanyahu told the US Senate in a speech he gave in 2002, 'If we do not immediately shut down the terror factories where Arafat is producing human bombs, it is only a matter of time before suicide bombers will terrorize your cities. If not destroyed, this madness will strike in your buses, in your supermarkets, in your pizza parlours, in your cafes' (Mearsheimer and Walt, 2008: 61).

And so began a new chapter in Israeli–Palestinian relations in which open season was declared against 'terrorism' and the states that harboured or supported it. As President Bush explained in the National Security Strategy of the United States of America:

> In many regions, legitimate grievances prevent the emergence of a lasting peace. Such grievances deserve to be, and must be, addressed within a political process. But no cause justifies terror. The United States will make no concessions to terrorist demands and strike no deals with them. We make no distinction between terrorists and those who knowingly harbor or provide aid to them.
>
> *National Security Strategy of the United States of America*, 2002: 5

On 24 June 2002, Bush called on the Palestinian people 'to elect new leaders, leaders not compromised by terror', which was a direct reference to Arafat, who had become an 'obstacle to peace' (Bush, 2002: 133). Bush's speech was considered so extreme it prompted one of Prime Minister Tony Blair's advisers to comment that the speech could 'have been written by Likud' (Kampfner, 2003: 189). But Arafat's fate was already sealed. In the White House he had become persona non grata. As Abrams explains, 'Israel had sought a peace partner for years but instead had found in Arafat a terrorist' (Abrams, 2013: 43).

Israel disengages from Gaza

On 11 November 2004, Arafat died in a French hospital in mysterious circumstances,[3] thus finally removing the obstacle from Mahmoud Abbas' path to power. Abbas had resigned as prime minister after only six months following a power struggle with Arafat, after Arafat had appointed him prime minister under American pressure the previous year. The plan to reduce Arafat's powers had been the brainchild of Ephraim Halevy, then director-general of Mossad. As Halevy explains in his memoir, 'The idea was to leave [Arafat] with his title of president, but to devolve his power in such a way that he would become a titular head of state, comparable ... to the Queen of England' (Halevy, 2006: 213). As McGeough explains, 'It was ...a classic maneuver from the playbook of American foreign policy interventions from Vietnam to Central America – the quest for a cooperative or puppet leader' (McGeough, 2009: 280). Arafat's (still unexplained) death followed the assassinations of Hamas leader Sheikh Yasin on 22 March 2004 and 'Abd al-'Aziz al-Rantisi, his successor, some three weeks later (Shlaim, 2014: 770–3).

With Arafat gone, and with Abu Mazen installed as prime minister, it was time to end the Intifada and prepare for new presidential and parliamentary elections. But first Sharon wanted to redeploy Israeli troops from the Gaza Strip in order to activate the 'Gaza First Plan', and despite bitter opposition from within his own party, especially from Netanyahu, who had resigned and was itching to challenge Sharon for leadership of the party (Abrams, 2013: 137). But Sharon wanted something in return from Bush before he would agree to disengage from Gaza. He got it in the form of a letter from the US president, with Bush declaring that, 'In light of new realities on the ground, including already existing major Israeli population centers, it is unrealistic to expect that the outcome of final status negotiations will be a full and complete return to the armistice lines of 1949' (Bush letter, 14 April 2004).[4]

Following the publication of the Bush letter, Sharon persuaded his cabinet to pass the Revised Disengagement Plan on 6 June 2004, which provided that in any future permanent status arrangement with the Palestinians, 'there will be no Israeli towns and villages in the Gaza Strip'. However, on the other hand, the Plan made it 'clear that in the West Bank, there are areas which will be part of the State of Israel, including major Israeli population centers, cities, towns and villages, security areas and other places of special interest to Israel' (Revised Disengagement Plan, 2004).

The Fatah–Hamas divide deepens

In 2003, when Sharon first considered disengagement, no one thought that Hamas would take over within a few years. Fatah, and especially Dahlan, their strongman in Gaza, was expected to crack down on Hamas as Arafat had occasionally asked him to do in the 1990s. The problem, as Abrams soon realized, was that Dahlan had only 2,000 reliable men in Gaza. Dahlan told Abrams, 'Don't be misled by the impression we have created that [sic] the PA is strong: Hamas and Palestinian Islamic Jihad and the gangs are stronger' (Abrams, 2013: 135). Indeed, on 7 September 2004, Musa Arafat, Yasser Arafat's cousin, one of the most powerful security officials in Fatah in Gaza, was murdered (Abrams, 2013: 140).

On 9 January 2005, less than two months after Arafat's death, presidential elections were held in the West Bank and Gaza. Hamas and Islamic Jihad boycotted the elections. Predictably, Abbas, having been nominated by Fatah to run, and with Hamas not participating, was elected with 62 per cent of the popular vote, ahead of his nearest rival, Mustafa Barghouti, with 19 per cent of the vote.[5] After a delay due to Fatah infighting, and despite Hamas' objections, Palestinian parliamentary elections were scheduled for 25 January 2006. This time, and after much internal debate, Hamas decided to run, and President Abbas insisted that they should participate, perhaps confident that Fatah would win despite Israel's and Abrams' initial opposition to Hamas' participation in the elections.[6] After all, promoting democracy in the Middle East had been a major policy goal of the Bush administration. Just four months before the legislative elections, Condoleezza Rice told Salam Fayyad, the PA's Finance Minister, that

> GOI [Government of Israel] said it would not facilitate the elections if Hamas were involved. We responded that it must. But the reality is that it is hard to make them swallow the idea that they have to support an armed group that still plots to kill Israelis. I am not so sure we would either.
>
> Palestine Papers, 22 September 2005

But under US pressure, Israel shifted its position, albeit reluctantly. In a meeting between Palestine's chief negotiator, Sa'ib Erekat, and Shimon Peres in Tel Aviv, Erekat insisted that Hamas participate in the elections: 'They will be the turning point in Middle East history, and in Palestinian history and if Israel or the US stops these elections we will have the Algerian model.' Peres replied, 'We need a face saving way to change [our position on Hamas]. In general we know the elections are going ahead . . . and we do not want to stop them' (Palestine Papers, 14 October 2005).

Despite polling by Khalil Shikaki's Centre for Policy and Survey Research in Ramallah which showed Fatah leading Hamas by a comfortable margin (Crooke, 2007: 4), there were contrary indications in the first weeks of January that Hamas might win more seats in the legislative council. According to documents disclosed by WikiLeaks, Israel's Ministry of Defence and the domestic Security

Agency Shin Bet believed that Hamas was going to win the elections because it had done better than expected in the municipal elections (that took place on 15 December 2005). On 12 January, Abrams and David Welch, Assistant Secretary of State for Near Eastern Affairs, met with Shin Bet chief Yuval Diskin in Tel Aviv. Diskin told them that Hamas had done well in the recent municipal elections, and that 'the most probable result is Hamas winning 35–40 percent'. Diskin also said that senior Fatah officials had asked for his help. According to the account of that meeting in the cable cleared by Welch and Abrams for Washington,

> ... these activists want the GOI [Government of Israel] to 'do their dirty work' and postpone the elections. For example, Diskin said, a worried Muhammad Dahlan came to see him a few days earlier seeking help from Israel's political leadership in postponing the elections... Meanwhile a confident Hamas wants the elections to take place on schedule.
>
> WikiLeaks, 13 January 2006

Dahlan's fears and Hamas' confidence proved to be well founded. Hamas won 74 seats in the 132-member Legislative Council to Fatah's 45 seats. This meant that Hamas won 56 per cent of the seats to Fatah's 34 per cent. Voter turnout was 77 per cent (Youngs and Smith, 2007: 10).

Just before the elections, the Middle East Quartet had called on those parties that wanted to be part of the political process to 'renounce violence, recognize Israel's right to exist, and disarm' and 'expressed its view that a future Palestinian Authority Cabinet should include no member who has not committed to the principles of Israel's right to exist in peace and security and an unequivocal end to violence and terrorism' (Quartet statement, 28 December 2005). Rice discloses in her memoir that as early as November 2005, the Quartet had agreed to include language in its statement about disarmament as a condition for participation in the elections, but Abbas was worried that 'such a statement would be seen as an effort to exclude Hamas' (Rice, 2011: 415). However, following Hamas' victory in the elections, the Quartet hardened these demands and insisted that 'A two-state solution to the conflict requires all participants in the democratic process to renounce violence and terror, accept Israel's right to exist, and disarm, as outlined in the Roadmap' (Quartet statement, 26 January 2006). These additional demands prompted Alvaro de Soto, the UN representative to the Quartet, to observe:

> [I]t was one thing to take positions before the elections, when we all assumed an outcome that would preserve Fatah's majority, and another to take positions in the face of an outright Hamas victory. The people had spoken in free and fair

elections whose holding had been encouraged by the international community, and their wishes should be respected.

de Soto, 2007: 18, para. 46

Strikingly, the Quartet's conditions were issued as a result of American pressure *after* the teleconferences between the Principals in December (i.e. the meeting between all of the members of the Quartet). Moreover, the conditions were virtually identical to the benchmarks that had been demanded by Israel's National Security Council. We know this because WikiLeaks has disclosed the report of a meeting in Tel Aviv, dated 25 January, one day before the Quartet's 26 January statement, between Giora Eiland, the Director of Israel's National Security Council, his deputy, Eran Etzion, and Robert Danin, Deputy Assistant Secretary of State for Near Eastern Affairs. In addition to calling on the US government and the Quartet to accept Israel's red lines, Israel's National Security Council told Danin that they also wanted the US administration to ask Cairo and Riyadh 'to pressure HAMAS to accept certain conditions – including recognition of the state of Israel, renunciation of terrorism, and disarmament – as a price for joining a Palestinian coalition government' (WikiLeaks, 26 January 2006). Accordingly, what began as Israel's benchmarks became US benchmarks, and subsequently Quartet conditions.

Given Hamas' founding ideology, these conditions were totally unrealistic, as Welch and Abrams and the other members of the Quartet must have understood. Moreover, the Quartet's demands on recognition, renouncing terrorism, and disarmament, came with a sting: until they were met, the US and the EU would cease their aid to the Palestinian Authority and Israel would cease transferring tax revenues. In addition, and under pressure from Washington and other capitals, the world's banks refused to process the electronic movement of funds to Gaza. By the middle of 2006, Hamas complained that various Arab banks had frozen more than $300 million that had been donated by Iran and several Arab regimes (McGeough, 2009: 331). However, unlike Fatah, which was heavily dependent on Western aid, Hamas was able to resort to surreptitious means to bring in donations from Iran and Qatar. Indeed, as explained below, one of the unintended consequences of the sanctions is that they weakened Fatah and strengthened Hamas.

Hamas' victory threw American and European policymakers into a quandary as they had been trumpeting the spread of democracy in the Arab world – hauntingly foreshadowing the events that would rock the region in 2011 when Ben Ali, Mubarak and Qaddafi were overthrown in popular uprisings. Instead of coming to terms with its new opposition role, explains McGeough, 'many senior figures in Fatah immediately began plotting the overthrow of the newly elected government. They spoke in terms of being at war with Hamas, and they urged the United States and other foreign donors not to bail it out' (McGeough, 2009: 324).

On 31 March, Abrams, Welch and Lieutenant-General Keith Dayton, the US Security Coordinator for the PA, had a meeting with Erekat, where he urged them to find ways to restart permanent status negotiations with Israel. Abrams voiced scepticism about the conditions for moving forward with permanent status issues because the US government and the international community could not ignore Hamas' victory in the legislative elections. When the subject turned to US support for the Presidential Guard, Erekat emphasized that 'when the confrontation with Hamas happens' Abu Mazen will need a force of about 10,000 men that is well trained, properly equipped and capable of protecting him. To emphasize this point, Erekat explained that under the PA's Basic Law, if 'anything happened to Abu Mazen Hamas PLC speaker Aziz Dweik would assume the presidency'. Dayton responded by explaining that the US government would need further details on the training and equipment needs of the Presidential Guard, noting that providing assistance to the PA security forces would be difficult for the US administration at this point.

When Welch and Abrams met with Ministry of Defence Bureau head Amos Gilad later on 31 March, Gilad warned them that 'despite all possible efforts on security, in time the Palestinians will "do something" (i.e., a terror attack)' that he said would 'force a "spectacular" response out of the GOI' (WikiLeaks, 4 April 2006). On 25 June, the time for that spectacular response arrived when Hamas captured Israeli soldier Gilad Shalit in a pre-dawn operation through a tunnel (Milton-Edwards and Farrell, 2010: 273). Israel swiftly launched operation 'Summer Rains' and snatched sixty-four Hamas officials, including eight cabinet ministers and twenty members of the newly elected parliament (McGeough, 2009: 339). Additionally, airstrikes knocked out the main Gaza power station, several bridges and a series of government buildings, including Hamas Prime Minister Haniyeh's office and the Palestinian Ministry of Foreign Affairs (McGeough, 2009: 340).[7]

Hamas takes over Gaza

In his memoir, Abrams rejects the accusation by 'Hamas and its supporters' that Hamas' takeover of the Gaza Strip in 2007 was to prevent Fatah forces from crushing Hamas with arms and training provided for that purpose by the Americans (Abrams, 2013: 228). However, in his End of Mission report, de Soto claims that 'the US clearly pushed for a confrontation between Fatah and Hamas – so much so that, a week before Mecca [where the first national unity government was declared], the US envoy declared twice in an envoys meeting in Washington how much "I like this violence", referring to the near-civil war that was erupting in Gaza in which civilians were being regularly killed and injured, because "it means that other Palestinians are resisting Hamas"' (de Soto, 2007: 21, para. 56). While the envoy's delight at intra-Palestinian violence does not amount to an admission of US involvement in such violence, McGeough claims that a group of Palestinian businessmen had been taken aback when they met with Abrams in Washington because he had stressed the need for the United States to provide guns, ammunition and training to enable Mahmoud Abbas' Fatah forces to wrest control of the West Bank and Gaza from Hamas (McGeough, 2009: 351).

But at the time Fatah was concerned about security not only in Gaza, where they feared for Abbas' safety (WikiLeaks, 24 February 2006), but also in the West Bank, where Fatah's forces had been pulverized by Israel during the Second Palestinian Intifada. On 3 October 2006, Shin Bet director Yuval Diskin told Richard Jones, the US Ambassador in Tel Aviv, that

> Fatah's ability to act against Hamas is limited to the West Bank, where Fatah owes its comparative strength primarily to ongoing GOI [Government of Israel] operations against Hamas activists. He added that if GOI operations against Hamas in the West Bank ceased, the situation would soon reflect a more realistic power relationship, with Hamas on top.
> WikiLeaks, 4 October 2004

Diskin also told Jones that

> Shin Bet now had sensitive information that Hamas recently smuggled 20 Russian-made Koronet anti-tank missiles into Gaza, of the kind used successfully by Hezbollah against IDF Merkava tanks.[8] Hamas militants are currently holding the missiles, and are waiting for training on how to deploy them ... this was one of the reasons why Shin Bet opposed openings of the Rafah crossing.
> WikiLeaks, 4 October 2004

On 12 October, Diskin told Dayton that Israel supported the strengthening of President Abbas and the Presidential Guard, but thought it more important to strengthen Fatah as a movement rather than the personal position of the president. Diskin also warned Dayton that although a Palestinian civil war was still remote, 'if Abbas were to do something which would cause Hamas to feel their hold on the government is in jeopardy, the situation could deteriorate and make things worse than they are today' (WikiLeaks, 12 October 2006).

Amidst the deteriorating security situation in Gaza, with almost daily clashes between factions loyal to Fatah and Hamas, King Abdullah of Saudi Arabia summoned President Abbas and Hamas leader Khaled Meshaal to Mecca, where they concluded a reconciliation pact on 8 February 2007. To the astonishment of the Americans, who had not been given prior notice of this development, the Mecca agreement provided for the establishment of a national unity government, which they had been trying to prevent. As Rice recalls:

> When word came that there was a deal [at Mecca], it was a devastating blow. My trusted interpreter Gamal Helal rushed down to my office. He'd been on the phone with Abbas's people and had been following the Al Jazeera coverage as well. 'How bad is it?' I asked. 'It's a piece of sh–t!' he exclaimed, quickly apologizing for his language. Hamas would enter into a unity government with the Palestinian Authority, and the party's putative leader in Gaza, Ismail Haniyeh, would become prime minister. With that agreement, the distinction between moderate Fatah and extremist Hamas factions was immediately blurred since the Palestinian Authority would now allow officials from a group that we, the Europeans, and the Israelis listed as a terrorist organization into the Palestinian government.
>
> Rice, 2011: 551–2

The power-sharing agreement negotiated at Mecca gave Hamas nine cabinet seats to Fatah's six (Milton-Edwards and Farrell, 2010: 276). Desperately hoping for a unity dividend, Abbas called for the resumption of Western aid and for the hundreds of millions of dollars confiscated by Israel in tax payments. Norway announced that it would lift its sanctions, and the United Kingdom indicated that it might begin contacts with non-Hamas ministers[9] (Milton-Edwards and Farrell, 2010: 277). On 20 February, Israel's prime minister, Ehud Olmert, explained that he had cautioned Dahlan not to join the new PA cabinet in the forthcoming national unity government (WikiLeaks, 21 February 2007), probably because this would make continued Israeli contacts with him difficult, due to the Israeli boycott of Hamas. Dahlan heeded this advice, having 'disavowed interest in the Deputy PM position in a statement issued to the press on February 19' (WikiLeaks, 23 February 2007).

On 2 March, 'An Action Plan for the Palestinian Presidency' was drawn up by the State Department. The agreement was subsequently leaked to the Jordanian weekly *al-Majd*, where it was translated into Arabic and published on 30 April.

The Action Plan is worth highlighting because it garnered a lot of press attention in the Arab world following its publication in *al-Majd*, and might have contributed to Hamas' decision to attack Fatah in June. The document also forms one of the central pieces of evidence in a sensational story published in *Vanity Fair* which claimed that the White House and the State Department backed an armed force under Dahlan to overthrow Hamas in Gaza (Rose, *Vanity Fair* online, 31 March 2008). In the interview with Michael Hogan accompanying the exposé, David Rose, the article's author, described the Action Plan as 'a blueprint for a full-blown coup against Abbas's own unity government' ('The proof is in the paper trail', *Vanity Fair* online, 31 March 2008).

According to the Action Plan, which is available online (Action plan, 2 March 2007), the credibility of President Abbas suffered after the Mecca Accord and the failure of the national unity government to fulfil the Quartet's conditions. In the absence of efforts by Abbas to keep the presidency as 'the centre of gravity', the international community's support for his government and efforts to establish a Palestinian state would erode. Accordingly, Abbas needed to present 'a concrete, meaningful, and performance-based action plan that would render him more credible' ahead of discussions with the Israelis and Secretary of State Rice later in March. The document cautioned Abbas to avoid 'wasting valuable time on accommodating Hamas' ideological conditions and turning the clock to the pre-Madrid context'. The objective of the plan was to provide political and economic support for Abbas so that he would be in a position to enter into negotiations with Israel, and call for early elections to support the peace process. The presidency was expected to control the security institutions and impose order to deter attempts at escalation by Hamas. In this connection, the document alludes to security commitments that had already been agreed upon between the Palestinians and the Israelis, and refers to Dayton and Dahlan by name, and the understandings reached between the Arab Quartet (Egypt, Jordan, Saudi Arabia and the UAE) and the US. A brief description of the transformation of the Palestinian security forces is included in the Annex. According to the Annex, the Palestinian Authority was to transform the Palestinian security forces to ensure law and order over a 6–12 month period, which included the appointment of a national security adviser to follow up on the reform programmes. The document explained that camps were to be prepared for training, which would also include specialized training abroad. The entire action plan was subject to approval by Israel. The costings for the action plan came to a staggering total of $1.27 billion, but significantly no money was earmarked in the costings for security equipment – whether lethal or non-lethal.

Although the unauthorized publication of this document would have aroused Hamas' concerns and contributed to further distrust between Fatah and Hamas, it hardly amounted to a blueprint for a coup. First, the plan had to be approved by Israel, and second, the money had to be appropriated by Congress, neither of which could be taken for granted. As Dahlan admitted in his interview with Rose, the cash never arrived: 'Nothing was disbursed.' As Rose concedes, 'Any notion that the money could be transferred quickly and easily had died on Capitol Hill, where the payment was blocked by the House Subcommittee on the Middle East and South Asia. Its members feared that military aid to the Palestinians might end up being turned against Israel.' Rose was also forced to admit that efforts to obtain aid from Arab states came to very little. Dahlan told Rose, 'the Arabs made many more pledges than they ever paid' (Rose, *Vanity Fair* online, 31 March 2008). The publication of the Action Plan by *al-Majd* did, however, put Hamas on notice that if it did not act against Fatah soon, Fatah's security forces would become stronger over time, once the plan had been approved by Israel, and once the monies had either been appropriated by Congress or obtained from other sources. At this point, Fatah would be in a stronger position to dictate terms and confront Hamas. When Abbas appointed Dahlan National Security Advisor to the newly created National Security Council (NSC) on 8 April, Hamas' suspicions would have intensified, as Dahlan was, in the words of one Hamas minister, 'the man who burnt our beards and tortured us' (Milton-Edwards and Farrell, 2010: 280). Moreover, only two of the ten men appointed to the NSC – Ismail Haniyeh and Ali Sartawi – were from Hamas (WikiLeaks, 16 April 2007).[10]

Dahlan was also part of a top-secret programme to train Palestinian security forces in Egypt to prevent smuggling through Rafah. The programme was disclosed in the unprecedented leakage of documents from meetings of the PLO's Negotiations Affairs Department by Al-Jazeera and the *Guardian* in 2011. The disclosure included two memoranda addressed to Sa'ib Erekat, in his capacity as a member of the National Security Council, with summaries of the meetings of the Quadrilateral Security Forum between Israel, the United States, Egypt and Fatah. The memoranda are dated 11 March 2007 and 3 April 2007 respectively. Dayton headed the American team, Amos Gilad the Israeli team, and Dahlan the Palestinian team (it appears the Egyptians sent different people to each meeting). The purpose of these meetings was to discuss the security situation in the Gaza Strip. The rules of engagement outlined in the first meeting made it clear that the meetings were top-secret and that 'any leakages would immediately result in the cessation of the use of this forum and the projects being aborted'. The memorandum explained that the forum was backed by 'the highest political echelons of each government represented' (Palestine Papers, 11 March 2007).

We do not know how many meetings took place before they were aborted. The Palestine Papers only disclosed two meetings. The first meeting took place in Tel Aviv, where the Israeli team gave a presentation on the use of tunnels in Gaza to smuggle advanced weaponry, and send fighters to be trained aboard, particularly in Iran. 'Hamas is seen to emulate the Hizbollah model, which in turn is based on the Iranian model. They use Rafah to move militants and money' (Palestine Papers, 11 March 2007). The Palestinian team agreed that this may be part of the analysis, but made it clear that each team was to assume responsibility for restabilizing the security situation in the Gaza Strip: 'Palestinians cannot do this alone.'

The next meeting of the Quadrilateral Security Forum took place on 3 April 2007 in Egypt. In welcoming the participants, General Kinawi said that he spoke on behalf of Omar Suleiman, the director of the Egyptian General Intelligence Directorate, who sent his apologies. The meeting was chaired by Dayton who opened the meeting by explaining that President Bush had directed him to speak to the Saudis, the Emiratis, the Egyptians and the Jordanians: 'The purpose of these meetings is to prevent Hamas from using the NUG [national unity government] as a means of gaining more powers and building up more arms' (Palestine Papers, 3 April 2007). General Kinawi then interjected saying that Egypt would judge the national unity government based on its actions, meaning the extent to which Hamas cooperated with Abbas and stopped rocket fire into Israel. For the time being, it was Egypt's view that the US position on the national unity government was 'premature'. By contrast, Amos Gilad had no qualms about the US position and expressed Israel's concern that Hamas would use its position in the Ministry of the Interior in the national unity government as cover for its forces, before they were unleashed against Fatah. Rashid Abu-Shbak, the PA's Internal Security director-general, spoke on behalf of President Abbas for the Palestinian side. He explained that the president fully backed the forum, and hoped that the Israelis would not delay things since the removal of the tunnels and ending the smuggling was a collective effort. Israel also needed to do more to help Abbas, since only by supporting Fatah would Hamas be weakened. Palestinian general Jamal Kaid then delivered a presentation on plans for the deployment of three battalions along the Philadelphi corridor between Egypt and Gaza. General Kinawi thought the Palestinian proposal to deploy Palestinian forces east of the Rafah crossing was reasonable, with barbed wire, towers, lighting and communication equipment, subject of course to Israeli approval. Kinawi explained that 'Egypt has been training and will continue to train Palestinian security elements to help create professional and effective bodies that can control the situation on the ground.' But he emphasized that this training required financial support, indicating that resources for this support had not yet been allocated. In response, Gilad said that Israel would have to study these proposals carefully, 'which will take time'. Dayton suggested that the Palestinian proposal to stop the smuggling through Rafah needed to be approved by Palestine's NSC and endorsed as policy for approval by President Abbas: 'If the President approves, this will help convince people in Washington and Tel Aviv that the NSC is a serious tool that will provide security to the Palestinians.' Significantly, Dayton suggested that this would necessarily entail reaching an agreement with Prime Minister Ismail Haniyeh as he was the deputy chair of the NSC.

On 4 April 2007, the new PA interior minister, Hani al-Qawasmi (an independent), published a 100-day security plan to enforce domestic law and order in the West Bank and Gaza. The head of the Technical Team for Reform, Basil Jabr, told the American policy office at the Consulate General in Jerusalem[11] that al-Qawasmi was responding to public pressure to improve law enforcement and that the plan was published without either the consent of President Abbas or any coordination with the NSA. The publication of the plan caused concern to Hamas, with former Interior Minister Sa'id Siam insisting that Hamas' Executive Force was the only force capable of performing its functions in Gaza and would not be disbanded (WikiLeaks, 6 April 2007). In any event, on 7 April the cabinet approved the security plan. Although the plan scarcely addressed deploying Palestinian security forces in Gaza and assumed the full involvement of Hamas' Executive Force in security operations, it did envisage amalgamating the PA security forces with the Executive Forces at some point in the future. There was, however, a division of opinion between al-Qawasmi and President Abbas on the role of the Executive Forces, with Abbas taking a harder line and insisting the Executive Forces be disbanded as it was illegal. In the ensuing power struggle between al-Qawasmi and Abu Shbak, who was close to Dahlan, al-Qawasmi threatened to resign if he was not given authority over the internal security forces and if Abu Shbak was not dismissed. Al-Qawasmi had tried to resign on 23 April, but this was rejected by Haniyeh (WikiLeaks, 3 May 2007).

Uncannily, the State Department's Action Plan for the Palestinian presidency, described earlier, was published in the Jordanian weekly *al-Majd* during the power struggle between Fatah and Hamas over the incorporation of the

Executive Forces into the PA's Security Forces, which had been exacerbated by the tussle between al-Qawasmi and Abu Shbak. When, five days later, *Ha'aretz* published details of another leaked document, the US-sponsored 'Benchmarks for Agreement on Movement and Access', along with its security protocol (*Ha'aretz* online, 4 May), Hamas' fears of a plot to launch a coup appeared to be unfolding. This was especially so as the security goals outlined in the benchmarks agreement provided that the PA's Security Forces were to enforce law and order, fight terrorism, stop the launching of Qassam rockets and 'address smuggling of terror-related weapons and materials and cash destined for Gaza' (*Ha'aretz* online, 4 May). The security forces were also expected to improve their coordination with Israel, take control of the Palestinian side of the border with Gaza, and destroy the tunnels. Effectively, *Ha'aretz* had just published a plan to cut off Hamas' lifeline to the outside world. Why *Ha'aretz* chose to publish the story at this particular moment in time remains a mystery, as does the agency that disclosed it. Nor do we know who leaked the document to *al-Majd*.

Then, to compound matters, on 10 May, Fatah deployed 500 men in Gaza, after their entry was approved by Israel. This was done without coordinating their deployment with Hamas or even with the PA's own interior minister, al-Qawasmi (*Washington Post* online, 18 May 2007). Dahlan told Rose that these were new recruits that 'had been on a crash course for 45 days. The idea was that we needed them to go in dressed well, equipped well, and that might create the impression of new authority' (Rose, *Vanity Fair* online, 31 March 2008). But instead of creating the impression of new authority, the 500 recruits created feelings of insecurity in Hamas, given the revelations in *al-Majd* and *Ha'aretz*, amid rumours of weapons being transferred through the crossing with Egypt. On 15 May, al-Qawasmi resigned after less than two months on the job. Haniyeh took on the interior portfolio until a new minister was named (*Los Angeles Times* online, 15 May 2007).

In the days and weeks that followed, relations between Fatah and Hamas deteriorated sharply, amid tit-for-tat killings. According to the US Consul General's analysis of the fighting from 13 to 18 May, Hamas held the initiative in all significant clashes, while the PA's security forces' successes were limited to defensive actions. Hamas focused on eliminating Dahlan's dreaded special forces, which sustained heavy casualties, and the al-Aqsa brigades, whose leader, Baha Abu Jarad, was killed. The PA's Security Forces in Gaza, which largely refrained from fighting, frequently complained of inadequate rifles and pistols and chronic ammunition shortages, whereas Hamas appeared to have plentiful ammunition. The Kalashnikov 7.62mm rifle was the principal weapon used, although a number of MI6 rifles stolen from Israel and sniper rifles were also used. 'Security contacts report Hamas used sniper rifles at night in some instances, suggesting a small number of starlight scopes or other first generation night-vision sets' (WikiLeaks, 25 May 2007). Both sides possessed 12.7mm heavy machine guns, but only Hamas used these in an offensive role.

On 22 May, Richard Jones, the American ambassador to Israel, had his first meeting with Pinchas Buchris, the new director-general of the Israeli Ministry of Defence, who expressed concern that Hamas was gaining control of the Gaza Strip, and might take complete control of military forces in the area. He was frustrated that neither President Abbas nor Dahlan was in control of events in Gaza. Astonishingly, despite Fatah's setbacks, security officials in Israel were, even at this late stage in the fighting, opposed to transferring weapons to Fatah in Gaza. Pinhas explained to Jones that while the Karni crossing[12] was open on the Israeli side, there was no one on the Palestinian side to receive the weapons once they passed through the crossing: 'We do not want the equipment to go to Hamas so that it can be used against us.' Jones responded by saying that most of the weapons were small arms, and that if Fatah did not receive help, Hamas would gain total control of Gaza (WikiLeaks, 25 May 2007). But despite Jones' pleas, Israel refused to send weapons, including small arms – even though Dayton had gone through a pre-prepared list.

On 11 June, one day before Hamas gained complete control of Gaza, Ambassador Jones met with Diskin, the director of Shin Bet, who told Jones that Fatah was on its last legs. Diskin criticized Dahlan for attempting to lead his loyalists in Gaza by remote control from abroad. 'We are not even sure where he is,' he claimed, amid reports that Dahlan had been spotted in Cairo and Amman.[13] Diskin told Jones that security forces loyal to Abbas had been penetrated by Hamas and that Hamas had stolen some 'Doshka' heavy machine guns from the Presidential Guard. This was why Diskin opposed Dayton's proposal to supply ammunition and weapons to Fatah: 'I support the idea of militarily strengthening Fatah, but I am afraid that they are not organized to ensure that the equipment that is transferred to them will reach the intended recipients.' Diskin observed that the new generation of leaders in Fatah were facing a moment of truth: 'They are approaching a zero-sum situation, and yet they ask us to attack Hamas. This is a new development. We have never seen this before. They are desperate' (WikiLeaks, 13 June 2007). With Israel refusing to come to their aid, Fatah's forces soon crumbled and the basic weapons and training that had been provided by Dayton 'counted for nothing' (McGeough, 2009: 373). As Abrams rues in his memoir, 'Once again, Dahlan had proved to be better at paddling the payroll than taking risks or inspiring his troops' (Abrams, 2013: 229).

As the tide began to turn against Fatah, Abbas declared a state of emergency, sacked Haniyeh as prime minister and appointed Fayyad in his place. Abbas then retaliated for the loss of Gaza by ordering a round-up of key Hamas figures in the West Bank, driving much of the Islamist leadership underground as their institutions were torched ahead of orders that more than one hundred Hamas agencies must fold (McGeough, 2009: 377–8). On 24 June, Haniyeh gave a speech at a rally in Gaza in which he accused Israel of working to deepen the divide between Palestinian factions by restricting movement from Gaza and by releasing clearance revenues only to the West Bank. Haniyeh claimed that Hamas' takeover of Gaza was a pre-emptive strike in response to the pressure on Hamas related to international restrictions, the arrest of PLC members and Fatah attacks against Hamas personnel and interests. He displayed a letter at the rally addressed to Abbas warning of a 'planned explosion' due to Fatah's violations of the Mecca agreement (Haniyeh speech, Gaza city, 24 June 2007).

Abbas' dissolution of parliament, and the appointment of Fayyad without parliamentary approval, provoked strong criticism from the drafters of Palestine's Basic Law – lawyer Anis al-Qasim and the late Anglo-Palestinian judge and jurist, Professor Eugene Cotran – who told reporters that the law did not grant Abbas 'the power to appoint a new government without legislative approval nor the right to suspend articles of the Basic Law ... to spare new premier Salam Fayyad the need to win a vote in parliament' (Reuters online, 2007).[14] A spokesman for Fatah responded to the criticisms from al-Qasim and Cotran by insisting 'the President's word was law' (Reuters online, 2007). But Cotran retorted, telling Reuters that 'Ruling by decree doesn't mean he can suspend or change the constitution.' But Abbas has ruled by decree ever since.

Conclusion

So do the claims by Crooke and Rose stack up, or are we to believe the accounts by Abrams and Rice? The difficulty with writing about an alleged coup is, of course, its clandestine nature. The evidence is scanty, as one would expect. Yet the unprecedented disclosure of US diplomatic cables by WikiLeaks and the disclosure of the Palestine Papers indicate that while there was no master plan for an armed coup to overthrow Hamas, there were plenty of reasons for Hamas to believe that there was a coup in the making.

The Quartet's conditions that Hamas recognize Israel, abandon violence, disarm and abide by previous Israel–PLO agreements,[15] which were all demands by Israel's National Security Council, placed Fatah and Hamas in an untenable position. This was especially so when the funds began to dry up and when Palestine's banks were unable to process electronic payments. The message this pressure sent was as clear as it was damaging: there was no place for Islamists in democratic politics. Hamas had, after all, agreed to participate in the elections under an agreement the PLO had negotiated with Israel, which arguably amounted to indirect recognition of Israel, and the US insisted that the elections take place despite full knowledge of Hamas' refusal to surrender its weapons.

The sanctions ultimately backfired. Once the funds dried up, the PA and President Abbas became even weaker, while Hamas, which was not dependent on Western aid, became stronger. Without money, including the monies collected from the taxes that Israel withheld from the PA, the PA was unable to pay its employees – including those employed in the security sector – for almost one year. Hamas, in contrast, was able to mobilize local resources from *zakat* committees (charities) and from its patrons in Qatar, Iran and Syria. Six weeks after Fatah's rout from Gaza, Dayton told Shaykh Hazza, the UAE's national security advisor, that Hamas' armed wing had received much more money and training than Abbas' forces. Iran sent Hamas $150 million and Qatar $400 million, in addition to training and equipment. Hazza agreed with Dayton's analysis, but told Dayton that the supporters of Abbas had tried to balance Hamas, rather than destroy it. Hazza explained that Abbas had refused to take sides, even when Hamas attacked the national security forces. Abbas only called on both sides to stop the fighting, which equalized both parties. Hamas never attacked the Presidential Guard, and the Presidential Guard never fought Hamas. Its commander has since been charged with high treason (WikiLeaks, 30 July 2007).

The claim of Crooke and Rose that there was a plan for a coup d'état in Gaza by Fatah, Israel and the US is difficult to sustain. The documents disclosed in *al-Majd*, *Ha'aretz* and *Vanity Fair* do not provide evidence of a plan to launch a coup. No money was earmarked for the provision of weapons to Fatah in the State Department's Action Plan for the Palestinian presidency, and no money was appropriated by Congress. The plan was predicated on Israel's consent, and envisaged Fatah returning to power in the next election, which is why the plan placed so much emphasis on boosting the economy, capacity-building, safeguarding the rule of law, negotiating an end to the conflict and creating a Palestinian state. A close reading of the documents disclosed by WikiLeaks reveals that Dayton was more concerned that Hamas would try to take over Gaza and the West Bank before the next elections, if Fatah did not get its act together. While the Arab Quartet pledged to send money to Fatah, very little was disbursed. In the Quadrilateral Security Forum on Gazan smuggling, Egypt wanted to give the national unity government a chance to prove itself, describing the US position that Hamas was seeking to take over Gaza as premature. The training programme in Egypt was to stop the smuggling of weapons into Gaza from Egypt, not a conspiracy to overthrow Hamas. Moreover, the plan to stop the smuggling of weapons through the tunnels under Rafah had to be approved by the PA's NSC, where Haniyeh, the prime minister, was the deputy chair. The Egyptians were always concerned about upsetting the Muslim Brotherhood in Egypt, which is why, prior to 2013, they did not want to be seen to be close to Israel in making life difficult for Hamas.[16] Dahlan, the alleged mastermind of the coup, was nowhere to be found. If Dahlan was plotting to overthrow Hamas, he would have made sure that he was in Gaza directing his forces in the midst of battle. But Dahlan had been absent from Gaza for weeks, convalescing from knee surgery. Moreover, Dahlan told Rose that 'even when we asked [the] Israelis to release our own money that was frozen ... that we need[ed] to pay for our security, [the] Israelis did not allow us to use our own money' (Dahlan interview transcript with Rose, December 2007). It was as if Israel was setting up Dahlan to fail. Israel refused to transfer weapons to Dahlan's forces, even when the US ambassador urged Israel to send weapons to Gaza as late as 12 June, when Hamas was on the verge of seizing control of the whole of the Gaza Strip.

Palestine is a small place where rumours – real and imagined – spread like wildfire and where nothing is ever what it seems. Claims, whether or not they are based on evidence, are largely irrelevant. What counts are perceptions. Even though no money was earmarked for the provision of weapons to Fatah in the Action Plan, the plan was designed to hollow out Hamas' election victory. If the security regime in the West Bank is any guide, where Fatah keeps Israel well informed about what is going on and coordinates its activities with Israel, Fatah's cooperation with Israel to end the tunnelling through Rafah would have looked to Hamas as though it was an attempt by Fatah to take over Gaza, especially after the revelations in *Ha'aretz*. When we take into account the opacity of Dayton's efforts to train Dahlan's security forces, the complicity of the Egyptians in that training, and the appearance through the crossing at Rafah, with little if any warning, of newly trained military personnel in new uniforms, however slapdash their training, there existed a rich body of elements to create suspicion. Unwittingly, the allegations that the US, Israel and Fatah were planning to take over the Gaza Strip and expel Hamas with the aid of friendly Arab states opposed to the Muslim Brotherhood contributed to the climate of mistrust between Fatah and Hamas that was exacerbated by misguided American policies (that were actually Israel's policies) following the elections that fanned the flames in Gaza. The question is, who was spreading these rumours and why?

One hint as to who might have been spreading these rumours was given by Amos Yadlin, head of the Directorate of Military Intelligence (Aman) at the height of the conflict between Fatah and Hamas, when he confided to Ambassador Jones that some people in the Israeli government preferred having Gaza controlled by Hamas. This might sound counterintuitive, as Israel did not support a coup d'état in Gaza, but as Yadlin explained, in the event of a coup, one of the advantages of having Hamas control Gaza was that it 'would enable the IDF to treat Gaza as a hostile country rather than having to deal with Hamas as a non-state actor' (WikiLeaks, 13 June 2007). And this is precisely what happened, when Israel's security cabinet declared Gaza 'hostile territory' three months later ('Security Cabinet declares Gaza hostile territory', 19 September 2007).

Following the dismantling and evacuation of the settlements in Gaza in 2005, Israel no longer needed a security interlocutor to protect settlements that had now been abandoned. In contrast, a security interlocutor was still necessary in the West Bank where there are many settlements. Prior to 2005, Gaza was a security nightmare for Israel and a graveyard for many soldiers who had stopped foot patrols in Gaza city and the teeming refugee camps in 2004 because they had become so dangerous, which is why Israel's air force had resorted to air strikes or 'extrajudicial killings' (Goldberg, *The Times of Israel*). Despite the redeployment of Israeli military personnel to Gaza's perimeters, Israel is able to contain Hamas in Gaza because it is hemmed in to the north and east by a security barrier with Israel, by the Mediterranean Sea to the west, by a wall with Egypt (controlled by Israel) to the south, and by controlling Gaza's airspace (Li, 2006: 38–55). By treating Gaza as 'hostile territory', Israel can hold Hamas responsible for armed activities in Gaza and justify its armed attacks against Hamas in Gaza as acts of 'self-defence'. Declaring Gaza hostile territory also provided a basis for economic sanctions against Hamas, which has enabled Israel to limit the provision of fuel and supplies to Gaza and enforce a maritime blockade over its coastal waters. Finally, the rout of Fatah from Gaza divides the Palestinians into factions in a further blow to national unity, and administratively separates Gaza from PA institutions in the West Bank, diminishing the prospects of establishing an independent and viable Palestinian state. It also allows Israel to argue that should it ever leave the West Bank, Hamas might take over, because

Fatah is not capable of controlling them. All the more reason for Israel to stay in the West Bank.

By taking control of the whole of the Gaza Strip in 2007, Hamas accomplished what its founder, Sheikh Yasin, had refused when Israel asked Hamas to take over the administration of Gaza in 1988. While we may never know who leaked the documents to *al-Majd* and *Ha'aretz*, one thing is for certain: the fallout from their publication has been an unmitigated disaster for the Palestinian people.

5

Hezbollah and the Lebanese State: Indispensable, Unpredictable – Destabilizing?

Peter Sluglett

In 1969, Michael Hudson published the first edition of a book about Lebanon, based on his doctoral fieldwork, called *The Precarious Republic*, a skilful analysis of the Lebanese political system at the time.[1] In the book, Hudson imagined the possibility of the formation of a 'country-wide, left-of-center social democratic party', by which he probably meant something like the German SDP, the French Parti Socialiste or the British Labour Party, which would be multi-sectarian (or non-sectarian). In the forty-eight years since Hudson's book first appeared in 1969, and especially since 2005, the Lebanese republic is as precarious, if not more precarious, than ever, and sectarianism remains as large and, one might say, as destructive, a factor in Lebanese politics as it has ever been. With the passage of time, and particularly with the collapse of the left in the 1990s, the idea of forming a non-sectarian political party remains, and as far can be imagined, will remain, a pipedream, especially in the context of the growth of ever more extreme forms of sectarianism in recent years.

Largely as a consequence of its long-standing political structure,[2] Lebanon is a 'weak state', that is, one that is institutionally weak, with a government that often has only tenuous, partial or intermittent control over the national territory.[3] Hence militias, or violent non-state actors, funded from a variety of internal and external sources, have long been a regular feature of Lebanese political life. The structure of Lebanese politics is built around religious confessions as corporate actors in the system, rather than around the 'conventional' role of citizens in the modern state. The political leaders of the communities act as decision-makers in national politics, regardless of their formal positions in the state.[4] The various confessional militias, mostly[5] the product of the civil war (1975–90), have generally been too powerful for the state's armed forces to be able to control them. Before the appearance of Hezbollah, which forms the subject of this chapter, the best-known Lebanese militia was *al-Kata'ib*, founded by the Maronite politician Pierre Jumayyil.[6] *Al-Kata'ib*, a political formation with a conventional political wing and an extra-parliamentary militia, has 'been around' since the late 1930s, that is, long before the foundation of comparable organizations in other parts of the world like ETA in the Basque Country (1959), the FARC in Colombia (1964), or Sendero Luminoso in Peru (1970).

Like *al-Kata'ib*, Hezbollah, founded in 1982, thinks of itself as the defender, or upholder of the interests, of the Lebanese state, as well as, obviously, advancing or reflecting the interests of its own members. Hezbollah has a particular vision of the Lebanese state as a spearhead of resistance against US and Israeli aggression in the region, as well as a perennial commitment to the liberation of Palestine. It sees itself as an embodiment of Lebanese patriotism rather than as a challenger, or an alternative, to the state, a stand that was buttressed enormously by its strong performance during the Israeli invasion of 2006, and throughout the war for Syria as the main defender of the Lebanese state in the struggle against extremist Sunni (= *takfiri*) groups.[7] The current structure of Lebanese politics means that it would not be possible for a Shia political party to 'take over' the state, or for its leader to become president, an office to which the Maronite Pierre Jumayyil could and did quite reasonably aspire during his long political career.[8]

The rise of the Shias as a 'significant force' in Lebanese politics

In the evidently flawed Lebanese census of 1932,[9] the Maronites and other Christians formed over 50 per cent of the population, Sunnis 22 per cent and Shias 20 per cent. More recent and more accurate statistical sampling suggests a 64/36 Muslim/Christian divide, with 29 per cent Shias and 28 per cent Sunnis, with Alawis and Druze forming the remaining 7 per cent of the Muslim population.[10] What is important here is that no single sect is or is ever likely to be sufficiently numerous to be able to dominate all the others on its own, a partial although perhaps not sufficient explanation for the coming into being of the unwritten National Pact of 1943. The Pact set the stage for a series of Christian–Muslim power-sharing partnerships entered into essentially by the leaders of the Maronite and Sunni communities between 1943 and the outbreak of the Lebanese Civil War in 1975. The Shias did not do so well out of this arrangement: reflecting their relative lack of political power at the time, they were given the speakership or chairmanship of the National Assembly.

The influence of the Shias has increased immeasurably since the 1932 census, partly due to their demographic growth and gradual social advancement (*promotion sociale*), and partly due to a process of institution-building initiated during the French mandate, with the official recognition of Lebanese Shiism as a *madhhab* in 1926 and the subsequent development of a Ja'fari court system.[11] This was accompanied by the more thorough-going politicization of the Shias in the 1940s, 1950s and 1960s,[12] and the concomitant decline of the political influence of the great Shia landlords (such as the As'ads and the 'Usayrans), who had been important members of the national political elite between the 1920s and the 1950s. By the end of this period, large amounts of Shia money, made mostly by migrants from the Biqa' and Jabal 'Amil in Beirut, West Africa, the Gulf or South America, were beginning to circulate in Lebanon. This injection of new capital and its various ramifications gradually led to the rise of a new Shia middle class with a new political consciousness, and the lifting of significant numbers of the community out of poverty. Other factors in the acquisition of greater influence by the Shias in the 1970s and 1980s included the dynamic role played by Imam Musa al-Sadr, the formation of both Amal and Hezbollah and the immense impulse given (to Twelver Shias everywhere) by the Iranian Revolution.

Norton has chronicled the widespread Shia (and of course other Lebanese) disenchantment with the clientelism and corruption that has always characterized Lebanese politics, particularly in the late 1960s and 1970s.[13] Like many other Lebanese at the time, left-leaning secular Shias were attracted to the non-sectarian parties (communist and – though to a lesser extent – Arab nationalist, Syrian Nationalist and Ba'thist) that flourished during those years. The mass of Shias, not all of whom shared in the upward social mobility experienced by some of their co-religionists, accounted for a disproportionate share of the casualties in the Civil War (1975–90). In the late 1970s, Imam Musa Sadr founded Amal, a Shia militia attached to *Harakat al-Mahrumin*, the Movement of the Deprived, which he had founded with the Greek Catholic Archbishop of Beirut, Grégoire Haddad.

Sadr, who had arrived in Lebanon from Iran in the 1950s, was a well-connected figure from a famous Iranian clerical family of Lebanese descent – he was related to Ayatollah Khomeini by marriage and was a cousin of the revered Ayatollah Muhammad Baqr al-Sadr, who would be murdered in Iraq by Saddam Hussein in 1980. Amal and Musa Sadr were close to Fatah, which trained the Amal militia, but Amal's relations with the PLO (and the Lebanese left in general) became strained after Sadr supported Syria's invasion of Lebanon in 1976, a move aimed against the leftist Lebanese National Movement and its Palestinian allies (with whom Amal was associated at the time). This morally questionable alignment with Syria has dogged Amal and its younger but much more powerful cousin Hezbollah to this day, although the Iran–Syria–Hezbollah axis had still to be forged in 1976, and Sadr disappeared during an official visit to Libya in August 1978 before being able to see it come to fruition. As Norton points out, although Sadr enjoyed a loyal following, most politically minded Shias still preferred to join the older-established secular parties. Amal's main achievement in Sadr's lifetime was to weaken the power of the traditional Shia *zu'ama* of southern Lebanon.

Before we leave Musa Sadr – presumably in an unmarked grave somewhere in the Libyan capital, a victim of Gaddafi's brutal security forces – he should be remembered for two other achievements that resonate to this day. First, he encouraged steps to enhance the general respectability of the 'Alawis, the somewhat negatively perceived minority sect from which the rulers of Syria since 1970 originate. In 1972, the Iranian Ayatollah Hasan al-Shirazi visited the 'Alawi communities in Lebanon and Syria and pronounced them 'true Shias', while in 1973, Sadr, who was on good personal terms with Hafiz al-Asad, issued a *fatwa* in his capacity as head of the Supreme Islamic Shia Council in Lebanon, declaring that 'the Alawis were an authentic part of Shia Islam'.[14] While this declaration probably achieved little in the sense of making other Lebanese or Syrians 'think better' of the 'Alawis, their new status, together with al-Sadr's close relations with Asad, facilitated the strengthening of ties between the Syrian regime and the opposition to the Shah (both inside and outside Iran). This formed the basis of an alliance that has endured for some forty years, from before the Iranian Revolution, through Iran's war with Iraq and the rise of mass Shia political parties in Lebanon associated with Iran and Syria.[15]

The Israeli invasion of Lebanon in June 1982 played a crucial role in the consolidation of Hezbollah, and set it on a trajectory on which it quickly became more attractive to religiously committed Shias than the more secular Amal (from which many members of Hezbollah originated). In the 1980s, Hezbollah was responsible for a series of kidnappings and killings, most notable the bombing of the US and French marine barracks in Beirut in October 1983, which resulted in the deaths of some 300 people.[16]

Of course, given the Iranian Revolution, there is every reason to think that Hezbollah, as a movement of Shia Islamists (for want of a better word) would have developed 'anyway', but its unequivocal resistance to Israel became a hallmark of its mission. This led to its pulling away from Amal, which was essentially a secular party composed mainly of Shias led, then as now, by Nabih Berri, whose relations with Israel at the time were somewhat ambiguous. Israel continued to occupy south Lebanon all through the Lebanese Civil War and beyond, on the ground that it was defending itself against 'terrorism'. Given the illegality of the occupation, it is hardly surprising that Hezbollah and other groups, including the PLO, should have chosen to resist it.

Both the Amal and Hezbollah militias were supported by Syria and Iran, although of course Iran had many other preoccupations in the early and mid-1980s. Syria too, always deeply involved in Lebanese politics, had profound internal problems, partly the result of the deeply divisive policies of its regime and partly by politico-religious opposition from Sunni/Muslim Brother dissidents, funded by Jordan and Saudi Arabia and supported, if indirectly, by the United States.[17] Thus in 1982, an attack on the Syrian regime by cohorts of the Muslim Brotherhood based in Hama led to a devastating riposte by the regime, in which between 10,000 and 40,000 were killed.[18]

It is hard to overstate the enormous influence of the Iranian Revolution at the time, especially, but not only, for young Shias in Lebanon and Iraq, to whom it brought new vision and a new sense of purpose. In an open letter in February 1985, Hezbollah expressed its profound hostility to world imperialism, Israel, the US, the USSR, the Lebanese Forces (a Maronite militia, not the Lebanese army) and the Maronite establishment in resoundingly uncompromising terms.[19] Inevitably, many opportunists have joined Hezbollah over the years, but it seems to have retained a hard core of profoundly committed 'true believers', now (2017) in their forties and fifties, who came of age during the Lebanese Civil War and for whom the organization has profound religious resonance. Inevitably, Hezbollah was obliged to soften its more extreme sectarian tone when it decided, with Iran's blessing, to enter the hurly-burly of Lebanese politics (by forming a political party which would contest seats at the parliamentary election) in July 1992.[20] At that point, or perhaps earlier, it played down its emphasis on the doctrine of *vilayet-i faqih*, which was not especially relevant in a pan-Lebanese context, and moderated its stance in many other ways.[21] By the 1990s the kidnappings of foreigners and hijackings had stopped, and there were no repeats of incidents comparable to the killings of the marines in October 1983. It did, however, maintain its opposition to Amal, in any case something of a spent force by the 1990s, which (in company with many other Shias and other Lebanese) it considered corrupt and unprincipled. Hezbollah has also come to accept, over the years, that few members of the new Shia middle class want to live in an Islamic Republic of Lebanon.

The Civil War and its consequences

Although it is not possible to go into the Lebanese Civil War in any detail, fifteen years of the most profound misery ended with very little change in the political structures of the country, in spite of the fact that this was the goal for which many of the participants had fought and sacrificed their lives. A more or less equal number, of course, had made similar sacrifices in order to maintain things as they were. The fighting in Lebanon was emblematic of other struggles taking place in the region at the time, with proxies and militias funded by various external interests (such as Iran, Iraq, Israel, Libya, Saudi Arabia, the Soviet Union and the United States) fighting each other, although the various proxies often changed sides. Syria wanted as far as possible to maintain the status quo, since the appearance of a secular pro-Palestinian democratic Lebanese state might call the legitimacy of the Syrian Ba'thist state into question. In addition, Asad wanted to pre-empt the possibility of 'more leftist' Lebanese or Palestinian groups being able to set themselves up in Lebanon to attack Syria, or, perhaps even more dangerous for regional stability, to give Israel an excuse for an all-out attack on Syria and/or Lebanon. Hence Asad's decision to send troops to Lebanon against the Lebanese National Movement and the PLO in the spring and summer of 1976.

Largely because of the damage that the PLO had inflicted on the Shia community in southern Lebanon (either directly or because of the retaliation its activities aroused from the Israelis), Amal was generally opposed to the PLO and Fatah, while Hezbollah – partly, at least, following Tehran – broadly supported them, was more visibly opposed to Israel, opposed Amal and was almost certainly the major factor bringing about the end of twenty-two years of Israeli occupation in 2000.[22] Ten years earlier, it had also driven Amal from most of the areas it occupied in Beirut. At that time Syria was generally more inclined to support Amal than Hezbollah, since Hezbollah was more powerful and potentially more threatening. Of course the United States supported Israel, and in a somewhat lukewarm way, as it had done for many years, the Soviet Union supported Syria and some of the 'leftish' Lebanese political factions. Israel wanted to contain Syria and restrict its activities in Lebanon; it also made sure that Hezbollah and Hamas continued to be labelled 'terrorist organizations' by the US and its allies after 9/11.

It is difficult to dispute the notion that the long war achieved little beyond first, the perpetuation of the status quo, a weak state with parliamentary representation based on sectarian quotas, often with little reflection of socio-economic realities, second, a slight adjustment (in favour of the Muslims) in the number of seats allotted to Christians and Muslims in the national parliament; and third, the institutionalization of stronger Syrian control of Lebanon. Perhaps the most significant aspect of the Ta'if accord in 1989, the formal instrument which brought most hostilities to an end, was that while all the other militias were obliged to disband, the forces of Hezbollah were not, on the grounds that they were a national defence force committed to ending the Israeli occupation (and, as has already been noted, they would be instrumental in bringing about the evacuation of Israeli forces from Lebanon some ten years later). As already noted, Hezbollah decided to participate in the national elections in 1992, a generally popular move, although it did not participate in government until 2005. Here is an apt comment by Sune Haugbølle on the political regime that emerged in post-Ta'if Lebanon:

> It incorporated many of the warlords and politicians who had risen to high positions during the last phase of the war [including Elie Hobeiqa (killed in 2002), Nabih Berri and Walid Jumblatt] ... Those responsible for massacres, theft, war crimes and the displacement of civilians under their command became responsible for rebuilding the country.[23]

Post-Ta'if Lebanese governments also favoured what Haugbølle calls a 'strategy of oblivion' (70), that is, that the horrors of the past should, as far as possible, be forgotten, following the mantra of no victor/no vanquished, *la ghalib, la maghlub*, which may seem an easy way of 'going forward', but inevitably leaves gaping wounds and solves little in the long run. Experience elsewhere shows that programmes that specifically attempt to achieve some degree of national reconciliation after civil war (or apartheid, or long periods of military dictatorship), although inevitably imperfect, such as the International Criminal Tribunal for the Former Yugoslavia, or the Truth and Reconciliation Commission set up in South Africa in 1995, have tended to be at least partly successful, especially the various bodies set up in Latin America.[24]

There is also the notion, which seems to have been borne out in post-civil war Lebanon, that instead of being a symptom or expression of developmental *malaise*, civil war may be an 'instrument of enterprise, and violence a means of accumulation'. In other words, while a civil war may bring about the collapse of the existing system, it can also usher in a new one that may well benefit some sections of the population and impoverish others. In addition, globalization facilitates the flow of capital and services around the world economy, and those running the militias (who, as has been noted, mostly remained in power, or gained power, after the war) always had access to the international arms market.²⁵ Huge sums of money were involved in Lebanon: Roger Dib, second in command of the Lebanese Forces in 1989, reported that the cost of his militia's equipment and salaries was around $40 million, and General 'Awn's 'liberation war' in the same year is said to have cost $1 billion. Other estimates suggest that the various patrons of the militias (the neighbouring states or the Lebanese diaspora) spent around $700 million every year in support of their protégés.²⁶ Inevitably, however dreadful the accompanying circumstances, those who succeeded in siphoning off this money had little interest in staunching the flow. This kind of corruption continued unabated after the end of the war, and the Syrians in particular showed no interest in abandoning the golden egg-laying goose that they had created for themselves by occupying Lebanon.²⁷

One final note on the end of the civil war: the signature of the Ta'if agreement late in 1989 coincided with the fall of the Berlin Wall, followed some two years later by the imploding of the Soviet Union. The echoes of these momentous events reverberated around the world, in ways that had mostly negative repercussions for leftists and progressives. Of course the Soviet Union and its allies had played a highly ambiguous role in promoting progressive causes in the Middle East and elsewhere – think of the Iraqi communists in the mid-1960s, whom Moscow more or less forced to enter a front with the Ba'thists, who had slaughtered them in large numbers in the previous years.²⁸ On the other hand, in many other important ways, the *vision* of the Soviet Union and the states of Eastern Europe had been attractive to many Arabs, Iranians and Turks between the end of the Second World War and 1990, and its demise produced a sense of aimlessness and loss of intellectual bearings among many leftists. It is also of some interest that Middle Eastern conflicts thought in some ways to relate to aspects or factors in the Cold War (Palestine, the Kurds) continued unabated well after its end.²⁹ So some Sunni leftists eventually became Islamists, and some Shia leftists became religious militants – with all the necessary caveats against lumping these categories of people together. Presumably the anti-imperialism both of Iran and of the more radical Sunni groups – such as al-Qaeda and its affiliates, and later Islamic State – proved a strong attraction for some former leftists.

In spite of these developments, Syria, although in so many ways the great betrayer of leftist aspirations, was still waving the banner of anti-imperialism in the post-Ta'if period, and it continued to play this role until and well beyond 2005. In many ways the promise of Syrian protection, or Syria's guarantee to support the flimsy structures of the Lebanese state, was the last resort for many

Lebanese who were pro-Palestinian and anti-establishment, and thus bitterly opposed to the US–Israeli axis and the machinations of Saudi Arabia and its allies, which they saw as far more threatening than the Syrians. And of course Hezbollah's handling of the war launched by Israel in 2006, and the speed and efficiency with which it got a reconstruction programme underway (aided by funding from Qatar[30] and by the strong social service networks that it had created over many years) provided yet more evidence of its capacity as the defender and rebuilder of the state.

The period between the Israeli withdrawal from Lebanon in 2000 and the war launched by Israel in 2006 was a time of relative calm on the Lebanese–Israeli front, to the extent that many Lebanese, not just Hezbollah and its supporters, came to believe that the deterrent posed by Hezbollah was 'working'. In February 2005, following the assassination of the prime minister, Rafiq Hariri, the Lebanese political system experienced what became less of a sea change than a clearer redrawing of the boundaries, although other observers may regard that as a somewhat optimistic description of what happened. By 2005, Syrian forces had been in occupation of much of the country for more than twenty years. Syria controlled Lebanese political institutions and a large part of the Lebanese economy, particularly smuggling and the drug trade based on crops grown in the Biqa'. Hariri, who had brokered the Ta'if Agreement in 1989, was an immensely wealthy businessman who had made his fortune in Saudi Arabia and subsequently played a major role in Lebanese politics, becoming prime minister in 1992 and being elected again in 2000. He had also played a major part in the reconstruction of Beirut in the 1990s, during which he amassed even greater wealth.

The assassination of Rafiq Hariri

Although generally opposed to Hezbollah and its activities, Hariri acknowledged the importance of its role in freeing Lebanon from Israeli occupation in 2000. He also accepted the 'inevitability' of Syria's role in Lebanon, but began to distance himself and Lebanon from Syria in the early 2000s,[31] and these efforts had not gone unnoticed both by the regime in Damascus and by Damascus' representatives in Beirut.[32] Hariri's assassination on 14 February 2005 – which involved massive amounts of explosive and which also killed twenty-two members of his entourage[33] – was widely believed to have been carried out by individuals close to the Syrian regime (or by Israel, according to some versions). Several other outspoken opponents of Syria were assassinated over the next weeks and months, including Samir Kassir (6 June), George Hawi (22 June), Gebran Tueni (12 December) and Pierre Amin Jumayyil (21 November 2006).[34]

Hariri's assassination triggered huge anti-Syrian demonstrations in Lebanon in February and March, probably the largest turnouts in the streets that the country had ever seen. Some anti-Syrian protestors also called for the return of General Michel 'Awn, a prominent military strong man who had defied the Syrians in 1990 (with Iraqi support) and had been in exile ever since. However, these large anti-Syrian demonstrations were themselves dwarfed by *pro*-Syrian demonstrations on 14 March: protestors accused Israel and the United States of meddling in Lebanon's internal affairs. The Hezbollah leader Hasan Nasrallah declared that 'The resistance will not give up its arms...because Lebanon needs the resistance to defend it,' a reference to calls for all militias (including Hezbollah) to give up their arms in response to UNSC resolution 1559 of September 2004. Large pro-Syrian demonstrations were held in other Lebanese cities over the next few days. The Syrian response was to promise that Syrian troops would leave Lebanon, which they did by early April.

The dates of the demonstrations (8 and 14 March) produced the parliamentary blocs that now characterize Lebanese politics. The post-2005 political scenario is as follows: the 14 March alliance (generally anti-Syria and anti-Hezbollah) consists of Rafiq Hariri's son Sa'd's *Tayyar al-Mustaqbal*, or Movement of the Future; the (Maronite) Lebanese Forces, headed by the former militia leader Samir Ja'ja'; *al-Kata'ib*, the long-established Maronite party now largely reduced to a fiefdom of the Jumayyil family; the Hunchak Party, consisting broadly of Armenian conservatives; and Walid Jumblatt's mainly Druze PSP. The 'other side' is the 8 March alliance, generally pro-Syrian and pro-Hezbollah, now consisting of the Maronite ex-General Michel 'Awn's *al-Tayyar al-Watani al-Hurr* (Free Patriotic Movement) – which attracts other Christians as well as Maronites – Amal; Hezbollah; the Tashnaq (Armenian Revolutionary Federation); the SSNP; and the Ba'th. In broad terms, this configuration of forces was somewhat lopsided, given that a strong Maronite president should ideally be balanced by a strong Sunni prime minister, and Sa'd Hariri's relative youth and inexperience (b. 1970) in the early 2000s left the Sunni community bereft of a political leader with wide national appeal.

Michel 'Awn, once a bitter opponent of Syria, formerly commander-in-chief of the Lebanese army, and prime minister and acting president between 1988 and 1990, returned to Lebanon in May 2005 and founded *al-Tayyar al-Watani al-Hurr*, the Free Patriotic Movement (FPM) in September 2005. However tongue in cheek, a stated aim of the (mostly Maronite) FPM is to establish a secular democratic state in Lebanon. On 6 February 2006, five months before the outbreak of the July war, and to the surprise of most Lebanon-watchers, General ʿAwn and Sayyid Hasan Nasrullah met at St Michael's Church in Shiyyah, in the southern Beirut suburb of al-Dahiya, to sign a Memorandum of Understanding, containing a series of declarations about joint approaches to the various problems besetting Lebanon.[35] One of these was Hezbollah's right to keep its weapons: ʿAwn cited Israel's continuing occupation of the Shabaʿa farms, which Lebanon claimed were part of its territory.[36] The accord made Hezbollah less isolated politically and gave it greater national legitimacy.

Of course a formal alliance between the main Shia political organization and what had become the most popular Maronite movement marked a major turning point in Lebanese politics. It also split the Maronites politically, with ʿAwn, FPM and Hezbollah in the 14 March alliance, and the *Kataʿib* and the Lebanese Forces (Jaʿjaʿ) in the 8 March, together with their Sunni partners. These marked the first serious undermining of the National Pact between the Sunnis and the Maronites since its inauguration in 1943. These political combinations formed the main political divisions in Lebanon on the eve of the Israeli invasion. In 2011, Walid Jumblatt and the PSP switched sides and joined 8 March. Jumblatt has veered between supporting Syria and Hezbollah and being a vocal critic of the Syrian regime since the war for Syria began in 2011. In October 2016, with the assent of Saʿd Hariri and his followers, ʿAwn was elected president of Lebanon, a development that marked the end of a deadlock that had lasted some twenty-nine months.

Israel's incursion into Lebanon, July–August 2006

After the Israeli withdrawal from southern Lebanon in 2000, there were occasional incidents involving Hezbollah, IDF soldiers and civilians on both sides of the border, but a kind of modus vivendi evolved in which '[t]he rules were so well established . . . that officials on both sides were periodically quoted as saying that such and such a military action was within "the rules of the game."'[37] In 2003, there were fears (assiduously spread by the Asad regime) that the early successes of the US in Iraq might be followed by attacks on Syria (and possibly on Hezbollah); these came to nothing, but the political landscape of the Middle East changed irrevocably with America's encouragement of a Shia ascendancy in Iraq. Almost inevitably, this artificially induced support for the Shias, which included the introduction of sectarian quotas in political and administrative office, caused a revival of sectarianism not only in Iraq but also in Syria, where the regime, whose most significant members were Alawite, was seeking to delegitimize any opposition to it either in anti-imperialist or Salafi/jihadi terms.

In the spring and early summer of 2006, there were constant calls from the Lebanese right for Hezbollah to disarm, which were countered by what were beginning to sound less and less credible assertions on its part of the need to remain armed to defend Lebanon against Israel. However, in June and July the situation on the border became increasingly tense, and the 'normal' tit-for-tat responses spiralled out of control. The question of which side bore the major responsibility for the sudden widening of the conflict is largely irrelevant, but the fighting, when it began in mid-July, drew immediate condemnation of Hezbollah from the United States and its conservative Arab allies. However, in the course of the campaign (which lasted some thirty-five days), Hezbollah managed not only to gain the upper hand and force the Israelis to withdraw, but also to regain much of the standing it had lost, not only in Lebanon, but on the Arab street, particularly in Egypt, Iraq, Jordan and Syria. The war ended with about 1,100 deaths in Lebanon (mostly civilians) and billions of dollars' worth of infrastructural damage; it also took place at a time when Lebanon had been trying, with some success, to revive its tourist industry.

This devastating attack by Israel did not occasion any intervention on Syria's part, although Hezbollah received crucial reinforcements of Iranian missiles and artillery delivered to bases in Syria.[38] In addition, the war revealed the utter unpreparedness of the Lebanese armed forces after so many years of Syrian occupation; similar inadequacies became clear in the summer of 2007, when the Lebanese army struggled for over four months to wrest control from a group of Islamic radicals who had taken over Nahr al-Barid Palestinian refugee camp, ten miles north of Tripoli. In May 2008, after some eighteen months of political stand-off and occasional violent incidents, a week of fighting between (essentially) pro- and anti-Hezbollah groups in Beirut and other Lebanese towns caused the deaths of several dozen people. This episode ended in the Doha Agreement of 21 May, a rather unequal 'national reconciliation',[39] after which Michel Sulayman, commander-in-chief of the Lebanese armed forces, was elected president of the republic, thus ending another political stalemate. The Agreement was widely regarded as a victory for Hezbollah and its allies, and thus, indirectly, for Syria and Iran. Hence, 'while Syria was indeed forced out of Lebanon [in 2005], it used its Lebanese allies to make sure that its most significant interests there would be protected'.[40] Furthermore, in April 2010, only weeks after diplomatic relations had been restored between the US and Syria, the US confirmed Israeli claims that Syria was supplying Hezbollah with ballistic missiles, made either with Russian or North Korean technology.

Hezbollah's role in Syria

I will conclude with a brief look at Hezbollah's role in Syria since 2011. Given Hezbollah's and Nasrallah's strong vocal support of the nationwide protests which overthrew the regimes in Tunisia and Egypt early in 2011, as well as even more energetic support for the anti-regime protests in Bahrain, Hezbollah's steadfastness on the side of Bashar al-Asad naturally appeared somewhat inconsistent. It was clear that the 'liberal' opposition in Syria was fighting the excesses of a dictatorship which was every bit as bad as (if not even worse than) the Ben 'Ali regime in Tunisia and the Mubarak regime in Egypt. According to David Lesch, with the violence growing out of control in late 2011, 'seeing the real possibility of a vital ally falling from power, [both Iran and Hezbollah] began openly to encourage Bashar al-Asad to implement the necessary reforms in order to stem the tide of protest; they urged the Syrian government to curtail the violence, and deal calmly with the opposition'.[41]

When it was clear that the Syrian regime was not going to yield, or reform itself, those elements of the Syrian armed forces that favoured change broke off to form the Free Syrian Army (FSA), the main opposition to the regime in 2011 and much of 2012. Hezbollah 'got round' what might seem to be its contradictory stance by appealing to a certain core constituency both among its own members and among many Lebanese: the notion that Asad was facing opposition from an Israeli and US-backed movement to overthrow him, which Hezbollah had to try to help to stop. As the fighting continued, and as it became increasingly difficult to conceal Hezbollah's quite considerable involvement, in terms of both 'martyrs' and matériel, Nasrallah's and other members of Hezbollah's rhetoric (daily on its TV station, al-Manar) stressed the importance of combatting *takfiri jihadis* in Syria and preventing the conflict spilling over to Lebanon. This line of argument became more vigorous after the fighting in Qusayr (on the Syrian–Lebanese border) in June 2013, when Syrian government forces received crucial support from Hezbollah in retaking the town from the rebels who had occupied it for more than a year. A fair number of Hezbollah fighters were killed during the battle, and their very public funerals in Lebanon testified to the extent of the group's involvement. From an examination of funeral announcements and other open sources, around 900 members of Hezbollah were killed during the fighting in Syria between 2011 and May 2016.[42] Saʿd Hariri and the Future Movement accused Hezbollah of not 'matching words with deeds – of speaking out against sectarianism yet escalating sectarianism through its violent involvement in Syria … in practice Hizbullah was undermining the authority of the state by intervening in the Syria crisis without being sanctioned to do so by the government [of which it was part]'.[43]

While this kind of rhetoric did appeal to a certain core constituency, revelations of the various atrocities committed by the Syrian government have made the Syrian-state-as-bulwark-against-imperialism into an increasingly less credible hand for Hezbollah to play, especially after the terrible scenes enacted daily on television screens around the world of the last few weeks of the Russian/Syrian siege of Aleppo in late 2016–early 2017.

Epilogue: the present situation

As always, the Lebanese political system managed to relaunch itself, with the election of ʿAwn as president in October 2016, although it still leaves a great deal to be desired in terms of functionality and credibility. In the Lebanese system the president is elected by a quorum of members of parliament, so that the absence of a functioning parliament meant that there could be no presidential elections. The present parliament was elected in 2009, and preferred to prolong its mandate illegally rather than pass an appropriate electoral law under which the next parliament could be elected. The 'traditional leadership' is mostly pretty elderly: Michel ʿAwn is 80, Nabih Berri is 77, Amin Jumayyil is 74, Walid Jumblatt a sprightly 66, Tammam Salam, prime minister since February 2014 and acting president since May 2014, is 70.

There are very large problems requiring immediate attention. There are a million Syrian refugees, mostly Sunnis, in Lebanon; most public services (education, health, social welfare and so on) are not functioning because they have no proper budgets – obviously this has a more profound effect on the poor and lower middle class who do not have access to private insurance or private education. Places like Arsal and Tripoli have become breeding grounds for jihadis, especially since the takeover of Mosul by Islamic State in June 2014. Sunni–Shia tensions are rising, although the worst knock-on effects of the Maliki regime in Iraq – which came to a long awaited end in August 2014 – seem to have been somewhat mitigated by his successor, al-Abadi. Wealthier Iraqi,

Lebanese and Syrian Christians are leaving the Middle East in droves. More immediately, the piles of uncollected rubbish all over the country are an eloquent testimony to the paralysis of the 'system'.[44] One of the more hopeful aspects of the present crisis has been the very large apolitical/non-sectarian demonstrations that have taken place since August 2015, protesting not only against the failure to remove the rubbish but against the system as a whole. Another baby step that has already been mentioned is the grudging alliance between the Future Movement (*Tayyar al-Mustaqbal*) and Hezbollah against Sunni extremists. In general:

> What is special here is the ideological and political position of Hizbullah as the only Shia mass movement to have contracted a series of alliances with non-Shia groups or non-Muslims on a basis of equality, combining Lebanese nationalism, Pan-Islamism and Shia identity.[45]

Of course, what those who seek to control Lebanon fear most is any lasting alliance across the sects (against Israel, against Syria, against Saudi Arabia, to name only a few). Such coming together in Lebanon and elsewhere in the Middle East, incidentally, was one of the greatest fears of the Saudis and their clients in 2011.[46] Sectarianism, as we know, is not a fixed entity; it is a tool that can be, and has been, manipulated to create or perpetuate divisions, which is exactly what most parties to the present conflict in Syria and other parts of the Middle East are doing at the moment. Although Hezbollah's activities in support of the present Syrian regime may be judged questionable, its widely admired capacity to check Israel's activities in Lebanon, as well as its efforts to combat *takfiri*/jihadi groups in alliance with non-Shia groups (Sunnis, Christians) suggest a shrewd appreciation of the value of a pluralistic outlook that transcends sectarian boundaries. This kind of pragmatism, a welcome change from the narrow perspectives of some of the movements studied in this book, is one of the few positive political signs in the contemporary Middle East.

6

When the State Becomes a Non-State: Yemen between the Huthis, Hirak and Al-Qaeda

Daniel Martin Varisco

Introduction

The aftermath of the Arab Spring that led to the fall of Yemen's President 'Ali Abdullah Salih also signalled the start of a struggle between multiple groups to form a new state. In the previous two decades the focus of attention had been on al-Qaeda in the US War on Terrorism, but in fact there were several groups that were emerging as non-state actors. In the south the secessionist movement of Hirak campaigned actively against Salih's government; its political arm of the Southern Transitional Council has recently established de facto control over most of the southern governorates. In the north the Huthis, a movement that gained notoriety during 2004 for protests against Salih in Sana'a, eventually staged a successful coup against the interim government. All of these competing groups are politically directed, non-state actors attempting to gain power after the fall of the last official government, now reduced to being a ghost entity in exile.

The definition of what constitutes a non-state actor is as fraught with complexity as determining what factors make up a state. The most basic sense is 'an organized political actor not directly connected to the state but pursing aims that affect vital state interests' (Pearlman and Cunningham, 2012: 8), but this does not necessarily imply the use of violent means to overthrow a state. Violent non-state actors include a range of armed groups, including paramilitary groups, liberation movements and crime cartels. In the case of Yemen, certain tribes need to be considered as non-state actors since they often act independently of the central state and have their own militias. Historically Yemen has always had a range of non-state actors, given the lack of a strong central government that could maintain control over the entire territory.

Al-Qaeda, Hirak and the Huthis are only the most recent examples. The Republic of Yemen, formed by the unification of two earlier states in 1990, struggled to become a viable state from the start. President 'Ali Abdullah Salih's decision not to join the alliance against Saddam Hussein's invasion of Kuwait a few months after Yemen's unification led to a major economic blow as some 800,000 Yemeni workers in Saudi Arabia were sent home. After an initial democratic process that involved all political parties, Salih soon consolidated his control with a civil war in 1994 that guaranteed northern hegemony over the former socialist-run south. By 2007 this led to the formation of a southern secessionist movement known as Hirak (al-Hirak al-Janubi). The attack on the USS *Cole* in Aden harbour in 2000 indicated the growing presence of al-Qaeda, leading to the formation of AQAP (al-Qaeda in the Arabian Peninsula) in 2009. Salih was already fighting a rebel movement known as the Huthis or Ansar Allah in the north, launching six small wars there after the murder of the group's leader, Husayn al-Huthi, in 2004. After Salih was removed from power by a GCC sponsored plan in 2011, the Huthis gained followers, entered the capital Sana'a in September 2014 and soon forced the ouster of interim president 'Abd Rabbuh Mansur Hadi. For the past three years a Saudi-led coalition has waged war on the Huthis, creating what the UN calls the worst humanitarian crisis in the world.[1]

The relevance of this recent political history is obvious, but it is also important to consider the historic sweep of Yemen in the Arabian Peninsula to recognize that understanding the dynamics of Yemen's past three millennia is equally important for analysing the present. One myth that needs to be put to rest is the common stereotype that Yemen was an isolated backwater to events in the region until the 1960s. There is no doubt that Yemen has remained terra incognita in academic circles compared to the extensive travel and scholarly output on many other parts of the Middle East. But this is a reflection of the lack of Western engagement, apart from the limited British control of the port of Aden from 1837 to 1967, rather than a region cut off for centuries from regional and global events.

Historically there were major reasons why Yemen was an important place to control, given the essential role of the port of Aden in the lucrative Red Sea–Indian Ocean trade network (Margariti, 2008). It is noteworthy that Britain held on to its Aden Protectorate for two decades after India received independence. Had oil been discovered in Yemen as early as it was in the Arab Gulf, it is hard to imagine that the British would ever have abandoned its relationship or that the Americans would have bestowed their petrol favouritism solely on the Saudis.

The fact that Yemen has some profitable oil and gas, with perhaps more to find near the Saudi border, is obviously as important a factor to consider as the current political rivalry between Saudi Arabia and Iran. The potential of reviving Aden, one of the best natural ports in the world, is also worthy of consideration for understanding the Emirati interest in Yemen. It can be argued that the past is not only a prologue in an abstract sense, but is directly relevant for thinking about what a future Yemeni state might look like, especially after the current crisis.

While the chronological digest of Yemen's history has an inevitable focus on wars and dynastic change, it should be noted that a major reason why there was never a centralized state over all of ancient southern Arabia is its geographical diversity, especially the high mountain ranges that make communications difficult. This is also true for the Islamic era, starting in the seventh century CE. Although legend claims that Yemen received the message of Islam from 'Ali, the Prophet Muhammad's nephew and son-in-law, the conversion of Yemen to Islam was not immediate. The early Umayyad caliphate was able to subdue Najran and Sana'a as early as 660 CE, but this brief foray did not establish hegemony, even with the appointment of governors sent out from both the Umayyad and 'Abbasid courts. One of these local officials, Muhammad ibn Ziyad, established his own fiefdom in the coastal town of Zabid in the early ninth century, but had to share space with the Yufirids, who ruled in the northern highlands between 847 and 997, as well as with pockets of Ismailis. At the end of the ninth century the first Zaydi imam, al-Hadi ila al-Haqq (r. 897–911), a descendant of 'Ali, entered Yemen from the north and established an imamate that lasted there, through many vicissitudes, until its official demise in the revolution of 1962.

In addition to its homegrown polities, Yemen became a prime target for expanding empires throughout its Islamic history. In the late twelfth century the Egyptian Ayyubids were able to control much of Yemen's coastal region and southern highlands for over half a century, eventually being replaced by their mercenary emirs, the Rasulids, shortly before the Mamluks ousted the Ayyubid sultans from Egypt. The Egyptian Mamluks made inroads into Yemen in 1517 just before the Ottoman conquest of the region. Ottoman suzerainty lasted for a century after 1538 and was reimposed, very sporadically, in the last quarter of the nineteenth century until the end of World War I. It should be clear that the control of Yemen as a geographical space has always been contested and has never been immune from outside intrigue, a fact readily recognized for the entire region.

Successfully challenging the state: the rise of the Huthis

On 9 September 2004, in the rugged mountains near the northern city of Sa'da, a group of soldiers from the Yemeni national army sent north to find the so-called rebel leader Husayn al-Huthi murdered this charismatic man, who had challenged the dictatorial rule of 'Ali 'Abdullah Salih. Thus began a series of short wars culminating in 2009 with an operation appropriately labelled 'Operation Scorched Earth' (*'amaliya al-ard al-mahruqa*). What started out as yet another of Salih's attempts to eliminate a rival for power eventually erupted into a crisis that brought in a Saudi-led bombing campaign and military intervention that many consider a proxy war between the Saudi regime and Iran. Today Yemen remains mired in a maelstrom of insecurity, with a relentless bombing campaign and counter-insurgency that has created an unprecedented humanitarian crisis.

What makes the Huthi insurgency of special interest is that a movement to replace the government of 'Ali 'Abdullah Salih later evolved into a Faustian alliance between the Huthis and Salih in an attempt to rebuild a new state out of the ashes of the failed state. It is this alliance that made them a non-state actor capable of creating a new state, tentative as it may be. The story of the rise of the Huthis dates back to 1979 when a Yemeni scholar named Muqbil bin Hadi al-Wadi'i returned to Yemen after studying in Saudi Arabia, where he was introduced to Wahhabi Salafism.[2] On his return he established a Salafi madrasa known as Dar al-Hadith in Dammaj, a town in the heartland of traditional Zaydi Islam. Al-Wadi'i was a quietist, refusing to follow the violence advocated by al-Qaeda and a critic of Khomeini's revolution in Iran. He preached against the tenets of Zaydi Islam, as well as against Yemen's traditional Shafi'i and Isma'ili schools, in the process irritating many Yemenis in the north. Al-Wadi'i found a patron in Salih since he followed the Salafi directive that in a Muslim state even a corrupt and sinful ruler must be obeyed. Throughout the 1980s and 1990s, Salih, himself of Zaydi origin, used al-Wadi'i and his followers as a wedge against those Zaydis whom he suspected of working against his regime in Sana'a. At the same time his political party, the General People's Congress, was closely allied with the anti-Zaydi party Islah, including its Muslim Brotherhood-leaning leader, Sheikh 'Abdullah Majid al-Zindani.

During this time, Badr al-Din al-Huthi, a senior Zaydi theologian, was studying in Iran with his sons Husayn and 'Abd al-Malik. There they were exposed to Iranian twelver Shia theology, which had not been present in Yemen. As his writings show, Husayn was particularly influenced both by the Ayatollah Khomeini and by Husayn Nasrallah of Hezbollah. Out of this also came a deep distrust and antagonism to the policies of the United States. On his return to

Yemen, Husayn al-Huthi served as a member of parliament from 1993 to 1997 for the Zaydi al-Haqq party, founded in 1990 by several respected Zaydi scholars, including Husayn's father. Husayn's anti-American rhetoric and opposition to Salih made him persona non grata to the Salih regime. Reacting against Salafi criticism of Zaydism, Husayn and other Zaydis critical of Salih joined a movement known as Believing Youth (*al-shabab al-mu'min*), which created a revival in Zaydi theology with a political edge. It also attracted the attention of tribal leaders in the north, since many of them were increasingly frustrated by Salih's lack of investment in the region. Salih resorted to his influence technique of giving financial support to both the Salafis and Islah. As noted in the RAND report, this 'strategy of patronage as a means of cooptation and control of multiple, conflicting groups engendered latent tensions in the small local society of Sa'da' (Salmoni et al., 2010: 101).

In January 2002, first in Sa'da and later in Sana'a, Husayn pronounced his rallying cry or *sarkha* that has become the rhetorical icon of the Huthi movement: death to America, death to Israel, a curse on the Jews and victory for Islam (*al-mawt li Amrika al-mawt li Isra'il al-la'na 'ala al-Yahud, al-nasr li-al-Islam*). This politicized mantra was clearly influenced by his experiences in Iran and anger at the US invasion of Iraq. In his written work and speeches he even referred to America as 'the Great Satan'.[3] The stage was now set for confrontation, starting with government forces engaging the Huthi militia in June 2004. After the death of Husayn, his younger brother 'Abd al-Malik became the leader of the insurgency. There were several attempts to mediate the violence, including an offer of pardon by Salih in May 2005 and a temporary ceasefire in 2007 brokered by Qatar (Kamrava, 2011). Major fighting in 2008 led to thousands of deaths on both sides and the forcing of at least 70,000 Yemeni citizens from their homes. The final push in 2009 saw a major military engagement with losses on both sides and with tensions spilling across the border into Saudi Arabia. Like earlier efforts to destroy the Huthi resistance, this too ended in a stalemate, with continuing clashes in the north until the Arab Spring.

The ripple effect of the Arab Spring was felt in Yemen in January 2011, as thousands of protestors took to the streets calling for the overthrow of Salih. The decision by General 'Ali Muhsin al-Ahmar, who had previously led the attacks against the Huthis, to side with the protestors spelled the end for Salih. Huthi militia, primarily northern tribesmen, took effective control of Sa'da in March. In June, Salih was almost killed in a bomb blast at the mosque in his home in Sana'a. Brought back to life by doctors in Saudi Arabia, Salih eventually conceded control in a GCC-brokered agreement that called for a general election in

February 2012. The only candidate, former Vice-President 'Abd Rabbuh Mansur Hadi, was elected interim president, and a National Dialogue Conference was initiated. Although not involved directly, the Huthis supported the overthrow of Salih and gained support in the northern regions with their call for reform and against the endemic corruption of the previous government. Huthi representatives were involved in the National Dialogue Conference, although the assassination of a Huthi delegate, Dr Ahmad Sharaf al-Din, in February 2014, dampened participation. Hadi's decision to implement the restructuring of Yemen from thirteen governorates into six was rejected both by the Huthis, who would have their region landlocked, and the southern delegates. In a sense, Hadi never had a chance to form a unified government. He was unable to rid the military of loyalists to Salih and his administration was deemed to be as corrupt as that of Salih. As Tobias Thiel (2008: 129) concludes, 'the transition team failed to espouse popular demands for more transparent, effective, inclusive and rule-based public governance'. When the economic crisis led to a rise in fuel prices, the Huthi tribal militias and their allies among Salih's former troops were gradually able to gain control all the way south to Sana'a, driving out the Hashid Ahmar clan who had been major power brokers during the Salih years (Brandt, 2018: 167). On 21 September, five days before the commemoration of the 1962 revolution that had created the Yemen Arab Republic, the Huthi alliance took control of Sana'a, resulting in the resignation of Prime Minister Mohammed Basindawa and the effective loss of control by President Hadi.

Hadi was accused by the Huthis of aiding al-Qaeda, now known as *Ansar al-Shari'a*, and in January 2015 he was placed under house arrest, eventually leading to his forced resignation on 22 January. Soon the Yemeni parliament was dissolved and a new revolutionary committee was created to rule Yemen. Hadi was able to escape to Aden on 21 February, but the situation was too tense for him to remain there. On 25 March he fled to Saudi Arabia, arriving the next day as a Saudi coalition began Operation Decisive Storm to reinstate him and roll back the Huthi victory. Less than a month later, the Saudis symbolically declared victory on the military front, but by October 2018, after more than three years of an unending campaign, the Huthis still controlled the areas containing the majority of Yemen's population. Although news reports often refer to the majority of Yemen's territory as loyal to Hadi, in fact he is a figurehead with little support and regarded as a Saudi puppet. As a woman in Aden noted in 2016 after the power shortages led to deaths in the southern city, 'Government? What government? . . . They left us to die while they are enjoying air-conditioned hotel rooms in Riyadh.' (Dawsari, 2016: 29).

Prelude to the Huthi insurgency: Yemen's sectarian 'imam' 'Ali 'Abdullah Salih

> Whether Saleh comes or goes as appears likely or whether his successor lasts 10 years or 10 days, Yemen will still be Yemen. There 'the past is not dead; it's not even past'.
>
> Barrett, 2011: 104

The history of Yemen over the past four decades is very much the history of one man, 'Ali 'Abdullah Salih, who once described his tenure as dancing on the heads of snakes (Varisco, 2011). As an anthropologist planning to study traditional water resource use and highland irrigation for my doctoral research, I arrived in Yemen just before Salih came to power in the young Yemen Arab Republic. My wife, Najwa Adra, also an anthropologist, and I were looking for the ideal location for our fieldwork and waiting for the necessary government permission to begin. On 24 June 1978 we were still in Sana'a and walked daily past the *qiyada*, the military headquarters of then President al-Ghashmi. On this day we noticed a few more soldiers and a flurry of activity, but we walked on until we stopped at a local grocer for a bottle of water. We learned from this man, the 'street' as it were, that al-Ghashmi had just been assassinated and we should hurry home since no one knew what might happen. As newly arrived anthropologists, this was not the kind of news we wanted to hear. It did not take long for the army to settle on a new leader, a young colonel who was the governor of Ta'izz, 'Ali 'Abdullah Salih. He was appointed president and commander of the armed forces just as we moved to our field site in the central highland valley of al-Ahjur. At the time, few of our Yemeni friends expected him to last, given that the previous two presidents had been assassinated in less than two years. History has proven otherwise. Until his death in December 2017, Salih remained a central figure in the struggle to control what remains of Yemen.

It is important to assess how Salih used indirect power in order to understand how he survived for three decades in a country where the central state had very limited powers. There is no little irony in the fact that Salih followed the divide-and-conquer, or at least divide-and-keep-at-bay, tactics of the last two twentieth-century Zaydi imams, Yahya and Ahmad, towards Yemen's tribes. The 'revolution' after the death of Imam Ahmad in 1962 was only a quasi-military coup, as Yemen had no standing army to speak of, just a small and loose-knit guard taken from tribal ranks for periodic use by the imam. As had been true throughout the entire period of the Zaydi imamate, the tribes provided the main fighters, whether battling other Yemeni factions or in order to punish a given tribe. The two major tribal confederations in the north, Hashid and Bakil, were known as the wings of the imamate since they were the real power in Yemen, at least in the highlands.[4] With support from Egypt, the young republic was able to survive Saudi patronage of the northern tribes throughout a lengthy civil war.

Salih attempted to create a modern nation state by forming a national army that at its height reached a combined force of military and security of around 200,000. Yet this force was never able to exercise effective control of the whole country, even after unification in 1990. Salih was careful to appoint field commanders from his own tribe of Sanhan or from his family, creating a military elite that was more loyal to him than to the state. This is an important point to remember, since interim President Hadi never had control over the army, despite his alliance with General 'Ali Muhsin al-Ahmar (Salisbury, 2016: 24). As shall be seen, the ability of the Huthis to enter Sana'a and beyond was entirely due to support from Salih's troops, a major reason why the Saudi-led campaign was unable to win a quick war against the Huthis, The creation of a modern army, well equipped to an extraordinary degree, had altered the traditional role of the tribes as fighting units, although the army itself still reflected tribally based divisions. The current insecurity has reinvigorated the role of tribal militias, some of which are close to recently formed political groups such as *Ansar al-Shari'a*, the remake of al-Qaeda in Yemen.

Back in 1978, civil society in northern Yemen was tribal, in part the result of the long civil war in which both Saudi Arabia and Egypt attempted to buy the loyalty of the tribes, a loyalty that has always been temporary. If a realist perspective were to be downsized from national state building to more local levels, Yemen's tribes would be a prime candidate. These non-state actors have been as powerful a force as the state, and constantly intertwined with the state in many cases. Throughout history tribal structure has emphasized autonomy rather than an unbroken loyalty to a larger group. Hashid and Bakil were convenient macro-level tribal confederations, but local tribal groups would realign as circumstances warranted. Salih realized this, which is why he had to combine his desire to compel loyalty by force with the kind of diplomatic persuasion that had always characterized politics in the region. In this he was assisted by the paramount sheikh of the Hashid confederation, 'Abdullah al-Ahmar, who allied with Salih to provide tribal support when needed. Neither was master of the other, but both maintained an alliance of convenience. In many ways it was the longest and most stable alliance of potential rivals for either the north or south in the history of the two states born in the 1960s.

The oil wealth that began to flow into Yemen in the late 1980s allowed Salih to buy the loyalty of sheikhs, but as the revenues decreased and Salih's regional interference increased, so did the discontent of those sheikhs whose payments were reduced or stopped. In a way he sowed the seeds of his own destruction, by using the state treasury to coopt local sheikhs without being able to sustain the practice. The same problem had plagued Imam Badr in the late 1950s near the end of his father's rule, promising payments that the treasury could not afford and thus making enemies of potential allies. When push came to shove in the Arab Spring, Salih's support among select tribal leaders could not keep him in power. Even the Ahmar clan, led by Sadiq al-Ahmar after the death of Sheikh 'Abdullah in 2007, turned against him.

As is obvious from the current conflict, tribes maintain an important role in the ever-evolving politics of Yemen. During the 1960s civil war a number of northern tribal leaders around Sa'da were incorporated into the army as the so-called 'Colonel shaykhs' (Brandt, 2017: 57–61). These tribal leaders remained loyal to the central government through the system of patronage that Salih exploited. However, Salih's combined use of the formal military and irregular militia during the anti-Huthi wars after 2004 alienated many of the northern tribes. The brutal assaults by the army and Salih's allies were seen as violating existing tribal norms in conflict, as thousands of local people were displaced or killed. As Marieke Brandt explains, this policy 'ignores the fact that local tribal norms are orientated towards peaceful reconciliation, and hence towards the limitation and containment of conflict and violence' (Brandt, 2014: 116). Thus, local tribes began to side with the Huthis, who offered an alternative and more attractive agenda to the Salih regime. Those sheikhs who had supported Salih were mostly unable to stem the criticism against them; some were killed, others fled and their property was confiscated.

Like the imams, Salih was never able to supersede the tribal dynamics of the Yemeni highlands. Outside observers often look at tribalism as antithetical to state power, but this is largely due to the association of tribes with the history of nomadic Bedouin on the peninsula. In Saudi Arabia, although the state was created through the effective use of tribal militias, the militant spirit of such tribesmen had to be tamed in the late 1920s so that the Saudi family could create a stable regime and gain international recognition (Commins, 2006: 71–103). Similarly, tribalism in the Gulf has essentially become a symbol of heritage in which ruling families justify their rule as an outgrowth of local tribal history. In reality the Gulf states are better viewed as 'families with flags', kept in monarchical power by what has seemed to be an unlimited supply of oil wealth. Tribalism in Yemen has had a very different trajectory.

Throughout its history most Yemeni tribes have been sedentary farmers with only a few nomadic Bedouin on the fringes. As a diverse geographical region, the foothills and highland plains were especially conducive to agriculture, making this area known as the 'Verdant Yemen' (*al-Yaman al-khadra*') over the centuries. The primary areas of tribal dominance are in the central and northern highlands, which no external power has ever been able to conquer and effectively hold. The Ayyubids and Rasulids tried from the twelfth through to the fifteenth centuries, as did the Ottomans later, but the only viable civil society has remained tribal over two millennia. The first Zaydi imams were invited from the north in order to help mediate tribal disputes, forming an alliance that was mutually advantageous for a millennium. Although the British took possession of the port of Aden in 1839 as a refuelling station for their budding empire, they too never exercised control over the tribal areas in the south and Hadramawt. While areas along the coast were less tribal, in the formal structural sense, community structure was still largely based on self-help and alliances.

A key to understanding the persistence of tribal organization in Yemen over the centuries is the system of values known as *qabyala* and enshrined in tribal customary law. In her analysis of the tribal honour code *qabyala*, Najwa Adra (2011: 8) notes, 'More than genealogy, occupation or even military prowess, tribal self-definition rests on principles of action, which include courage, community responsibility, hospitality, and hard work, as well as a respect for individual autonomy.' Tribal customary law in Yemen was acceptable to Islamic jurists of both the Zaydi and Shafi'i schools as long as it did not directly contravene Sharia law. Thus most disagreements about land, water shares and agricultural contracts were settled by tribal customary law. Among the more important principles was the role of mediation at all levels of community conflict. This has long been the case in Yemen, with the Austrian traveller Eduard Glaser (1993: 16) noting at the end of the nineteenth century that 'South Arabians of the same tribe, and particularly Hashidi, start a conflict with words, and then they throw stones, and only reach for their rifles and jāmbiyyas [daggers] as a last resort.' In the absence of a strong central state, customary law kept the peace in what otherwise looks like a regime of anarchy.

Those who do not understand the nature of Yemeni tribalism assume that Yemen's tribes are a nesting ground for terrorism, although the opposite is the case (Koehler-Derrick, 2011). When al-Qaeda was first launched in Yemen, it found very few recruits, mainly a few Yemenis who had been with Bin Laden in Afghanistan and several Saudis who had migrated south. It is telling that the Yemen branch was renamed al-Qaeda in the Arabian Peninsula (AQAP) in 2009.

Although Salih claimed to be cracking down on al-Qaeda in order to obtain military aid from the United States, it was a half-hearted effort. It now seems clear that Salih was in fact willing to let al-Qaeda operate as long as they avoided targets within Yemen. The Huthis, however, were adamantly opposed to al-Qaeda, as they were to the Salafis who had been infiltrating Yemen from Saudi Arabia since 1980.

The insecurity surrounding the disintegration of Salih's regime created space for a new terrorist group to form. Although very limited in number, a Yemeni branch of the Islamic State was formally announced in November 2014, mainly in the south. It has carried out a number of acts against both the Huthis and the forces allied with the Saudi coalition. In March 2015 the Yemeni branch of ISIS claimed responsibility for a suicide attack on two Zaydi mosques in Sana'a that killed 142 people and wounded more than 351, one of the most deadly terrorist attacks in Yemen's history. There are continuing attacks by ISIS on government forces in Aden. Like its rival, al-Qaeda, ISIS has also destroyed a number of historic Yemeni shrines in the Hadramawt. Unlike al-Qaeda, however, ISIS is not a tribal phenomenon.

An outsider looking into the maelstrom of Yemeni politics may see the tribe as a causal factor of the conflict, overlooking the counterbalance of tribal mediation as a moderating force that has been practised in Yemen for centuries, usually in harmony with Islamic law as locally interpreted. Far from being a stimulus for terrorism or a hindrance to resolving the current Yemeni conflict, the principles of tribal customary law offer the best chance of negotiating an agreement and, moving forward, developing a new state. 'While not all aspects of tribalism are positive, tribal cooperative mechanisms and methods of resolving conflict through mediation are exemplary and currently being emulated in developed countries with robust state courts,' argues Adra (2011: 12). 'Following customary rules,' she continues, 'communities form an indigenous "civil society" that can, and has, realised development projects such as the building of roads, schools and health centers and the cleaning of cisterns.' The house that Salih built, appropriate for his own misuse and eventually brought down around him, will not be easily restored, but the long tradition of mediation remains the best hope for an eventual resolution of the current conflict.

The fallout of the proxy war

My brother was a sheikh and he resolved conflicts and tried to bring peace. They weren't even in an area near the clashes. They were in an area that is more than 40 kilometers away from the conflict zone. The men were in a hangar chewing *qat* [a mild narcotic leaf that Yemenis chew, usually in the afternoon, as part of their daily socializing]. They thought they were far from danger when all of a sudden, a missile hit the hangar. Ten men died immediately and one was severely injured. The women were in a nearby house that was destroyed as a result of the airstrikes but they survived only to live as widows and orphans for the rest of their lives.

Yemeni widow from Marib

It is no secret that Saudi Arabia has long had an interest in controlling, if not outright governing, its southern neighbour. By 1932, Ibn Saud had carved out a kingdom that covered most of the Arabian Peninsula with the exception of the British-protected states of Bahrain, Kuwait and Qatar, as well as the area then known as the Trucial States and now as the United Arab Emirates, Oman and Yemen. Imam Yahya was incensed that Ibn Saud, a Bedouin challenging his rule, had already taken over Asir from the traditional Idrisi rulers and was now assuming control over Najran. Ibn Saud's forces were able to capture the Yemeni port of Hodeidah in 1934 and attempted to advance on the capital Sanaʻa. With British diplomacy, the two sides eventually signed the Treaty of Taʼif, under which Hodeidah was returned to Imam Yahya, and Asir and Najran became part of the new Saudi kingdom, with the border issue to be renewed in the future. During the northern civil war in the 1960s the Saudis attempted to reinstate Badr, the son of Imam Ahmad, but to no avail due to Egyptian support of the new republic. Saudi monetary support for the northern tribes continued after the war and continues in the current conflict. During the 1970s and 1980s, Saudi Arabia provided substantial foreign aid to its poor southern neighbour, especially to the Ministry of Education, which brought conservative Muslim Brotherhood and Salafi schoolteachers from Egypt and elsewhere and distributed them throughout Yemen. A Saudi hand in the assassinations of YAR presidents al-Hamdi and al-Ghashmi is often rumoured.[5]

The current conflict in Yemen, pitting Saudi Arabia and an array of Sunni regimes against the Huthi coalition, reverses the earlier support for the reinstatement of a Zaydi imamate. Adding to the quixotic nature of the shifting alliances in the conflict is the fact that Salih and his army, which once hunted down the Huthi insurgents, subsequently joined forces against Saudi Arabia, which was responsible for saving his life after a bomb attack in 2011. These Faustian bargains go beyond irony to the realization that all alliances are potentially ephemeral when circumstances warrant and large egos vie with each other for political power. It is important not to overemphasize collective identity, but recognize the potential for fragmentation. As Pearlman and Cunningham (2012: 8) suggest, 'Attention to actor fragmentation reveals how different factions within the collective face different sets of opportunities and constraints, both vis-à-vis each other and vis-à-vis the state that they challenge.' This was clearly the case with the Huthi–Salih alliance, which led to Salih's last snake bite in December 2017.

The network of ostensible partners in the Yemeni fighting belies the notion of an alliance at grass roots level. The Huthis consider al-Qaeda and ISIS mortal enemies and vice versa. Yet the areas under nominal control by both terrorist groups are often lumped together with forces loyal to President Hadi and his Saudi backers. There are reports that the Emiratis have cut secret deals with al-Qaeda and even allowed the militants to leave the port of Mukalla safely before entering and claiming a victory (Michael, Wilson and Keith, 2018). By attacking both the Huthis and Hadi's supporters, both terrorist groups show that they are in this battle for themselves. There are also individual tribal and sectarian militias, a virtual ménage à troika that has created a total lack of security nationwide.

The decision of the Saudis to enter into formal warfare in Yemen came after a major regime change with the death of King 'Abdullah in January 2015 and the succession of King Salman, whose young son has made the war central to his personal quest for fame. Unlike the situation in the 1930s with Ibn Saud, the present conflict is less about formal conquest or even the conversion of Yemen to Salafism than it is about an exaggerated fear of post-1979 Iran on the part of the Saudi royal family and their advisers. As the Custodian of the Two Holy Mosques, the Saudi leaders have sought to use their wealth to promote themselves as the leaders of Sunni Islam. While the Shah of Iran, a fellow monarch, posed no threat, the export of the Iranian Revolution and Iran's subsequent support for Hezbollah heightened tension between these two major sectarian powers in the region. Saddam's war with Iran in the 1980s was bankrolled in part by the frightened monarchs of the Arabian Peninsula. When Saddam invaded Kuwait, it was clear that no one could be trusted and the Saudis began to rely on American military support to protect their interests. The Arab Spring further exacerbated Saudi worries, with the downfall of the dictatorships that they had usually been able to buy off and what they saw as the spread of Iranian support to prop up the Alawite regime of Bashar al-Asad in Syria.

Although the current conflict is in large part the most recent outbreak of the simmering proxy war between the Saudis and Iran, it is decidedly one-sided. Since starting the bombing campaign in March 2015, billions of dollars' worth of military hardware from Western powers have been bought and used against much of northern Yemen, especially Saʻda and Sanaʻa. These include cluster bombs, which have mostly killed civilians, as reported by human rights organizations and admitted by the United Kingdom's Defence Secretary. Most analysts resist accepting the Saudi contention, earlier stated by Salih himself, of a major direct Iranian involvement in the Yemen conflict (Sharp, 2015: 7). Thomas Juneau (2016: 647) argues that the Huthis 'are not Iranian proxies', adding that 'Tehran's influence in Yemen is marginal.' First of all, there is no natural border between Iran and Yemen, and providing any weapons through Yemen's neighbours, even Oman, would be very difficult. Oman has remained neutral in the conflict while maintaining a cordial relationship with Iran (Baabood, 2017). Even before the Saudi-led coalition initiated a blockade of Yemen's main ports, Salih was always able to intercept any major shipments of arms to the Huthi rebels (whom, it will be remembered, he was fighting at the time). In the brief period of Huthi control of Sana'a before the war began, Iranian flights to Sana'a airport appear to have been carrying mostly humanitarian aid. It should also not be assumed that Iran supports the Huthis merely because they are Shias, since the Huthi' Shiism is only distantly related to Iranian Twelver Shiism, and Iran has also worked with Sunni groups such as Hamas. The Huthis share the anti-American and anti-Israel sentiment of Iranian hardliners, but this has led to rhetorical support rather than the kind of direct military participation that Iran has endorsed in Iraq and Syria.

Complicating the Saudi interest in heading a Sunni coalition is the shift of Iraq from a sectarian regime under Saddam to a series of pro-Shia governments following the American invasion in 2003. The alliance of Iran, even if not formal, with Iraq and its support for Syria and for Hezbollah in Lebanon are seen by the Saudis as creating a Shia dominated fertile crescent. The politics of this ideological confrontation, which has almost completely sidelined the issue of Palestine, has global as well as regional significance. An unlikely, and likely temporary, alliance of Russia, the United States and Turkey in fighting ISIS in Syria demonstrates that the real issues in this proxy war are not theological but territorial. To the extent that the fighting is represented as a proxy war between Sunnis and Shias, however, the political manoeuvring is obscured. The assumption that the fundamental cause of the current region-wide set of conflicts can be traced back to an age-old rivalry that began at the Battle of Karbala in the seventh century is highly misleading. The Huthis did not and do not present a serious military threat to Saudi Arabia, at least before the current conflict, but the Saudi pursuit of regional hegemony seeks to influence the politics of all other countries on the Arabian Peninsula. In addition, crying 'Iranian wolf' is a convenient way of obtaining Western military and diplomatic support for self-preservation.

Further confusion over the current proxy war has been caused by rumours to the effect that the Huthis have converted to Iranian Twelver Shiism and abandoned their Zaydi heritage. 'Although there are Twelvers who are Houthis, and many of them are newly "converted", the vast majority of Houthis would still self-identify as Zaydi,' notes Abubakr al-Shamahi (2014). Their leaders insist they have not become a satellite of Iranian Twelver Islam. In fact, there are Zaydi theologians who see the Huthis as a threat and resolve to maintain their own tradition. Their voices, however, are drowned out in the media blitz that either defends the Huthis as the saviours of Yemen or demonizes them as Iranian puppets. The Huthi phenomenon is less about a specific family (Salmoni et al., 2010: 101–7), which is small, than the alliances that the leaders formed with local tribes and Salih's forces. Stressing the alliance as 'Huthi' creates the impression that it is more of a proxy war than a local struggle for power engaged with foreign intervention, led primarily by Saudi Arabia and the United Arab Emirates.

While the royal princes of the Al Saud sit in their luxury palaces in Riyadh and on the Riviera, the damage being done in Yemen has been catastrophic, creating an unprecedented humanitarian crisis that has received minimal attention in the news media. By June 2018, it was estimated that 22.2 million of Yemen's estimated population of some 28 million were in need of humanitarian or protection assistance (UNOCHA, 2018). The closing of schools and health centres, some of which were bombed by the Saudi coalition, added to the threat of famine due to a virtual blockade of food and medicine entering the Huthi areas. The attempt in June 2018 by the Emiratis to take control of the vital Huthi port of Hodeida has brought the situation to a critical turning point. Estimates of deaths from the war range as high as 40,000, with many more casualties. Unlike the situation in Iraq and Syria, Yemenis literally have had nowhere to flee to, especially since the blockade by air and sea.

In addition to the loss of life and injuries, the infrastructure in Yemen's north has been indiscriminately bombed, including factories, businesses, schools, clinics, government buildings and personal residences. Both the Saudi bombing and ISIS radicals have attacked worshippers in mosques and at funerals. The old city of Sa'da has been targeted as a military zone in defiance of international law, including bombing of the millennium-old mosque of al-Hadi ila al-Haqq, the first Zaydi imam (Amnesty International, 2015). Buildings in the old city of Sana'a, a UNESCO World Heritage Site, have been hit or damaged, as has the local archaeology museum in Dhamar, parts of the ancient Marib dam, the museum of Imam Ahmad in Ta'izz and the historic fortress known as al-Qahira overlooking Ta'izz.[6] Dozens of shrines in southern Yemen have been destroyed by al-Qaeda and ISIS since they gained nominal control over large parts of the area, including the 800-year-old tomb of the noted Sufi scholar Sufyan ibn 'Abdullah in al-Hawta, a major Yemeni pilgrimage site. Such crimes against world heritage are at least comparable with the destruction of parts of Palmyra by the Islamic State.

Beyond the humanitarian crisis, the proxy war has also increased instability in Yemen and threatens the wider region. One of the major benefactors of the bombing campaign against the Huthis has been al-Qaeda. The impact of al-Qaeda in Yemen began with the bombing of the USS *Cole* in Aden harbour in 2000. Soon after, President Salih worked with American intelligence, and many suspected al-Qaeda recruits were rounded up and jailed. The first US drone strike in Yemen killed Abu 'Ali al-Harithi, one of the ringleaders of the attack on the *Cole*. In February 2006, twenty-three prisoners escaped from the central prison in Sana'a, and by 2009 a small number of al-Qaeda operatives had regrouped as al-Qaeda in the Arabian Peninsula (AQAP). The United States stepped up its drone attacks, eliminating a few noted members such as Anwar al-'Awlaki in 2011, but these attacks also killed many civilians (Varisco, 2015). During the Arab Spring, when the army no longer controlled much of Yemen's south, al-Qaeda, now known as *Ansar al-Shari'a*, took over a number of cities and initiated draconian measures. By stopping Huthi attacks on *Ansar al-Shari'a* and ISIS, the Saudi coalition forces have allowed these two terrorist groups to gain ground and sympathy. Ironically, both were far more dangerous to Saudi interests than the Huthis.

The primary architects of the war on Yemen are Saudi Arabia's Muhammad Bin Salman and the UAE's Muhammad bin Zayed al-Nahyan. Each country carved out a zone of influence, with the Saudis controlling the aerial campaign and the Emiratis leading the ground assaults, mainly with mercenary troops. From the start there was a disagreement about the role of the Muslim Brotherhood, which is anathema to the UAE. Saudi Arabia, although in principle against the Brotherhood, supports the Yemeni variant Islah as part of its coalition against the Huthis (Bonnefoy, 2018: 198). The weakness of Hadi, who represents the fig leaf for involvement in the war to reinstate him, became apparent when Aden's governor, Aidarus al-Zubaydi, formed the Southern Transitional Council in May 2017 with Emirati backing (Dahlgren, 2018). President Hadi's attempt to fire al-Zubaydi had only encouraged the secessionist movement. In 2018, Hadi's weakness was further exposed when the UAE, dubbed 'Little Sparta' by US general James Mattis, attempted to build a military base on the Yemeni island of Socotra. Unless there is a brokered negotiation, neither side is in a position to dominate.

Sectarian rivalry has long political roots in Yemen, but this has generally been due more to local political gamesmanship rather than external interference. The first Rasulid sultan, al-Malik al-Mansur (r. 1229–49), was officially recognized as the ruler of Yemen by the 'Abbasid court, shortly before that court was wiped out by the Mongols, in order to counteract the Zaydis who did not recognize the caliph. The Rasulids, who were of Turkish mercenary origin, were far more interested in creating an empire for their own gain than in converting fellow Muslims. There was little rivalry along purely religious lines in Yemen, even when the Zaydi imams gained the upper hand in the early twentieth century over the majority Shafi'is in the southern highlands. Indeed, the work of Yemeni religious scholars like Muhammad al-Shawkani brought Zaydi views into much closer alignment with Sunni schools (Haykel, 2003). When I lived in rural Yemen in 1978 the local tribesmen would have been nonplussed if I had asked them if they were Sunni or Shia. Until the recent events after the Arab Spring, Zaydis and Shafi'is would pray in the same mosque without controversy. Historically, political and tribal allegiance trumped any sense of attachment to a sect. Much of this has been changed, as might be expected, by the current sectarian strife.

Rebuilding the Yemeni state and restoring Yemeni society

Freedom from fear and oppression must be established in order to build peace and understanding between the diverse cultural and political groups within Yemen. There is no social justice without respect for human rights and their promotion.

Amat al-'Alim Alsoswa, 2014

Dresden, Hiroshima, Aleppo, Sa'da: this stream of war-devastated cities demonstrates the wanton power of destruction of a bombing campaign. Major cities in the Middle East have been conquered and destroyed for several millennia, a telling (literally in an archaeological sense) reminder that no part of the region has ever truly been in a state of *felix*, including Arabia. The inhabitants of Baghdad in 1258 were as unlucky as those who have fallen victim to cluster and barrel bombs today. In all these previous cases, destroyed cities have either been rebuilt or turned into nostalgic reminders of past glory. What the future holds for Sa'da, now largely bombed into a ghost town, or Sana'a, which has withstood over three years of bombardment, or Ta'izz, which has been Berlinized and where entire neighbourhoods have been brought to rubble, is too early to predict. As various human rights organizations have verified, there have been war crimes committed by all sides, including the Huthis.[7] In terms of the scale of destruction, however, I believe that this is the most comprehensive devastation that Yemen has ever received, even if the number of casualties is still relatively small compared to the conflicts in Iraq and Syria or major ethnic cleansings elsewhere. Yemen remains in danger both from recent sectarian ethnic cleansing from the inside and carpet-bombing from the outside.

There are multiple scenarios for the future of Yemen, few of them promising given that the sectarian conflict between Saudi Arabia and Iran continues to have such an adverse impact on regional stability. Before looking at what might happen, it is important to take note of a fact that transcends the political manoeuvring of all parties: the future belongs to the youth of Yemen. First of all, the current child and youth proportion of an estimated population of 28 million is around 61 per cent, with some 40 per cent under the age of fourteen, and 21 per cent between the ages of fourteen and twenty-four. In 2016, Yemen's population growth rate at 2.37 per cent was thirty-first in the world, although the current conflict may have an impact lowering this. It is precisely this group that will inherit the mess bequeathed by the current generation of leaders and combatants. Given the humanitarian crisis since March 2015, children and their mothers are suffering from inadequate supplies of food, medicine and access to health services. Education has virtually ground to a halt with destruction of schools and the flight or detention of many university faculty members. There are few viable jobs for the younger population who should be entering the workforce. As a result, exploiting the money that funds the warring factions has become one of the most ready options for young men to survive. Given these difficulties, the road to recovery will not be easy.

Another social aspect relevant to any scenario of Yemen's future is gender. In both the Yemen Arab Republic, starting in 1962, and more effectively in the People's Democratic Republic of Yemen, beginning in 1967, women were granted rights and opportunities that many did not have before. The revolutionary spirit provided a sense of liberation, especially in urban areas, despite the cultural tendency to seclude women. In rural areas, women had traditionally played an important role in household production and decision-making (Adra, 1983). The influx of imported Salafi views has had a negative impact on female mobility and access to the workplace. Similarly, the extreme views of al-Qaeda and ISIS mitigate against any productive role for women in Yemen's future. While Saudi Arabia and the GCC states can maintain a rigid pattern of gender seclusion due to the welfare state created by oil wealth, poverty in Yemen cannot be alleviated without the active support and work of women in rebuilding the country as well as educating children and restoring social cohesion at the community level. It is instructive to note that women played a key role in the initial protests that led to the downfall of President Salih (Strzelecka, 2018: 49).

In 2005 I participated in drafting a *Country Social Assessment of Yemen* for the World Bank (2006). Since this report was issued just as the Huthi wars were beginning, it has obviously had a short shelf life in development aid circles. The main findings of the report help explain why opposition to Salih's rule reached a peak during the Arab Spring demonstrations. The major challenges included:

- inequality is becoming an increasing issue in Yemen;
- insufficient and haphazard integration of modern and customary norms are rapidly changing the rules for managing communal resources such as land and water;
- poverty, inequality and patronage also threaten social cohesion in Yemen.

There were also opportunities for increasing socioeconomic inclusion of Yemen's diverse population. These included:

- where social mobility in Yemen used to be based on social status, the cash economy and state-provisioned education are providing the means for the social advancement of historically marginalized groups;
- Yemeni society is still largely sensitive to religious and cultural values reinforcing traditional mechanisms of solidarity and conflict resolution mechanisms that recall principles of generosity, support for the weak, fairness, reconciliation and integrity;
- decentralization, if appropriately resourced, provides citizens with an opportunity for more equity and voice since it supports the power of local community institutions.

It is instructive to look at these findings more than a decade later, with Yemen having become a de facto failed state rather than a state heading toward failure. Inequality across Yemen's diverse population increased due both to Salih's preferential treatment of his cronies and the continued exploitation of Yemen's south following the 1994 civil war that had left Salih in complete control of the former PDRY (Brehony, 2014: 137). Students with little hope for meaningful employment or the opportunity to start a family took to the streets in the Arab Spring as a catalyst to the removal of Salih (Alwazir, 2015). Land grabs by the power elite and the overexploitation of Yemen's aquifers deepened the crisis in rural areas, reducing the cultivation of food crops. The patronage system that

Salih perpetuated brought about less social cohesion in tribal areas, along with the rise of insecurity due to the very half-hearted attempts by Salih to eliminate al-Qaeda and other extremist elements.

Given the reality of Yemen's current humanitarian crisis, the road to recovery will be long and difficult, no matter when the current conflict is resolved. Yemen is bankrupt, with only limited revenue potential from the known oil and gas reserves and virtually no viable taxation system. There are almost no opportunities for Yemenis to work outside Yemen. The infrastructure, including bridges and public buildings, has been devastated in the major cities. Numerous schools, health clinics, businesses, civilian houses, mosques and heritage sites have been destroyed or damaged. Water supply continues to run out, even as there is a greater need for local agricultural production. The war has brought about uncontrollable inflation that has wiped out most people's savings. On top of all of this there is the psychological damage and trauma that war produces. Defining a new normal will not be done overnight.

Remarks that are not a conclusion

> A meaningful political settlement will need to address a highly complex and interconnected matrix of issues, not least the hard power dynamics on the ground, the wide variety of demands from the different armed groups that have emerged during the war, and the interests of regional players who have become party to the conflict.
>
> Peter Salisbury, 2016: 41

'Ali 'Abdullah Salih was fond of saying that he danced on the heads of snakes. Salih survived the venom of his enemies until his death in 2017. If the metaphor of Yemen as a snake pit has merit, it is well to remember that many of those snakes have been introduced from outside. The problem with the metaphor is that it assumes only the negative serpentine sidewinding of power politics. While that is clearly an apt description of the current conflict, reconciliation and rebuilding require a different image. Perhaps a better local metaphor would be the blue agama lizard, which I suspect is more numerous than snakes in Yemen, that can find a way to blend in with the background and seeks the sunlight when it is available. If it is assumed that Yemen is a backward, primitive, tribal society that needs to be developmentally patronized by outsiders, then no scenario for the future will be promising. A closer look at Yemen's long history, embedded cultural values and previous development experience suggests that Yemenis can plot their own viable future if left alone by the venomous politics of their neighbours.

It is important to highlight the globalized stranglehold that has led to and perpetuates the current conflict in Yemen. As Vincent Durac (2015: 41) argues, 'Thus the problem of violent non-state actors in the Middle East requires solutions that are located not merely at the local level but also at the broader geopolitical levels.' First, Yemen has not been allowed to forge a national identity on its own, a situation that is hardly unique for most states of the Middle East. Its wealthy northern neighbour has sought for decades to control the political and cultural life of Yemen, buying the loyalty of tribes and promoting a Wahhabi Salafi version of Islam that is not native to Yemen. Second, the wave of terrorist extremism, realized in Yemen through al-Qaeda/*Ansar al-Shari'a* and ISIS, is a present reality throughout the region, but especially acute in areas with major insecurity and opposition to the central government like Yemen, Iraq and Syria. The Huthis, like the Americans, were attempting to eradicate al-Qaeda in Yemen, although they were angry with Salih for working with US intelligence. Third, the powerful GCC interest in establishing hegemony over the entire Arabian Peninsula threatens the establishment of any kind of democratic (or socialist) government in Yemen. Yemen was the only theoretically democratic state on the peninsula, surrounded by kingdoms and emirates. None of these issues are going to disappear soon and all are major obstacles to creating a stable, peaceful and productive Yemeni state.

A fourth factor is the unknown trajectory of all the non-state actors, but especially Yemen's tribes. Tribal authority in rural areas continued unabated throughout the Salih era, although Salih was adept at coopting tribal sheikhs into his set of cronies (Longley, 2010). The Huthi alliance is totally dependent on tribal elements in the north, including the tribal dimension of the army. But the high level of insecurity and inroads of al-Qaeda/*Ansar al-Shari'a* and ISIS have weakened the traditional tribal mechanisms of peacekeeping and mediation. A man in Marib confided to Nadwa al-Dawsari (2016: 28) that 'Before the war, a man would seek the protection of his tribe or another tribe. Now the tribe cannot even protect itself let alone provide protection to its members.' The breakdown in a civil society that has always been held in place by tribal values makes the prospect for resolution of the conflict more problematic. Yet the long trajectory of tribal influence, where most of the tribesmen own or have access to land, will be hard to stop. Sectarian divisions have indeed hardened, but they are not necessarily destructive of tribal identity, especially in the northern areas controlled by the Huthi alliance.

As problematic as the situation in the north is the future of the south, now that support for secession is stronger than ever. Memories of the violence that Salih perpetrated on the south, combined with anger at the Huthi encroachment, makes the idea of reunification extremely unpopular. Emirati support for the recently formed Southern Transitional Council takes advantage of the resentment southerners hold for Hadi in previously carrying out Salih's policies. Yet, as Helen Lackner (2017: 188) suggests, 'Southerners do not need deep knowledge of the history of the PDRY to have serious doubts about the political reliability and honesty of the separatist leaders.' Given the continuing presence of al-Qaeda and ISIS, as well as a number of independent local militias, non-state actors here will form a major stumbling block for whatever form of new state emerges.

When I first arrived in Yemen in the late 1970s, it was very much a terra incognita in academic circles and virtually ignored by political scientists focused on more pressing issues and conflict in the Middle East. The current conflict, which has lasted more than three years, has made Yemen into a *terra nullius*, a region without functional sovereignty and with far too many rival non-state actors. Whatever the future brings, Yemen will continue to exist in one form or another. Some 28 million people are not going to disappear overnight, nor are they easily incorporated into an expanding neighbour's ambitious policy of establishing hegemony, especially of a Wahhabi/Salafi variety. Historically, Yemen has survived internal politics and external invasions, finally achieving a unified state for the first time in 1990. As imperfect as that Republic of Yemen turned out to be, and as isolated as the PDRY became, the idea of a single state with regional diversity remains a compelling option for the future. However attractive the goal of a return to two separate states, sought particularly by southerners, it would hark back to the time warp of proxy Cold War partisanship, and is probably not viable in the long run.

The future of Yemen cannot be determined except in relation to other states of the peninsula. Yemen is the poor relative among its neighbours, who form a consortium of wealthy states that has been able to maintain political structures that favour elite family rule. Apart from this elite corner of the Middle East, royal families have largely become mascots rather than powerful decision-makers. Without the oil wealth, which has created at the same time a dependence on expatriate labour at all levels, the Arabian Peninsula would look far different. In addition, the future of Yemen cannot be isolated from the waves of conflict currently swirling through the entire Middle East. As the Saudi–Iranian rhetorical battle advocating their respective politicized Islamic agendas plays out, the entire region becomes more polarized. The frustration with American foreign policy and political unrest that followed the Arab Spring reflect region-wide concerns. The extent to which Yemen can return to being a state where different schools of Islam can coexist without overt political fallout remains to be seen, especially given the thrust of previous Salafi influence. Since Zaydi Islam came to be closely associated with the Sunni schools in the past, there is room for hope that the proxy sectarianism of Saudi Arabia and Iran can be deflected once the fighting is over. But this is a long-term issue, one that it must be hoped can eventually play itself out in terms of mutual respect and plurality, rather than by one side trying to eliminate the other.

One thing is certain, given Yemen's long political history: non-state actors will continue to play a role both in creating conflict and resolving it. The recent success of al-Qaeda and ISIS, which has yet to be fully analysed, has created new and less predictable actors, albeit with declining regional influence. Both al-Qaeda and ISIS, as well as the Huthis, view America as a great evil, the primary concern being the impact of American foreign policy in meddling in Yemen's politics. The fact that the United States, as well as Britain and France, sold billions of dollars' worth of military weapons to the Saudis and Gulf States for the current war will reverberate far into the future. All this will make the road to improving relations with the United States, important as that will be to any future state, difficult.

Yemen's problems in the short term are nothing short of catastrophic. It will take a tremendous amount of development aid to address the current humanitarian crisis and begin the process of restoring a viable state structure. The political strings that are bound to be tied to this aid will make success all the more difficult to achieve. Even with the best possible scenario of a peaceful settlement and a rapid influx of aid on all levels, there are two issues that must be faced. The first is a population that has outstripped its resources and produces youth who have few viable opportunities for making a living. Even with massive foreign aid into the foreseeable future, how can Yemen meet the needs of its expanding population? The second pressing issue is the looming lack of water to meet the needs either of the population or for agriculture. Sana'a may be the first capital in the world to literally run out of water (Boucek, 2009: 6). Appropriate forms of agriculture, including a return to successful dry farming, are the only viable economic alternatives for a country that has virtually no industry and few other viable income-producing occupations.

So I conclude with no prescient solution, no clear idea of what will happen, just musings on what perhaps could and even should happen. Yemen's future is tied to that of its neighbours, a situation which is problematic for all involved.

A century from now a historian will look back on the current history of Yemen and the Middle East and no doubt shake his or her head at the disastrous situations that were created in this cradle of civilization. I believe that no matter how desperate the hardship and how damaging the political and religious polarization forced from the outside, Yemen's people are highly resilient and will ultimately find a way to create a viable future in harmony with their neighbours. I can only wish that historian of the future a success story to document.

7

Violent Non-State Actors in Somalia: Al-Shabab and the Pirates

Afyare A. Elmi and Ruqaya A. Mohamed*

Introduction

After the Somali government lost the war with Ethiopia in 1977, a number of military officers attempted to overthrow General Mohamed Siyad Barre. However, the coup d'état failed and the Somali government began to collectively punish the clans to which its leaders belonged. As a result, Somalia's military government killed hundreds of civilians and displaced thousands in the central and northeastern regions of Somalia, mostly from the Majerteen clan. Therefore, 1978 marks the beginning of the Somali Civil War. Since then, violence and conflict have engulfed Somalia. At the time, some of the military officers led by Colonel Abdullahi Yusuf (who became president in 2004) established the Somali Salvation Democratic Front (SSDF) and organized military resistance from Ethiopia.

Furthermore, in April 1981, politicians and military officers belonging to the Issaaq clan created the Somali National Movement (SNM). In May 1988, the SNM attacked the major cities of Bur'o and Hargaysa. The military government again collectively punished civilians that belonged to the Issaaq clan, killing thousands and displacing hundreds of thousands. Subsequently, more armed factions emerged: the Somali Patriotic Movement (SPM), the Somali Democratic Movement (SDM) and the United Somali Congress representing Ogaden, Digil and Mirifle and Hawiye respectively also took up arms against the military government in the late 1980s.

These factions were the first violent non-state actors to have challenged the power and authority of the state in Somalia. The emergence of violent non-state actors has not only increased the instability of the state, but also chased out

---

*This research was made possible by NPRP Grant 5-1275-5-196 from the Qatar National Research Fund (a member of the Qatar Foundation). The statements made herein are solely the responsibility of the authors.

international organizations and increased the role of regional military forces in Somalia (Linke and Raleigh, 2011). According to Linke, 'in some cases, these organizations have successfully exercised sovereign control of internal territory, resulting in quasi-state administrations within Somalia' (Linke, 2008: 2).

In addition, Somalia is unique in the sense that the state collapsed in 1991, and that it has many violent non-state actors organized along regional, clan and ideological lines. Different clan militias have fought to control regions and important cities. In the past, Islamist groups have also armed themselves and fought against warlords and foreign intervention. In addition, a variety of armed gangs have acted with impunity for the last two decades, committing piracy, assassinations and kidnappings. Although there have been several attempts to create a national government that would monopolize the legitimate use of violence since 2000, these efforts have so far (2018) not succeeded.

The international community has also provided more than 20,000 African troops to support this goal. However, a number of groups remain armed and defiant, refusing to be subordinated to the state. In this chapter, while using the literature on the issue, we first explain the concept of violent non-state actors. Second, we examine two of the many violent non-state actors in Somalia: al-Shabab and the pirates. Third, we discuss the relationship between these two groups, if there is any. Fourth, we analyse the factors that have helped sustain al-Shabab and the pirates. Finally, we assess the strategies that have been used to eliminate these two groups.

Understanding violent non-state actors

As many scholars note, the state's monopoly of the use of legitimate violence has been challenged from multiple fronts (Williams, 2008). There are many cases where even so-called strong states do not have complete control over their territories. Mulaj (2010) suggests dividing the social and political goals of violent non-state actors into five categories: liberation movements seeking secession; guerrilla movements aiming to weaken the state; terrorist organizations seeking to create fear; militants taking advantage of weak states; and private security companies that sell security (2010). These include ethnic groups, tribes, warlords, insurgents, youth gangs, pirates and ideological groups (Islamists). As William Reno argues, at times these groups compete with the state while at other times they cooperate (directly or indirectly) (Reno, 2010). The case of Sudan is illustrative on this point. With respect to the motivation, the literature identifies two main factors: opportunity-driven and cause-driven violent non-state actors (Williams, 2008). Some of the groups see the weakness of the state and want to take advantage, while others seek to satisfy their ideological demands (whether Marxism or Islamism) (Mulaj, 2010; Williams, 2008; Varin and Abubakar, 2017).

Lack of legitimacy and/or capacity of the state contribute to the presence of these groups (Holsti, 1996). Phil Williams agrees: 'the more legitimate a state is the more it will rely on consent and authority rather than the use of force' (Williams, 2008: 4). Other scholars argue that the capacity of the state with respect to delivering basic services plays a significant role in the emergence of violent non-state actors. Williams (2008) adds the 'inclusivity' factor, meaning that even if the state is legitimate and has the capacity but excludes a group that shares a common identity (clan affiliation, language or faith), the chances are that the excluded groups will challenge the state.

Violent non-state actors differ in terms of their goals, scope, organizational structure and sources of funding (Mulaj, 2010). According to Thomas and Casebeer (2004), these actors not only threaten human and national security, but also spread violence across the international community. In other words, as Williams (2008) points out, violent non-state actors come into existence where there is a security deficit in the state. An example is the case of Somalia where political instability and more than twenty-five years of civil war have crippled the state's legitimacy and ability to exercise its authority. This environment has provided the conditions for violent non-state actors to play a major role in the political and social order in Somalia and allows pirates and al-Shabab to further their goals.

In addition, there is no consensus as to which group is included or excluded in the list of violent non-state actors. Some authors adopt a broad definition of the concept (Chaudhry, 2013; Williams, 2008; Mulaj, 2010; Menkhaus, 2010; Reno, 2010; Varin and Abubakar, 2017). We believe that pirates fall into the opportunity-driven category that takes advantage of the weakness of the states. In justifying the inclusion of a chapter on piracy in their edited book, Varin writes that pirates are 'motivated strictly by financial interests but have been prompted by political and economic circumstances beyond their control' (2017: 12). We tend to agree with this view.

Violent non-state actors in Somalia: al-Shabab and the pirates

After the collapse of the Somali state in 1991 many violent non-state actors emerged to fill the vacuum, with variations of the above groups taking root at different times in different regions of the country. Ken Menkhaus identified 'business groups, Sharia courts, warlord and clan militias, criminal gangs, regional and municipal polities, autonomous paramilitaries within the Transitional Federal Government and Islamist groups' (Menkhaus, 2010: 344). In addition, Menkhaus argues that private security groups are part of the violent non-state actors in Somalia. However, this chapter only examines the emergence of al-Shabab and pirates in Somalia.

Al-Shabab: origins, expansion and decline

Al-Shabab emerged as a sub-group of the *al-Ittihad al-Islami* (AIAI) organization (Elmi, 2010; Hansen, 2013). The AIAI was established after two Islamist movements (a faction of Jama'a Islamiya in the South and a faction of the Wuhda-Shabaab al-Islam in the North) decided to unite in 1983. The goal of the organization was to propagate Salafi Islamic *da'wa* and eventually Islamize the politics and institutions of the country. At the time, AIAI was not armed at all. However, this changed when the Somali state collapsed in 1991. Like many Somalis, the Islamist organizations were not prepared for an all-out clan civil war. Some of the leadership of AIAI decided to take up arms in order to change the prevailing conditions by force, while others within the organization rejected the idea.

As early as 1992, the AIAI fought against General Muhammad Farah 'Aydid on the Arare Bridge of the Lower Jubba region. When the AIAI lost the fight, they moved to Bosaso in the Puntland region. After a while, the Somali Salvation Democratic Front led by Colonel Abdullahi Yusuf, who later became president, fought against al-Ittihad. Subsequently, AIAI lost several major cities and moved to the Lasqoray district in the Sanaag region. In addition, it captured the Gedo region and created Islamic courts in most of the cities there in 1996 (Menkhaus, 2003; Elmi, 2010). The Somali faction that claimed the region, led by General 'Umar Hajji Muhammad with the help of the Ethiopian government, removed the AIAI from Gedo in 1995–6. By 1996, after losing many battles, the leadership of AIAI decided to lay down their arms and focus on education and development (Elmi, 2010).

Interestingly, the decision to stop using force was controversial among the AIAI leaders. Shaykh Hassan Turki, who was based in Raskamboni, rejected this move. In addition, most of the leadership of the AIAI made an exception for their branch in the Ogaden region, which was allowed to keep fighting since they believed that (Christian) Ethiopia had occupied this Muslim Somali region. The leadership encouraged young fighters in Lasqoray to either disarm or join the Ogaden branch. However, some of the fighters decided to remain in either Raskambooni or small pockets in southern Somalia. Al-Shabab leaders such as Ibrahim Hajji Jama and Adan Hashi Ayrow have roots in these events. By 2003, some of these leaders had moved to Mogadishu and established the first Salah al-Din training camp in the city, as well as sending some of their committed leaders to Afghanistan for training. Besides the Raskaambooni group, which was always active and armed, two other training camps (Nasruddin and El-Gras) emerged from the Mogadishu and Galgadud regions respectively.

By 2004, Mogadishu was witnessing many assassinations of Islamic activists, civil society leaders and military personnel. In retrospect, it became clear that al-Shabab and warlords were engaged in this war. Against this background, nine warlords in Mogadishu joined forces and declared war on what they called terrorists. The warlords' approach did not differentiate between the various Islamist movements, which were diverse. For instance, at the time there were several Islamic Courts that neighbourhoods and clans created for security reasons. The courts had the support of many people who did not know of the existence of the violent extremist groups (Elmi, 2010). Open war between the Mogadishu warlords and the ICU (including al-Shabab) broke out in 2006.

This was a great opportunity for what later became al-Shabab. They were more committed and more experienced fighters, and the movement was better organized than the other Islamist organizations that supported the ICU. Here al-Shabab members offered their services. In fact, even though leaders such as Sharif Shaykh Ahmad and Hassan Dahir Aweys represented the face of the ICU, the leaders of al-Shabab became instrumental in the military successes of the ICU. The ICU defeated the warlords, pacified Mogadishu and much of southern Somalia and opened the port and the airport of Mogadishu in 2006. By December 2006, Ethiopian forces had invaded Somalia, removed the ICU from power and began a military occupation of the country. Many of the ICU leaders left the country, joined forces with other Somali nationalist groups and created what they called the Alliance for the Re-Liberation of Somalia (ARS) in Asmara, Eritrea. Many of the ICU leaders created their own movement called *Muqawama* (Resistance), which was politically led by Shaykh Sharif Shaykh Ahmed who later became president. The military side of the movement was led by Shaykh 'Abd al-Qadir 'Ali 'Umar who became minister of the interior in 2009.

Al-Shabab rejected the move of the ICU leaders. They called for a meeting among the different factions in the Lower Jubba region that shared their extremist viewpoint. The Salahaddin, Raskambooni, Nasruddin and El-Garas groups formally joined forces and announced the creation of *al-Shabab al-Mujahidin* in early 2007. They also called for jihad against the Ethiopian invasion and accused the other Islamists of being cowards who had run away before the war began (Godane Speech, 2007). Gradually, the organization increased the use of violence against all the groups that had not joined it. It was not until 2008 that the US designated al-Shabab a terrorist organization (Ali 2010), the same year in which the organization pledged allegiance to al-Qaeda.

Al-Shabab was able to raise revenue from several sources and use the money to pay its members. The organization was often more efficient than the government in how it raised and spent its revenue. It controlled large parts of the country and relied on revenue from taxation (*zakat*) in the areas that it controlled (UNSC Report, 2015). It also collected money from illicit charcoal and sugar trading in southern Somalia. According to the UN Monitoring Group (2015), al-Shabab had collected between $400,000 and $800,000 from the sugar trade (Monitoring Group Report, 2015).

If al-Shabab had previously been a small group within the ICU, this changed permanently in 2007. The organization became popular among young people and to some extent among the general population. Several factors led to this popularity. The most important event was the 2007–9 Ethiopian invasion (Ali, 2010; Hansen, 2013; Elmi and Aynte, 2012), which killed more than 16,000 Somalis and displaced more than 1 million people from the capital. In fact, most of the population of Mogadishu moved to an area on the outskirts called Elasha Biyaha (Wells of Water), near Afgoye district. The invasion created huge grievances against the Ethiopian forces and allowed al-Shabab to recruit thousands of young fighters who believed they had a legitimate cause to fight against the invading forces. Moreover, the general public sympathized with the movement and assisted with the resistance to the occupation.

In terms of tactics, al-Shabab employs different methods such as assassinations, suicide bombings and guerrilla attacks. According to Urgo (2009), there was a rapid increase in al-Shabab's use of improvised explosive devices (IEDs) from a few incidents in 2006 to seventy-four attacks in 2007. Furthermore, Urgo (2009) explains that there are two common types of IEDs in Somalia: vehicle-borne (VBIED) and person-borne (PBIED). VBIED devices use a vehicle to transport the bomb, which is detonated by remote control (Global Security, 2011). PBIED devices require a suicide bomber to carry the explosives, which are set off once the carrier reaches the destination (Homeland Security Research, 2015). Both types of IEDs have recently been used in Somalia to trigger explosions.

Al-Shabab forces have also attacked AMISOM soldiers from Uganda, Ethiopia, Burundi and Kenya. In 2016, the group ambushed Kenyan forces

(KDF) in the town of El Adde. Al-Shabab and the KDF fighters fought for almost ten hours in three waves of attacks (Chweya, 2016). The attacks left 'an unknown number of soldiers dead, others missing and others being taken into captivity' (Chweya, 2016). Moreover, al-Shabab attacked other African forces, such as those from Uganda, Burundi and Ethiopia, multiple times in different parts of Somalia such as Bakol, Lower-Shabelle, Hiran and Galgadud regions.

However, al-Shabab soon lost its popularity among Somalis. According to Elmi and Aynte (2012), three factors led to its dwindling approval. First, after Ethiopia pulled out of Mogadishu in 2009, al-Shabab demanded that the AMISOM peacekeeping troops should leave Somalia and the Transitional Federal Government (TFG) should dismantle its powers (Elmi and Aynte, 2012). Second, al-Shabab began to attack civilians indiscriminately. For instance, they bombed a medical school graduation ceremony in Mogadishu in 2009, 'killing twenty-three people including ministers from the TFG, parents, students, professors and journalists' (IRIN, 2009). This attack was a 'wake-up call' for many Somalis and was followed by another attack in October 2011 in which al-Shabab 'claimed responsibility for the worst suicide bombings in Somalia's history ... [where] more than 70 people (mostly students waiting for a scholarship abroad) were killed' (Elmi and Aynte, 2012). According to the *New York Times*, in October 2017 a truck full of explosive material killed more than 300 people and wounded over 200 in Mogadishu. Third, al-Shabab expelled IGOs and NGOs from Somalia in the midst of famine and droughts. As a result of the drought, thousands of Somalis fled from the southern regions (Gettleman, 2011) to nearby cities and to Ethiopia and Kenya. This was the last straw for al-Shabab's popularity in Somalia (Elmi and Aynte, 2012; Gettleman, 2011).

The rise and decline of pirates in Somalia

Like al-Shabab, Somali pirates, another violent non-state actor, have taken advantage of the instability in the country. Piracy is a universal crime (Law of the Sea, 1982). According to the Law of the Sea Convention, an act is piracy if it takes place between two ships on the high seas and is committed for private ends (Law of the Sea, 1982). In Somalia, organized pirate groups emerged after the Somali state collapsed in 1991 in the areas of Bari, Nugaal and Mudug. Since 1991, Somali pirates have attacked about 1,100 ships, of which they have hijacked around 300 (IMB Reports). Scholars identified various causes for this phenomenon, including statelessness, poverty, illegal fishing by foreign vessels, toxic waste dumping by Western companies, and criminal opportunism (Elmi et al., 2015).

To provide legitimacy for their predatory behaviour, pirates have often employed grievance narratives and claimed that they were defending Somali territorial waters from illegal foreign fishing and toxic waste dumping (Bahadur, 2012; Hansen, 2008). According to Mwangura (2009), illegal fishing increased exponentially after 1991 when the Somali state collapsed. Furthermore, several factors encouraged violent non-state actors including pirates to flourish in Somalia, with the lack of jurisdictional clarity, favourable geography, local conflict and disorder, inadequate security and the promise of reward (Murphy, 2010).

Researchers broadly identify three pirate groups in the waters of the Horn of Africa: the Eyl, Harardheere and Jubba groups (Hansen, 2008; Bahadur, 2012). These groups were led by Abshir Boyah, Mohamed Hassan Afweyne and Garaad respectively. As Bahadur argues, the Eyl group popularized the 'saviors of the sea' narrative. This group has also successfully used the illegal fishing cause. Bahadur pointed out to some of the pirates he interviewed that some of the ships they hijacked were not fishing vessels or close to Somali waters. However, the pirates argued that the tankers and bulk carriers were legitimate targets, because the same countries that owned these ships also owned fishing vessels (Bahadur, 2012).

Pirate operations were carried out by one group or another. For example, in 2009, while the Haradere group hijacked the MV *Sirius Star*, a Saudi crude oil supertanker, the Eyl group attacked the *Maersk Alabama*. The ransom gained by the two pirate groups was used to fund the intelligence and weapons used in the hijackings (Bahadur, 2011). Furthermore, the main pirate groups in Eyl and Harardheere collaborated in their pirate activities. The leader of the Eyl group, Boyah, collaborated with the leader of Harardheere, Afweyne (calling it the Eyl–Harardheere joint collaboration) in the hijacking of the MV *Faina*, a Ukrainian transport ship (Bahadur, 2011). This event paved the way for the two groups to gain a reputation and credentials in Somalia and the international media, increasing the number of volunteers and funding. However, not all the pirate operations were carried out in collaboration. Each pirate group needed to establish a reputation with their individual hometowns, which meant they had to carry out separate operations, such as the hijackings of an American and an Arab oil tanker.

Four coastal towns became the pirate hubs: Eyl, Harardheere, Garacad and Hobyo (McKnight and Hirsh, 2012), though smaller groups of Somali pirates were scattered along the coast. At times, these groups concealed their pirate activities, transporting migrants to Yemen and then on their way back hijacking any ship they found or transporting weapons back to Somalia (Bahadur, 2011). Like al-Shabab, the pirate groups initially gained strength and popularity within the country. Gradually, the local population realized the potential revenue from the business of piracy, which was when piracy began to be supported by different actors (Bahadur, 2011). Moreover, the ransom paid to the pirates circulated within the pirate groups to fund their activities. This also helped bring in youth volunteers, many of them barely able to swim, to join the pirate groups (McKnight and Hirsh, 2012). With the hijackings, the ransoms obtained and the international media frenzy, they were able to establish piracy as a lucrative business.

Piracy, of course, has had negative implications locally, regionally and globally. The World Bank (2013) estimated the cost of piracy at $18 billion each year from 2008 to 2012. Furthermore, the impact of piracy has halted all food aid to Somalia. The World Food Program had predicted that the country would require 185,000 tons of food in 2008, but the insecurity of Somali waters has led to the WFP suspending shipments to Somalia. The international community responded with naval support, particularly from the European Union, to transport WFP aid to Somalia from November 2007 to June 2008 (AEDI, 2009).

Moreover, according to Liwang and Ringsberg (2013), something between 20,000 to 30,000 ships pass through the Gulf of Aden, transporting goods and oil between Asia and Europe and North America. This means that an increase in Somali piracy leads to an increase in the price of global commodities and oil. Furthermore, pirate attacks in the Gulf of Aden have increased the dangers and cost of the premium of insurance companies for ships travelling that route (Middleton, 2008). The increased expenses of ships led to increased prices in goods and oil, thus leading to the prospect of global economic insecurity. The Arab region, and in particular Yemen and Egypt which control the southern and northern entrances to the Red Sea respectively, have also experienced security and economic challenges during the peak years of piracy (Middleton, 2008).

Although some countries have resorted to using the route around the Cape of Good Hope, this also increased the price of commodities (Middleton, 2008). According to Mbekeani and Ncube (2011), the rerouting of oil tankers from the Gulf of Aden to the Cape of Good Hope costs around $3.5 billion in annual fuel costs. These increased costs incurred by diverting maritime routes and high insurance premiums inevitably increase the cost of products and decrease the competitiveness of products in African markets (Mbekeani and Ncube, 2011). Finally, piracy has negatively affected Somalia (Elmi et al., 2016; Weldemichael, 2018). It has worsened the humanitarian situation in the country as pirates have hijacked ships carrying humanitarian aid. The cost of living has also increased, because pirates have hijacked many ships that were carrying business goods to the country. Most importantly, it has permanently damaged the image of the Somalis, who are regarded as tolerating the torture and ransom of peaceful seafarers. Finally, pirates have corrupted the nascent institutions (Elmi et al., 2016; Weldemichael, 2018).

The international community adopted an offshore strategy in order to contain the crime of piracy in the Horn of Africa. Navies were sent to patrol the area. The American-led Command Task Force (CTF) 151, the EU combined Naval Force (EUNAVFOR) operation named ATALANTA and NATO-led navies have been patrolling the Gulf of Aden, the Arabian Sea and the western Indian Ocean (Chalk, 2010). In addition, many countries sent their own navies to the area, including India, China, Russia, Pakistan, Saudi Arabia, the Netherlands, Malaysia, South Korea, Japan and the United Arab Emirates (Chalk, 2010). The shipping industry also employed private security guards in order to protect their ships transiting the dangerous waters. The industry used best management practices that included the building of citadels (Affi et al., 2016). Furthermore, the United States, United Kingdom and European Union have entered into an agreement with Kenya, whereby Kenya acts as a third party to prosecute persons suspected of engaging in armed maritime crimes (Chalk, 2010).

The relationship between al-Shabab and piracy

Some argue that the lucrative business of piracy has funded al-Shabab. Speculation increased when a Greek-owned ship was captured and redirected to a southern port controlled by al-Shabab rather than heading to the usual pirate bases (Ross and David, 2009). According to Ross and David (2009), 'Islamic insurgents are benefitting from the pirates' success.' Jane's Terrorism and Security Monitor agreed and argued that the success of Somali piracy had a far greater impact than simply harming the shipping industry (2008). It said that the two violent non-state actors cooperated in three areas: arms trafficking, piracy investment and training (Jane's Terrorism and Security Monitor, 2008). Moreover, Pham (2008) argued that training is a two-way deal between the two groups. While al-Shabab provided military training to the pirates, the pirates trained the Islamist fighters to operate and spread violence via the high seas (Jane's Terrorism and Security Monitor, 2008).

The World Bank Report of 2013 argues that there is evidence of the two violent non-state actors in Somalia interacting and coordinating together in two main areas: financial flows and hostage-taking for political reasons (World Bank,

2013). In other words, al-Shabab was able to benefit financially from Somali pirates in the past. The al-Shabab organization could benefit from the ransoms that the pirates received by investing in weapons and military training, while capturing Western hostages could serve as a tool to achieve political goals. The latter was evident when Somali pirates threatened to sell one hostage to al-Shabab if their ransom demands were not met (Somalia Report, 2012).

However, other Somali leaders have expressed disgust with the actions of the pirates and have distanced themselves from this group, claiming their actions contradict the tenets of Somali culture (Hansen, 2011). Similarly, most scholars reject the theoretical linkage between al-Shabab and piracy, and argue that the different ideological interests of the two organizations contradict the thesis of a mutually beneficial relationship. The idea of cooperation between al-Shabab and Somali pirates is not a credible one, because their means of survival are different. While pirates rely on hijacking ships and demanding heavy ransoms to reinvest and survive as an organization, al-Shabab aims to destroy international trade and commercial markets (Chalk, 2008). According to a RAND Cooperation Report, 'the objectives of the two actors remain entirely distinct' (Chalk, 2008: 31), which is why they have not worked together. Some of the London-based lawyers interviewed for this research also knew nothing of any link between al-Shabab and the Somali pirates. Had that been the case, it would be illegal to even give ransoms to pirates (interview with legal expert, London, 2014).

Furthermore, the actions of the pirates contradict not only the principles of Somali culture but also the culture of Islam, which al-Shabab claims to protect. This means that the interest of one violent non-state actor contradicts that of the other. According to Hansen (2011), Somali piracy has had negative consequences such as 'inflation related to war premiums on food, the outright theft by pirates of food aid, as well as the spread of prostitution and HIV infection in pirate-dominated areas' (Hansen, 2011: 30). These consequences contradict the ideology of the al-Shabab organization. In other words, although both groups take advantage of the weak Somali state, their end goals are not aligned. This reduces the likelihood of al-Shabab and the Somali pirates working together.

Why have the pirates and al-Shabab persisted?

Since the collapse of the Barre regime in 1991, Somalia has been without a functioning central government. The forces that have perpetuated this statelessness have inadvertently prolonged the life of the violent non-state actors, including the pirates and al-Shabab. In particular, neighbouring countries' short-term, self-serving policies, the divisive politics of the Somali political class and general corruption are three main reasons for the resilience of these groups in general and al-Shabab and the pirates in particular.

Somalia has had long and problematic relations with its neighbours Ethiopia and Kenya that are rooted in territorial disputes. Both countries considered the Somali state to be irredentist and therefore worked together to undermine it. Ethiopia has been instrumental in the collapse of Somalia due to its arming of destructive factions within the state. It has also intervened in Somalia many times over the last two decades, particularly in 2006. Kenya has also been involved in the Somali conflict, albeit on a much smaller scale than Ethiopia. Like Ethiopia, it has organized a number of reconciliation conferences, supported some proxy Somali factions and has also sent its forces to parts of Somalia.

Furthermore, Somalia's political class has engaged in divisive and sectarian politics that has perpetuated the country's statelessness. This has allowed violent non-state actors to exploit the regional, tribal and business conflicts of these groups. For instance, many young disaffected clan members have joined al-Shabab.

Endemic corruption in Somalia is an enduring problem. Both al-Shabab and the pirates have succeeded because of corrupt politicians and government institutions. The UN Monitoring Group (2015) reported that al-Shabab received its weapons from Somali government forces. Pirates have also survived and thrived by corrupting government officials. In 2014, the UN Monitoring Group investigated acts of corruption that had undermined government institutions, including the illicit sale of fishing licences to foreign clients. This shows that piracy occurs in Somalia due to top-down corruption, with ministries redirecting revenues and selling licences to illicit foreign fishing companies.

According to Waldo (2009), Somali warlords issue fake licences to foreign fishing companies. Furthermore, the UN Monitoring Group (2015) stated that the illegal selling of fishing licences is also a major concern in Somalia, as it fuels corruption and even conflict. Since March 2015, 'the Ministry of Fishing and Marine Resources had sold eleven licenses mostly to China-flagged long liners fishing for tuna and tuna-like species, generating more than USD 180,000 in revenue' (UN Monitoring Report, 2015). The revenues received from selling illicit licences were transferred to banks outside Somalia. One transfer shows that a total of US$40,100 was sent to a Djibouti account in the name of the Ministry of Fishing and Marine Resources (UN Monitoring Report, 2015). These transactions have further destabilized the security of Somalia and weakened its democratic institutions.

Other internal dynamics have also enabled violent non-state actors in Somalia to grow and continue to use violence as a tool for achieving their goals. These internal dynamics include poverty, lack of employment and the loss of hope among young people. Al-Shabab exploits this situation by drawing in children and young adults through the provision of a small monthly payment. The dire context of conflict and poverty coupled with these payments have encouraged young people to participate in the activities of violent non-state actors. Hassan (2012) observed that five out of fifteen youths he interviewed said that unemployment was the main reason for joining al-Shabab, quoting one youth (19) who said that 'it was easier to join al-Shabab rather than languish in poverty with no chance to pursue something greater'. This shows that although al-Shabab was established ostensibly for religious or political motives, many join the organization simply because of their lack of hope for a better future.

The two violent non-state actors under discussion have exploited the above factors prevalent in Somalia, while al-Shabab in particular has benefited from the Ethiopian and Kenyan invasions by rallying opposition to these foreign interventions. For many Somalis, fighting against Ethiopia and Kenya on Somali territory is considered legitimate action. For this reason, al-Shabab reached the peak of its popularity when Ethiopia occupied Mogadishu and most of southern Somalia.

According to Jeffry Gettleman of the *New York Times*, many government officials were accused of collaborating with the Somali pirates and splitting ransoms collected from hijacking vessels. A captured pirate, Farah Ismail Eid, sentenced to fifteen years in prison, said, 'A lot of our money has gone straight into the government's pockets' (Gettleman, 2008). The report explained how the ransom was divided: '20 percent for their bosses, 20 percent for future missions (to cover essentials like guns, fuel and cigarettes), 30 percent for the gunmen on the ship and 30 percent for government officials' (Gettleman, 2008). This account, as well as others from dozens of captured pirates, explains how revenues are shared with the government and shows the corruption on the part of higher-level authorities.

Strategies for controlling violent non-state actors

The international community has employed several strategies to fight al-Shabab and the pirates. It kept the nominal Somali government on life-support, and employed external forces against these two violent non-state actors. Even though it cannot physically control its territory, the international community has provided support to the Somali government and other sub-national authorities. Somali leaders are still considered the official representatives of the state that collapsed in 1991. As the practice suggests, the international community engages the Somali government politically while it engages all other regional actors in the security, development and relief areas.

Additionally, in order to control al-Shabab and the pirates, the international community employed external forces such as naval forces and AMISOM, which has been recruited from the neighbouring countries of Ethiopia, Kenya and Djibouti and the other African countries of Uganda and Burundi. Although AMISOM increased its troop numbers and captured Mogadishu and other cities in 2010, al-Shabab regularly launches attacks on AMISOM bases and cuts routes to AMISOM-captured cities. Furthermore, several countries in the UN have participated in the counter-piracy task force, and have employed anti-piracy naval forces to combat maritime robbery. These forces include the American-led CTF-151, EUNAVFOR and NATO-led navies (Chalk, 2010).

The United States is also part of those combatting al-Shabab through drone strikes. Although the US says that the air strikes have killed al-Shabab leaders, they are at times similar to al-Shabab's indiscriminate attacks (Greenwald, 2016). Another state carrying out air strikes is Kenya. According to Ohikere (2016), an airstrike sent by Kenya had supposedly killed the al-Shabab head of intelligence, ten mid-level members of the organization and forty-two recruits at the Nadris camp. Al-Shabab denied this and claimed that the attacks had led to civilian deaths. So although the international community has attempted to defeat al-Shabab, it has been far from successful. However, even though the strategies used to control al-Shabab have not been successful, the pirates have largely been contained.

At sea, armed private security guards protect ships that are transiting the high-risk areas, which are also patrolled by the EUNAV, NATO and CTF fleets, creating transit corridors. These offshore-based initiatives have significantly contained piracy in the Horn of Africa, though arguably these are neither sustainable nor efficient methods.

Ironically, the mechanisms the international community employed to contain al-Shabab and the pirates have not been effective in eliminating the violence of these groups in Somalia. Instead, these two violent non-state actors still threaten the peace and security of the country, the region and the globe. In order to end these threats, a new strategy is necessary, one that will incorporate state-building and meaningful development. The issue of insecurity and the rise of violent non-state actors in Somalia can be tackled through the rebuilding of the security forces on land and sea. Furthermore, investing in internal economic development, employment, education, healthcare and technology would also decrease the number of potential fighters joining violent non-state actors in Somalia.

Conclusion

The state of Somalia is still very weak. For many violent non-state actors, this is an opportunity. In this chapter we have described the Somalia context and explained the factors that enabled the emergence of the first non-state actors in the country (Somalia's armed factions). In addition, we have examined the concept of the violent non-state actors, focusing on al-Shabab and the pirates, discussing and analysing each. Furthermore, we examined the relationship between al-Shabab and the pirates, arguing that these two non-state actors pursue separate goals. Finally, we have assessed the strategies used by the international community to defeat or contain them. We have concluded that although strategies used against piracy have largely succeeded in containing that threat, those that have been employed against al-Shabab have failed to control that organization. Therefore, we call for a strategy that combines state-building and development in Somalia.

8

'Being in Time':
Kurdish Movement and Quests of Universal

Hamit Bozarslan

The following article was written in 2015,[1] since when both the Middle East and the Kurdish space have gone through some important evolutions. The Russian intervention in Syria has ensured Bashar al-Assad's survival but also changed the global context. The United States abandoned a coherent policy in relation to Syria under Obama, but the election of Trump as president has created a totally unreadable and unpredictable picture, with the White House, State Department and Pentagon constantly making contradictory statements. ISIS, which is still active on the ground, has been defeated both in Iraq and in Syria and ceased to exist as a 'state'. The tension that existed between Russia and Turkey over Syria in 2015 has been replaced by an impressive rapprochement between two countries, while a 'cold war' has emerged between Turkey and the United States. Similarly, in spite of numerous differences between them, Iran and Turkey have achieved a regional rapprochement. Both countries have also adopted an extremely hard-line policy towards the Kurdish issue, both internally and regionally.

The ad hoc alliances between Russia, Iran and Turkey benefited the al-Assad regime, which could impose its military power on Aleppo, largely destroyed by Syrian and Russian air forces, as well as the Eastern Ghouta near Damascus, with Ankara's tacit agreement. The Kurds have been the main losers in this power play. Following the Kurdish independence referendum on 25 September 2017 (72.16 per cent participation; 92.73 per cent in favour), the Iraqi Shia militias in close coordination with the Pasdaran General Qassem Suleymani attacked and occupied the city of Kirkuk. Turkey has given her full support to Tehran and Baghdad for this occupation. But the Kurdish defeat was above all the result of internal division: one faction of the Patriotic Union of Kurdistan (PUK), whose peshmergas controlled the city, had secretly negotiated with the Iranians and, consequently, decided to withdraw without fighting.

The second setback occurred in Syria in the spring of 2018, with the prolonged and intense Turkish bombardment of the city of Afrin, which had been controlled by the Democratic Union Party (PYD) since mid-2012. Disconnected from the main Kurdish region of the country, the airspace of this zone, located to the west of the Euphrates, was controlled by the Russian air force. Moscow officially did not approve of the Turkish action, but refused to close Syrian airspace to the Turkish army and instead placed the blame for the tragedy on the United States. The Free Syrian Army, composed mainly of Jihadists, took control of Afrin and subjected it to an almost predatory plundering.

In spite of these setbacks, the Kurdish movement had managed to survive; for example, in Iraq, where the results of the independence referendum were ignored, Kurdish forces stopped a second offensive by the Shia militias. In 2018, when they were invited by Baghdad to fight the resurgent IS, Kurdish forces returned to Kirkuk and the so-called disputed territories. In Syria, the US has refused, at least for the time being, to withdraw its forces from the Kurdish region situated to the east of the Euphrates. But recognizing the possibility of an American retreat, the PYD has decided to negotiate with Damascus for some form of regional autonomy.

There is no doubt that compared to the past, the region-wide Kurdish dynamics of the end of 2010 remain quite strong and could contribute positively to the reshaping of Iran, Turkey, Iraq and Syria in the future. But what will be the ultimate outcome of the disintegration of Iraqi and Syrian society? What shape will the hegemonic designs of Iran and Turkey take in the future? What will be the future strategy of the United States and Russia in Syria and in Iraq? The fate of Kurdish society will depend on these as yet unanswered questions.

For many decades the Kurdish movement has been active in the Near East, and has recently acquired a new public profile thanks to the existence of de jure or de facto Kurdish entities in Iraq and Syria, and their transformation into the main frontline resistance to ISIS in 2014–15.

Analysing such a movement is not an easy task. First of all, like all societies, Kurdish society is multilayered, with a variety of political, social and cultural forms of expression, resistance, resilience and in some cases, also accommodation; in reality the term 'Kurdish movement', that is used in this chapter as a generic term, also designates a plurality of political and/or military movements. Second, if the Kurds are not the only 'stateless nation' divided between different countries, they constitute nevertheless the only group I am aware of to be divided between four countries: Iran, Iraq, Syria and Turkey. Their historical trajectory is determined by complementariness with, and opposition to, Arab, Persian and

Turkish cultural–linguistic influences, which for more than a millennium have been the dominant components of the Middle East. This complex political and cultural map demonstrates that the Kurds, and the Kurdish movement, are, simultaneously, unified and diverse.

To some extent, 'Kurdish national unity' was realized between the 1920s and 1940s thanks to the elaboration of a common national narrative, including an integrated historiography of the four parts of Kurdistan, a cartographic imaginary, a flag, a national Pantheon and a national anthem; on the other hand, the division of the Kurds between the states produced distinct political cultures and patterns, specific histories which have been determined by distinct 'national powers', and in some cases also antagonistic strategies. The Kurdish political space cannot ignore these legacies of the past; it is obliged to manage its unity at its best benefit and its divisions at the lower cost that it can afford. As a consequence of this dialectic of unity and diversity, one observes simultaneously an intra-Kurdish integration, which could not be stopped by the militarization of inter-state borders, and a second process of integration, this time with Iran, Turkey, Iraq and Syria, and broadly speaking the Middle East. As a consequence of this double integrative process, the Kurdish movements had to combine their distinctiveness – that is, the 'Kurdishness' which constitutes their ultimate *raison d'être* – with broader, universal worldviews, norms and ideologies. That means that throughout the past hundred years, they had to be in *their time* and in *their world*, a world that kept changing in the answers it offered to the human condition, and in the ideologies and utopias it proposed in order to change it for the better.

This chapter proposes a number of hypotheses to understand the ideological evolution of the Kurdish space since the end of the Ottoman Empire. The first section of the chapter will offer some comments on the concepts of 'minority' and 'nationalism' as they are usually applied to the Kurdish case. The second section will be devoted to the period of the 1920s–1940s, which was marked by the disruptive effects of the collapse of the Ottoman Empire, the formation of the mandate states in Iraq and Syria and the 'reconstruction' of Iran and Turkey in accordance with what one could call the Westphalian model of states. The third section will analyse the period of the 1960s–1980s, which has been dominated, in Kurdistan as in many other parts of the world, by the spread of left-wing ideas and aspirations. In the fourth section, I will focus on the reasons why in the 1980s, Islamism, which became the dominant political and axiological syntax throughout the Middle East, remained rather marginal in the Kurdish political space. The last section will be devoted to the present situation, marked by an ideological vacuum in the Middle East where two societies, Syria and Iraq, face the risk of a total collapse, Turkey is evolving under the hegemony of AKP (the Party of Justice and Development), and Iran is following a rather uncertain path. The limited prospects offered by this scenario of region-wide conflicts for any change to the Kurdish condition have left the Kurds to seek new sources of legitimization in the universal ideas and norms advocated in the wider world.

Given the plurality of Kurdish society and the extreme complexity of each period under consideration, this chapter will limit itself to just a few illustrative examples, eschewing the multiple ideological syntheses elaborated elsewhere in relation to Kurdistan and the rest of Middle East between Islam and 'Westernism' or between 'nationalism' and 'socialism'.

'Minorities', 'nationalism' and ideologies

Many scholars, including the author of this chapter, have used the concept of 'minority nationalism' in order to define a broad social, cultural and political contest whose aim is to reach a satisfactory degree of national autonomy, a federative status within the existing state-borders or a full independence and political integration of the different parts of Kurdistan. While bearing a heuristic meaning, both concepts of 'minority' and 'nationalism' are, however, ultimately problematic and require some explanation. The term 'minority' is widely rejected by Kurdish political actors, opinion makers and intellectuals, on the basis that demographically the Kurds do not constitute a minority but rather, to the contrary, an overwhelming majority in the areas inhabited by them. In this chapter, I will suggest that from a political and/or legalistic perspective, 'majorities' and 'minorities' are not determined by their demographic weight, but rather by the power relations that create and impose an official 'identity', integrate those who can relate to this identity and exclude the others either by depriving them of equal status with the 'majors' or by designating them as non-loyal subjects and therefore potential internal enemies. Political and juridical 'minorization' is a process that always goes hand in hand with mechanisms of domination, subordination, denial and coercion. This fact also has an impact on historical trajectories broadly speaking. In his comments on Ibn Khaldûn, Gabriel Martinez-Gros, a French scholar of Medieval Islam, suggests that 'the history of the dominated groups belong to the victors' who have subdued them.[2] Therefore, any 'national struggle' or any struggle waged by a 'subordinated group' is also a struggle to secure the right to determine one's own history. This is also true as far as worldviews and ideologies are concerned: generally speaking, these ideologies are not produced by the dominated groups but by the dominant ones, or are first 'imported' by them from Western countries; the dominated groups can only access knowledge, including dissident information, and ideologies, including the most subversive ones, through the language and sources of the dominant groups. But as many cases, including the Kurdish one, demonstrate, the 'dominated' are not only 'passive receivers' but also 'active users' of what they 'receive'[3]: they can radicalize the received models and ideas and transform them into tools and interpretative/legitimizing frameworks of their struggle. Basically all anti-colonial struggles have actively used the knowledge available in colonial society to fight against colonialism.

The term 'nationalism' is equally complex. Apart from a few historical examples dating back to the romantic period of the 'rebirth' of the Kurdish movement in the 1950s and 1960s, during which the 'Kurdist' elite had limited political and cultural 'capital', the term 'nationalism' has not been used by the Kurdish movements themselves. On the contrary, as far as I am aware, the term has always had a negative connotation in Kurdish political discourse, associated as it was with the ideologies and praxis of the oppressive and dominant states. Abdullah Öcalan, leader of the PKK, has even dismissed the Kurdish variety of national self-identity as a 'primitive nationalism'.[4]

This does not mean that this concept, which is widely used in the scholarly literature, has no analytical meaning. It is obvious that it defines Kurdish aspirations as well as movements that express them, as well as a set of symbolic resources (history-writing, national anthem, cartographic imaginary, national pantheon) or discourses that find their ultimate legitimacy in Kurdishness.[5] Still, one should acknowledge that this concept has, at best, a limited descriptive value, in the sense that Kurdish resistance has never defined itself *exclusively* in terms of unique or particular demands. In fact, in the Kurdish case, like those of many other ethnic minorities or colonized peoples, 'particularism' and 'universalism' always went hand in hand: universalism constructed particularism as a 'national' group entitled to be part of universal history, and particularism has always sought to legitimize itself as a part of a broader humanity.[6] Notwithstanding the problem of 'alienation' in nationalist discourses, 'becoming the other' through the 'universal' has always been the only way to remain oneself. This has allowed the constitution of a peculiar '*asabiyya* ('internal solidarity of a would-be-conquering group'), as well as a unique subjectivity with a specific historical narrative and symbols, and at the same time justified the national struggle as a *universal* struggle – a struggle fought by the oppressed nation for humankind in general.

This is also true in the Kurdish case. Only a universalistic *da'wa* (literally 'appeal to accept the uniqueness of God and the prophecy of Muhammad'; by extension, ideology) could enable the Kurds to regard their condition as the consequence of human injustice that *had to be* challenged. This equation and the tensions between the peculiar and universal, between the '*asabiyya* and the *da'wa*, has been the focus of study by Ibn Khaldun (1332–1406) and continues to provide an insight into many national struggles in recent history. For instance, many nationalist movements in the Balkans had clear 'socialist' inclinations before the 1912 First Balkan War, and only subsequently became exclusive and even aggressive nationalist movements. As Talinn Ter Minassian has convincingly argued in her work on Middle Eastern left-wing movements,[7] the Armenian movement (among others) was a 'bearer' of the socialist ideas in the 1920s, as was the case with the Palestinian movement in the 1960s and 1970s and to a lesser extent the Kurdish movement during the same period. For all these groups, the combination of 'particularism' and 'universalism', an intra-group '*asabiyya* and a supra-group *da'wa*, which required constant abnegation and enormous sacrifices, was fundamental to their existence.

The pre-World War II Kurdish movement

A chronological approach can show that while retaining its internal dynamics, which ultimately constituted its *raison d'être*, the Kurdish movement was among the losers in the dissolution of the Ottoman Empire, and yet has always been *in time*, that is, in the Middle East's *or* world's *ideological time*, following narrowly dominant doxa such as Westernism, Marxism-Leninism, Islamism, Liberalism and/or neo-Liberalism.

We will start our chronological survey with the collapse of the Ottoman Empire, which led, among other developments, to the formation of an extremely fragile yet long-lasting and plural *Kurdish* movement in the former Ottoman lands, as well as in Persia. This does not mean that there were no Kurdish/Kurdist initiatives prior to this period. Some of the Kurdish rebellions of the nineteenth century showed a clear awareness of their ethnic distinctions, and Sheikh Ubeydullah, who was the last Kurdish leader to lead an armed struggle in the 1800s (1881–3), envisaged a Kurdish entity both in the Ottoman Empire and Persia.[8] To some extent, these contests, which were influenced by the others going on in the Balkans or in Egypt, were of their time, and Ubeydullah notably claimed the right for the Kurds to enjoy an equal status 'with the other nations'; but these armed conflicts, which were the products of multiple factors, including the centralizing objectives of the Ottomans and the preservation of Kurdish/ Muslim superiority in the Eastern provinces of the Empire,[9] did not aim at the establishment of a Kurdish autonomy or entity. Likewise, the review *Kurdistan* (1898–1902) distinguished itself from the other 'Young Turk' periodicals as the outlet for a Kurdish voice in the Ottoman Empire – but its demands were limited to reforms *in* Kurdistan and *in* the Ottoman Empire, and did not pursue an autonomist agenda. This was also the case with the Kurdish uprisings of 1909–14: they clearly promoted an 'awareness of being Kurdish', but remained, by and large, anti-Armenian and, paradoxically, pro-Ottoman and were even supported locally by the Unionist military elite. Many of the leaders of these insurrections were more than happy to negotiate an alliance with the Committee of Union and Progress during the Armenian genocide and in spite of the Kurdish deportations of 1916–17, renewed later in the 'Kurdish–Turkish pact' with the Kemalist forces. It is true that in 1914, three Kurdish uprisings (in Barzan, Bidlis and Soran) expressed what one might determine to be Kurdish nationalist claims, but these rising were rather modest in their scale and, more importantly, relatively short-lived. A more or less structured Kurdish political movement emerged only after the collapse of the Ottoman Empire in autumn 1918 and expressed itself through the Kurdish intelligentsia in Istanbul or the Kurdish clubs across Kurdistan.

Post-1918 Kurdish nationalism is not easy to define, not least because it was largely pluralistic and polysemic. In some cases it could, as in the case of the Simko (1919) and Koçgiri (1921) rebellions, express, even locally (and in the case of the Simko rebellion, in association with the Kemalist forces), 'Kurdist demands', while in other situations, such as Mahmud Barzandji's resistance in the 1920s in what would become Iraqi Kurdistan, it could champion a distinct Kurdish entity, with a right to exert its own 'national sovereignty'; notwithstanding the relations it had with the nascent Kemalist power, Barzandji's short-lived 'kingdom' constituted a major landmark in the history of the Kurdish movement, with its publication of a series of 'Kurdist' journals such as *Roji Kurdistan, Bangê Kurdistan* and *Diyari Kurdistan*.

The first Kurdish uprising in the republican Turkey, led by Sheikh Said, a nakshibandi leader, in 1925, was another landmark event. Sheikh Said's discourses attest that during this period of reinforcement of the central authority in Turkey, which promoted a radical Turkish nationalism and a radical 'secularist' policy,

Kurdish nationalism could be tempted by an Islamic *and* a national definition of Kurdishness and the Kurdish struggle. It is fascinating to note that Sheikh Said quite deliberately employed the concept of the Kurdish '*asabiyya (asabiyyet)*,[10] a term which even then had largely disappeared from common usage, and at the same time presented the Kurds as the new representatives of the Islamic *da'wa*. This style of approach indicated that by 1925, in order to legitimize Kurdish 'particularism' it had to be placed in a broader 'universalistic' appeal or cause. In Sheikh Said presented Kurdishness as *the* force that could and should save Islam, whose flag 'has been abandoned' by the 'Turks', who had not only betrayed their promises to the Kurds, but also to Islam as a religion and as an *umma*.[11]

Official Turkish historiography has placed great emphasis on Sheikh Said's jihad proclamation in order to present his uprising as a 'reactionary' movement. Although contradicted by the tribunal which condemned him to death as a defender of the Kurdish cause,[12] this interpretation was widely accepted by historians in both Western countries and the Soviet Union. Yet notwithstanding the wide support he received from Kurdish religious dignitaries, Sheikh Said appears to be the only figure who sought to link the Kurdish struggle to the cause of Islam; the short-lived Azadi ('Freedom') Committee, which in fact was the main architect of the 1925 uprising,[13] had a Western orientation and its members shared basically the same intellectual background as the Unionists and the Kemalists. Some of the closest collaborators of Sheikh Said, such as Fehmi-ê Bilal or Hasan Serdi, were even reputed to be unbelievers.[14] Barely two years after the failure of the uprising, the Khoybun Committee ('Being-oneself/becoming-oneself'),[15] the first effectively organized Kurdish political and military organization (with separate leadership structures for these twin elements), employed an openly Westernized discourse – in sharp contrast to the worldview of Sheikh Said. For the Committee, whose civilian branch was dominated by members of the well-known Bedirkhani family, the Turkish government and 'Turks' in general represented 'barbarianism' and not 'civilization', as they pretended to; the Kurdish movement and the 'Kurds', in contrast, truly represented civilization and were ready to fight for it.[16] Here the Kurds are presented as fighting for their *own* emancipation while at the same time fighting 'barbarianism' in the name of *universal* civilization. It is true that facing as it did a strong state which was supported not only by Great Britain but also to a lesser extent by Iran, the Soviet Union and France, as the mandatory power in Syria, Khoybun was politically and militarily doomed to fail, but ideologically speaking, it was of *its time* and did attract moral support from a few French colonial officers in Syria, such as Pierre Rondot.[17]

The hegemony of the left

This link between particularism and universalism became even more explicit after the Second World War, with the formation, in 1946, of the Republic of Mahabad and the Democratic Party of Kurdistan (KDP).[18] These two entities, which largely overlapped, were not exactly left wing: the KDP was rather a conservative party in its discourses and praxis, and politically speaking, the 'Kurdish Republic' was far more moderate than the neighbouring (and also short-lived) Azerbaijan Republic, which, in contrast with Kurdistan, was occupied by the Soviet military and adopted a tough 'Soviet model'. The Kurdish Republic, led by Qadi (Qazi) Muhammad, a religious judge, introduced some social reforms but did not exclude the tribes from the political system and the state administration nor did it interfere in religious affairs. In spite of this conservatism, however, the 'Soviet umbrella' that made its existence possible, positioned this first Kurdish republic on the left side of the Iranian political spectrum. This short-lived republic became a reference point for the left-wing Kurdish movements of the 1960s and 1970s. Qadi Muhammad, who surrendered to Iranian forces in order to avoid bloodshed in Kurdistan, was executed on 19 January 1947, but the general upheaval in Mossadegh's Iran contributed to the radicalization of Kurdish militants such as Ghani Bilurian and other young intellectuals like Abderrahman Ghassemlo,[19] who adopted Marxist-Leninist ideas. The now left-wing KDP received 80 per cent of the votes in Mahabad in the 1952 elections, before the onset of a new period of harsh repression.[20]

In general, the period from the Mahabad Republic to Abd al-Karim Qassem's military coup in Iraq in 1958 in Kurdish history has not attracted detailed study; although some 'Kurdist' circles remained active on the ground, no uprising took place in this era, during which the Kurdish legal space of activity was also extremely restricted. Still, we know that during these long years some of Kurdish militants, such as Zinar Silopi (Kadri Cemilpaşazade), tried to get in touch with Soviet representatives,[21] but without achieving any concrete results, while many Kurds in Iraq and Syria were attracted to the communist parties of those countries.

Qassem's military coup, however, provoked a radical change in the Kurdish political landscape, specifically in Iraq. The head of the Kurdistan Democratic Party, Mustafa Barzani, who had been forced to seek asylum in Russia after the defeat of the Mahabad Republic in 1946, now returned with the proclamation of the Iraqi Republic in 1958. In spite of many years spent in the 'homeland of socialism' (or because of them), Barzani returned home more conservative than ever and with basically a Kurdist agenda. However, the new cadres of the party, including the likes of Ibrahim Ahmad, the party's general secretary and author of the well-known novel *Jan-i Gel* (Suffering of the People), and Jalal Talabani, his future son-in-law, were largely influenced by the left-wing ideas. Many of Barzani's *peshmerga*s, who launched with him a long-lasting guerrilla campaign in 1961, had a rural or even tribal background and were probably less receptive to left-wing ideas or the realization of a socialist revolution in Kurdistan or in Iraq; but those who had an urban background or were descendants of urban notables were at both Kurdish *peshmerga*s and left-wing *militant*s: some belonged both to the KDP and the Kurdish branch of the Iraqi Communist Party. The uprising itself was described as a *chorech*, a polysemic term denoting both an 'uprising' and 'revolution', while the party's representative in Europe, Ismet Cheriff Vanly, declared that in essence 'Kurdish nationalism [was] revolutionary'.[22] Although the Barzani rebellion was supported by both Israel and Iran by the 1970s, this 'Cold War configuration' did not alter the fact that the struggle in Iraqi Kurdistan was essentially part of what was then known as the 'Tri-continental'-wide contests of the 1960s, the anti-colonial/anti-imperialist struggles, that encompassed Indochina and Africa. The situation was similar in Syria, where the Kurds had a significant presence in the Syrian Communist Party and where, as evident in the poetry of Cegerwin[23] and Osman Sabri, 'Kurdist' militants espoused radical left-wing positions. In Turkey, too, many Kurds, who had left-wing ideas even before the 1960s,[24] participated in nascent left-wing organizations before creating their own organizations. To be sure, the Kurdish movement in Turkey included some 'conservative' figures, but even they were obliged to accept a 'left-wing' or at least overtly 'democratic' label.[25] The formation of the DDKO ('Revolutionary Cultural Hearts of the East'), which promoted a Kurdified version of Turkish left-wing discourses at the turn of the 1970s, was an important development in that it would represent a sort of 'blueprint' for almost all future Kurdish organizations. For the DDKO, 'socialism' was not only the solution to the Kurdish national issue, but it was a way to combat the 'feudalism', 'backwardness' and 'underdevelopment' that had been imposed on Kurdish society.[26] Their slogan was 'only socialism can save the East'.[27]

There are many reasons for the popularity of the left-wing ideas, symbols and forms of axiology in Kurdistan in the 1960s. One was that the world of the 1960s was saturated by a left-wing vocabulary, graphics, heroes, legends and narratives that were not simply abstract symbols and concepts, but closely linked to the ongoing struggles in Africa, Asia, Latin America, and, last but not least, Europe.

A second reason for the popularity of the left was that the authoritarian regimes of the 1960s in Iran and Turkey were supported by the United States. In both countries not only the term 'socialism', but also those of 'freedom', 'liberty' or even 'social' were associated with the 'imminent communist threat', thus any meaningful opposition could but formulate itself through 'anti-imperialist' discourses and axiological forms. In contrast, in Syria and Iraq – allies of the 'Eastern Bloc' if not fully subordinated to the Soviet Union – left-wing ideas occupied almost the entire political terrain, allowing no legitimacy to 'right-wing' opposition; in these two countries any political opposition had to present itself as 'true' left-wing movements challenging the powers that had 'perverted' 'true' socialism.

A third reason for the prevalence of left-wing ideology was the messages that Marxism-Leninism sent to the 'oppressed nations': it was the only ideology that promised them the right to determine their own fate. There is no doubt that the 'real socialism', that is, socialism as it originally existed in the former Eastern Bloc, was highly oppressive, and in some cases even totalitarian in the countries in which it was experienced, and was no less repressive than the 'capitalist system' vis-à-vis the minorities and 'oppressed nations' submitted to its rule; but it is also obvious that elsewhere in the world, namely under authoritarian pro-Western governments, 'socialism' or 'communism' presented a horizon of emancipation both for the 'oppressed classes and nations'. The fact that almost all anti-colonial movements adopted left-wing discourses and ideologies only reinforced this perception. As Franz Fanon wrote it in his comments on Africa, 'America' could have won the hearts and the minds of the African peoples if it had been prepared to tolerate communism in this context and had 'recognized their independence'.[28] This quest for independence, or at least some degree of genuine autonomy and representation, also explains the attraction that left-wing ideas exerted in Kurdistan. Kurdistan was, once again, in its time and its world's time, flowing with a world-wide hegemonic current.

A fourth reason for the popularity of a left-wing approach was the vibrancy of Kurdish cultural activities in the Soviet Union (including a Kurdish radio station, a newspaper and many publications), which was seen as proof of socialism's genuine support for the 'oppressed nations'.

However, one should also take into account the sociological changes in the Kurdish urban landscape at this time. During the 1960s, the old elites and urban dynasties were still quite strong and generally continued to monopolize political and economic power, but as in the Arab societies, so in Kurdistan, such groups lacked the imagination to meet new political challenges. A new intelligentsia, which was very distinct from the late Ottoman intelligentsia, became the most dynamic actor, proposing an integrated reading of the past, the present and the future in a teleological framework. This section of society, which constituted to some extent the world's 'intermediary elite' during the 1950s and 1970s, was able to adapt its conceptual and analytical tools from the applied sciences, such as physics, medicine or chemistry, or from law, to the new social reality, and elaborate new axiological forms. More importantly, thanks to its intermediary position, it could have an impact on both the upper and the lower classes. It obliged the children of the upper class to 'renounce' their privileges in the name of the 'people', the 'nation' or the 'cause', and it offered the lower class a discourse as well as a space for expression and action, and therefore, the possibility of autonomy, which they had never before experienced.

The left-wing radicalization of the 1970s

This intelligentsia, which was dominant in the entire 'Tri-Continental' space throughout the 1950s and 1970s, was able to accommodate two other groups in the decades that followed: a technocratic elite, whose spread was closely linked to the formation of the middle classe; and the plebian actors, who were propelled towards the historical scene as a consequence of the rapid urbanization of the 1970s and 1980s. The plebian actors would emerge in the Kurdish case much earlier than the middle class, which only really began to have an impact after 2000: this was because the 'Kurdish 1970s' were characterized mainly by state coercion, violence and/or Kurdish uprisings as well as defeats. The 1971 military coup in Turkey constituted a serious blow to any hope of change through constitutional reforms and democratization. It also destabilized the Kurdish intelligentsia, which has been accused of being far too pacifist by the younger and massively politicized generations. After the end of the military regime in 1973, the collapse of the Barzani rebellion in 1975 marked yet another set-back, leading the younger generation or more radical components of the KDP to accuse not only Barzani but also the former Kurdish elite of betraying 'the national cause'. Just before its dramatic end, the rebellion, which involved some 110,000 active and reservist *peshmerga*s, seemed to be on the verge of a military breakthrough – but its was dependence on Iranian support left it weakened when that support was withdrawn as a result of the Algiers Agreement between Iran and Iraq on 5 March 1975. This inevitably advanced Kurdish 'anti-imperialist' sentiment, represented by the most radical militants of the PDK, including Jalal

Talabani, the future leader of the PUK (Patriotic Union of Kurdistan), and the assessment that any national resistance movement supported by 'imperialism' and 'reaction' was doomed to fail. Finally, after 1977, Iran became a theatre of revolutionary conflict which greatly motivated Kurdish youth. Here again, one could see internal diversity in operation: under the leadership of Abdurrahman Ghasemlou, who was influenced by the idea of Alexander Dubcek's 'socialism with a human face', the PDK of Iran, probably Kurdistan's most influential party, began to shift in this period from rigid Marxist-Leninist positions towards a more social-democratic stand. However, other organizations, among them Komalah, were radicalized partly as a consequence of the failure of the Barzani rebellion and partly in the wake of the revolution itself.

No wonder thus that during this decade almost all the Kurdish political actors accepted Marxism-Leninism (or one of its multiple varieties, including Maoism, 'Enverism' and Trotskyism)[29] as the only relevant doctrine in terms of 'ideological availability'[30] for Kurdistan. Even the PDK of Iraq adopted a left-wing/anti-imperialist discourse during its 're-foundation', in the second half of the 1970s, and formulated a rather harsh self-criticism of its past performance.[31] This conversion to Marxism-Leninism was largely an 'indigenous' one and could not be explained by any support from the Soviet Union (and even less from China and Albania, who were probably oblivious to much of what was happening in Kurdish political life).

It is difficult to evaluate the knowledge that the Kurdish elite had of the 'classics' of Marxism-Leninism, which it could mainly read in Arabic, Persian or Turkish. One should remember, however, that this elite acted in a context of defeat and 'axiological urgency' of the 1970s where both the intelligentsia and the plebian youth felt the necessity to act *hic* and *nunc*. 'Marxism-Leninism', as an 'integrated' and 'complete' doctrine having an answer to any major social, political, economic and 'national' question, appeared to be the *only* doctrine that could explain to the Kurds the reasons for their past or recent failures, the opportunities and constraints presented by their present conditions and offer them in a broader universal horizon. Most importantly, it could enable 'the oppressed Kurdish nation' to envision its emancipation not as an isolated group, but *in alliance* with the 'oppressed classes' of 'oppressing nations', allowing it to negotiate a kind of universal emancipation of 'humankind'. Particularism and universalism continued therefore to reinforce rather than exclude each other.

With the emergence of the PKK between 1975 and 1978, this radicalization reached a new peak, and eventually led to bifurcation of the Kurdish movement. Attracted neither to the Soviet model nor to Maoism, the PKK did not abandon

Marxism-Leninism but redefined and radicalized it by adding quite a high dose of Fanonism, while explaining the enslavement of the Kurds by their lack of resistance and presenting them as co-responsible for their situation. In his *L'An Cinq de la Révolution algérienne* (Year Five of the Algerian Revolution), published in 1958, Frantz Fanon had advocated what we might call 'positive violence', aimed mainly at the emancipation of the colonized world; he was, however, largely disappointed with the decolonization of black Africa, which altered neither the structural inequalities between the former colonial powers and the newly independent states, nor the power relations within the decolonized societies, where new 'indigenous' elites had confiscated power. Thus, in his famous *Les damnés de la terre* (The Wretched of the Earth), finished shortly before his death in 1961, Fanon called for violence that would lead not only to decolonization but to the invention of a decolonized human being, violence that potentially had no limits. Likewise, from the very beginning, Öcalan dismissed Kurdish history as a history of the enslavement of the Kurds, and urged Kurdish youth (and Kurds generally) to use violence not only as an instrumental or rational means for liberating Kurdistan, but also for liberating the Kurdish being from his interiorized enslavement. Similarly, for him, a socialist Middle East could and should be constructed through the Kurds' sacrificial efforts. It is obvious that Öcalan didn't use Khaldunian concepts and probably was not familiar with Ibn Khaldun's work; still, from his perspective, the Kurdish '*asabiyya* – in other words, the dynamic force of an 'oppressed people' – was to be transformed into the instrument that would realize a universal *da'wa*. In a sense, although no founding text of the PKK indicates it explicitly, the Kurds had to take the place of the Palestinians as the vanguard of the 'revolution' (*thawra/chorech/devrim*) across the Middle East. It is obvious that the prevailing conditions at the beginning of the 1980s were not conducive to the realization of such an ambitious project, and ultimately the Kurds remained in a subordinated position in the following decades. But for Öcalan, the time would come for the Kurds not only to be in *their time*, but to position themselves *ahead of their time*.

1980s–2010s: facing the domination of Islamism

After the major events of 1979 (the Iranian Revolution, the occupation of Afghanistan by the Red Army, the Second Camp David Agreement which confirmed Egypt's recognition of Israel, the Islamist uprising of Juhayman al-Utabi in Mecca), left-wing ideas lost their hegemonic position in many parts of the Middle East,[32] but still remained attractive in two supra-territorial or trans-state spaces: Palestine and Kurdistan. By the 1980s, however, Abdallah Azzam, the well-known theoretician of the Afghan jihad and the precursor of al-Qaeda (who would be killed in 1989), was playing a distant but influential role in the Palestinian camps through the diffusion of his radical messages.[33] In Palestine, it was easy for Islamism to become an ideology of resistance against a non-Muslim enemy and to some extent overshadow secular Palestinian movements even if they did not entirely disappear from the political scene. In the Kurdish case, too, Islamism won some popularity and gave birth to many organizations, including both pacifist and violent ones. Mella Krekar (alias Fattah Najmaddin Faraj), a former student of Azzam, for instance, played an important role in the formation of Ansar al-Islam, which, after 9/11, became the nucleus of the future al-Qaeda branch in Iraq, while Hezbollah, strongly supported by the Turkish secret service, remained active in Turkish Kurdistan. Still, Islamism, broadly speaking, could not determine the overall evolution of the Kurdish political space.

This remained the case in the mid-2010s, some thirty-five years after the dramatic upheavals of 1979: in Turkey, Hüda-Par (Hür Dava Partisi – the Party of Free Cause), founded in 2012 and the legal representatives of Hezbollah, remains a marginal electoral force even in its strongholds such as the city of Batman, and the ruling AKP could mobilize some 50 per cent of the Kurdish electorate only thanks to its 'Kurdist' cadres. Although we lack reliable information, the Kurdish Muslim Brothers seem to remain weak in Iranian Kurdistan and probably also in the Syrian one, while the two Kurdish Islamist parties of Iraqi Kurdistan (the Islamic Party of Kurdistan and the Islamic Union of Kurdistan), which are non-radical and exist in coalition with non-Islamic parties, obtain hardly more than 15 per cent of the votes.

This sociological weakness can partly be explained by the fact that non-Islamist actors have structured the Kurdish political space over many decades and capitalized on their legacy as either national resistance movements or 'state-founders', thereby building up elaborate networks of allegiance (and in the Iraqi Kurdish case, clientelistic ones) and political and military structures. But one could also argue that, in contrast to previous left-wing ideology, Islamism neither presents a universalistic perspective to the Kurds nor contains any promise of 'national emancipation'; at best, it recognizes the ethnic entities as legitimate parts of the larger *umma*, which should be governed according to the principle of the organic unity of Muslims. In contrast to the Palestinian case, Kurdish Islamist actors thus fail to establish their legitimacy in relation to both Kurdish society and Islamic/Islamist transnational movements.

The vacuum of the 2000s–2010s

Since the beginning of the 1980s, but particularly in the years since 2000, the Kurdish movement has generally evolved independently of 'Middle Eastern time'. However, this does not mean that it can stand on its feet and create an autarkic universe. It is true that in the 2000s-2010s, the Kurdish movement had either no 'counter-partners' or only weak ones in the Arab world, Turkey and Iran with whom it could build alliances, and thus had to re-invent itself in a context where 'universalism' itself seems to be hard to reinvent. In Iraq and Syria, not only have the left-wing movements vanished, but the societies themselves are at risk of total destruction. Even fifteen or twenty years ago, it was possible to translate the Syrian and Iraqi domestic conflicts into Kurdish political language and establish some bridges between the Kurdish claims of autonomy or federalism and Iraqi and Syrian Arab opposition groups' fight for democracy in those countries. The Social-Darwinist reconfiguration of the sectarian, Alawite-Sunni or Shia–Sunni conflict in Iraq and Syria has not only accelerated the process of disintegration of these *Arab* societies, but also destroyed any common Kurdish–Arab political language, preventing the Kurdish political elite, and public opinion, from making any sense of these conflicts.

While the Kurdish movement still has some links with the Turkish and Iranian left-wing or democratic opposition movements, and the possibility remains of establishing bridges between Kurdish demands and those formulated by the dissident segments of both societies, it is also true that such connections are much weaker than what they were in the 1970s and cannot constitute a 'nationwide' political alternative. In Turkey, for instance, there are close contacts between the Kurdish movement and the Turkish left-wing movement; yet the Kurdish and Turkish processes of mobilization and demobilization, radicalization and deradicalization have been dissociated for many years. While Kurdish participation in the 2013 Gezi-Park protests in Istanbul was somewhat limited, the Turkish left did not match the level of mobilization of the Kurdish movement in 2015. The Kurdish political space, where the 'political family' comprising the PKK and BDT-HDP (the Party of Peace and Democracy and the Democratic Party of Peoples) enjoys an almost hegemonic position, is differentiated from the Turkish one, which is almost entirely dominated by the AKP. Any regime crisis in Iran might be expected to lead to similar developments, highlighting the differences between the Kurdish, Azeri and Baloudj political spaces and the Persian/Iranian ones.

The Kurdish movement can deal with this hegemonic but constrained isolation partly by using the plurality of Kurdish society as a resource and partly by legitimizing itself through new international expectations. The plurality means that the trans-border Kurdish political space, which also includes a strong diasporic component, has to accept that it is both unified and divided by different political cultures, patterns and genealogies imposed on it by history. There is no doubt that for more than a decade, two major actors – the KRG (Kurdistan Regional Government, dominated by the PDK of Massud Barzani) and the PKK (led by Abdullah Öcalan) – have played the role of *primus inter pares* in this political space, though not its sole actors.[34] The PYD (Party of Democratic Unity) and the PJAK (Party of the Free Life in Kurdistan), for instance, are not simply extensions of the PKK, but the result of intra-Iranian or intra-Syrian Kurdish dynamics. It is due to these dynamics that the PKK has been accepted as a model or a 'core-organization' by some segments of Iranian and Syrian Kurdish society.

As far as international expectations are concerned, one should note that since the fall of the Berlin Wall, which ended the socialist bloc as a worldwide reference point, new international points for 'norm-setting' have emerged: in Brussels, Washington and various European capitals. In contrast with the protagonists of the Cold War period, the new norm-setters fix the horizon of a new universalistic model, but also allow criticism of the norms that they themselves advocate. For instance, there is no doubt that neo-liberalism, or at least some variety of 'economic liberalism', has become a universal 'norm', and Kurdish actors in Iraq, but also in Turkey, have no great quarrel with this reorientation. At the same time, however, these norms are also criticized in the name of political liberty, radical universalism, feminism, ecology and local democracy, a development that is echoed in the programme of the PKK and its allies, PYD and PJAK.

Thus, as in the 1920s–1930s and the 1960s–1970s, the Kurdish movement can once again pretend to be in *time*, or in the *world's time* or even to position itself *ahead of this time*, not only because it accepts what the 'world' defines as norms, but also because it can criticize these same norms in the name of a 'better humanity' and not just of a 'better' or 'emancipated' Kurdish society. Certainly, Kurdish political praxis in the 2000s–2010s has been half-democratic and half-patrimonial in Iraq, and half-representative and half-hegemonic in Turkey and Syria, but Kurdish political parties, beginning with the PKK (and to a lesser extent those of Iraq) had to accept that their hegemonic or patrimonial constructions could only be maintained if they fulfilled the promise they made to Kurdish society, including to respect its internal plurality. They are also aware that they have unleashed a new dynamic that they are not necessarily capable of mastering. Compared to the situation that prevailed in the 1980s or even 1990s,

Kurdish society has experienced important changes, with the emergence of a middle class and changes to the sociological profile and expectations of young people: in Turkish Kurdistan, for example, constant mobilizations dating back to the 1960s not only allowed intergenerational continuity and transformation, but propelled young men, and more importantly, young women, into the frontline.[35] There is no doubt that these groups – the middle class, youth, women's movements – are committed to the Kurdish cause and sympathetic to the PKK, but they are not necessarily linked to the party or the armed struggle through partisan or organic ties and cannot be transformed into simple soldiers of a 'national cause'.

In post-2003 Iraqi Kurdistan and in post-2012 Syrian Kurdistan, Kurdish actors imagined that they could operate in widely pacified frameworks, able to establish a 'national time' and master the 'national space'. Despite lacking an administrative framework, including either autonomy or genuine decentralization, this was also true in Turkish Kurdistan, where the war stopped in 2012 in order to give the so-called 'peace process' a chance. The de facto margins of manoeuvre for Kurdish actors have never been so great in this country.

Since ISIS (the Islamic State in Iraq and Syria, renamed Islamic State) attacks on the Kurdish territories in Iraq and Syria in the summer of 2014 (Shengal-Sincar, Kobane), however, this trust in time and space, which characterizes state-building processes,[36] has been challenged by the new conditions in the Middle East, which reintroduced violence to the heart of its societies, including Kurdish society, which was forced once again to militarize itself. The context of this remilitarization is entirely new in the sense that in both Iraq and Syria the Kurds are no longer fighting an existing state through guerrilla tactics, but rather defending a 'national territory' as de facto state-entities. The Kurdish space has thus experienced an accelerated process of internal integration, and the struggles of the summer of 2014 have become an important part of the Kurdish national narrative and to some extent redefined the Kurdish cause. However, during this process, Kurdish authorities and organizations have also been obliged to add a Spartan dimension to their 'neo-liberal' 'feminist/ecological' models of a 'pacified society' by once again placing military mobilization at the heart of their activity.

But this evolution is itself in complete accordance with international expectations and can ultimately allow the Kurdish movement to reinforce its claim of being once again *in time*.

Afterword

Abdullah Baabood

Since the seminal book *Violent Non-State Actors in World Politics* by Kledja Mulaj (2009), this important topic has attracted less academic attention than expected. The various contributions in this volume deal with diverse actors, adding further vital contributions to our understanding and providing indispensable knowledge as to why violent non-state actors play such a key role in the political field in the Arab world.

This book came about due to institutional cooperation between the Middle East Institute (MEI) of the National University of Singapore and the Gulf Studies Centre (GSC) of Qatar University following the signing of a memorandum of understanding between Qatar University and the MEI to sponsor joint academic conferences, symposiums and workshops. Two workshops were held: 'Crisis in the GCC: The Gulf Cooperation Council in its Regional and Global Environment' and 'Violent Non-state Actors in the Arab World'. The first was the brainchild of Professor Michael Hudson and the second was initiated by the late Professor Peter Sluglett, who took over the MEI directorship but sadly passed away before the publication of this book. Peter's passing is a big loss to academia in general and to Middle East studies in particular, and to all of those who knew him and worked with him, as is reflected in Toby Dodge's foreword and in Victor Kattan's preface.

Following the untimely passing of Peter, his colleague Dr Victor Kattan, a Senior Research Fellow at MEI, with the support of the incumbent director, Professor Engseng Ho, thankfully completed the task that Peter had started, ensuring that the second workshop commitments were fulfilled. Victor has tirelessly followed up with the presenters and carried out the required amendments to ensure that the academic community and the public at large benefit from these important contributions.

The high-quality contributions in this book have been produced by renowned experts in the Middle East and deal with a number of Middle Eastern movements (such as the PLO and Hamas in Palestine, Jabhat al-Nusra in Syria, Hezbollah in Lebanon/Syria, the Huthis in Yemen, al-Shabab in Somalia) and other transnational actors (such as Islamic State and the Muslim Brotherhood). These contributions provide illuminating insights into such groups' aims, scope, history, motivation and modus operandi.

The various chapters show that there are some discernible common features among these movements, such as a general disregard for democracy, human rights and the rule of law, while institution-building is notably absent in contemporary Middle Eastern state structures. There are also some signs of outside links and support, financial and otherwise, from other regional states or transnational movements involved in regional rivalry and proxy wars, deploying violence to achieve their aims.

Despite these commonalities, there are many stark differences between the groups and movements studied here, ranging from their aims and the scope of their operations to their motivation and ideology and modus operandi, making it difficult to draw any simple conclusion, classification or categorization or to arrive at any generalized assessment. Any attempt to deal with or counter these groups must be approached with extreme caution and a careful understanding of their diverse natures. While the various chapters in this book are wide-ranging and cover several groups, they are by no means comprehensive, as there are other movements that remain outside this study. The hope is that this volume will provide several case studies of some of the most prominent groups in the Middle East and inspire others to carry forward research into those that are omitted. The phenomenon of these non-state actors has been present in the Middle East for some time and there is no indication that it is about to disappear anytime soon, despite global efforts at confronting the issue. Understanding the underlying reasons and motivation for the formation of these groups and their fundamental ideologies creates the possibility of formulating the right strategies for confronting them. Military and security confrontation, without dealing with the root causes of their existence, has failed to get rid of these violent non-state actors, which have proven to be resilient and able to mutate or disperse, but not disappear.

May the soul of Peter rest in peace, having inspired and accomplished this important work, adding to his many achievements and credentials. Thanks to the MEI, GSC and the other contributors involved for making this possible, and to Victor Kattan and his colleagues for their enormous efforts in bringing this work to life, with the hope that its readers find it to be both beneficial and illuminating.

Notes

Introduction: Violent Non-State Actors in the Arab World – Some General Considerations

1 And, of course, in many other parts of the world.
2 In the region, a number of Kurdish groups have had, or have, secessionist or quasi-secessionist aims; perhaps the Kurdish Regional Government in northern Iraq has gone furthest towards achieving this since 1991, although during the upheavals in Syria, the Kurds of northern Syria have carved out an (ever-expanding) self-governing enclave along the border with Turkey, the Federation of Northen Syria – Rojava. The KRG has been in existence since 1991, and its militia, the *peshmerga*, well before that. It is also recognized de facto by most of its neighbours, while Rojava, despite its remarkable state-building efforts, is battling the Syrian state, the forces of Islamic State, and Turkey at the same time, and thus fits more neatly into the category of 'violent non-state actor'. See Dirik Dilar, Michael Taussig and Peter Lamborn Wilson (eds), *To Dare Imagining: Rojava Revolution* (New York: Autonomedia, 2016).
3 The classic text is Richard P. Mitchell, *The Society of the Muslim Brothers* (London: Oxford University Press, 1969 (and later editions)). For a more recent assessment, see John Calvert, *Sayyid Qutb and the Origins of Radical Islamism* (London: Hurst, 2010).
4 'Unlike the powerfully sovereign nationalist frame of the US, the nominally sovereign spaces of the modern Middle East remain heavily mediated by Western imperialism. This mediation matters intensely for the nature of the wars fought there ... Geopolitics, far more than the presence or absence of democratic traditions or allegedly age-old sectarian identities, shape the limits of the political horizon. It is this horizon, as well, that transforms and entrenches the significance, and thus the meanings and implications, of religious and sectarian identifications in the modern Middle East.' Ussama Makdisi, 'Diminished Sovereignty and the Impossibility of "Civil War" in the modern Middle East', *American Historical Review* 120, no. 5 (2015): 1751–2.
5 James Gelvin, *The Modern Middle East; a History*, 4th edn (New York: Oxford University Press, 2016), Chapter 5.
6 For the experience of interwar Syria, see Michael Provence, *The Last Ottoman Generation and the Making of the Modern Middle East* (Oxford: Oxford University

Press, 2017); Daniel Neep, *Occupying Syria under the French Mandate: Insurgency, Space and State Formation* (Cambridge: Cambridge University Press, 2012). For Iraq, see Toby Dodge, *Inventing Iraq: The Failure of Nation Building and a History Denied* (New York: Columbia University Press, 2003). See also the various chapters in Nadine Méouchy and Peter Sluglett (eds), *The British and French Mandates in Comparative Perspectives/Les mandats français et anglais dans une perspective comparative* (Leiden: Brill, 2004).

7 Roger Owen, *State, Power and Politics in the Making of the Modern Middle East*, 3rd edn (London and New York: Routledge, 2010), 10.

8 Nelida Fuccaro (ed.), *Violence and the City in the Modern Middle East* (Stanford, CA: Stanford University Press, 2016). See especially Banko on Nablus, Bashkin on Baghdad, and Fuccaro on Kirkuk.

9 With the exceptions of Egypt, Morocco and Tunisia, which had deeper historical roots as 'national states'.

10 For example, see my 'Will the "real nationalists" please stand up? The political activities of the notables of Aleppo, 1918–1946', in Nadine Méouchy (ed.), *Les Ambiguités et Les Dynamiques de la Relation Mandataire: France, Syrie et Liban, 1918–1946* (Damascus: IFEAD, 2002), 273–90.

11 See the quotation from Ussama Makdisi in note 4, above.

12 Members of the Iraqi Levies were refugees (or the sons of refugees) from Ottoman ethnic cleansing in eastern Anatolia and Iran during the First World War who had managed to reach Iraq.

13 See Victor Kattan, *From Coexistence to Conquest: International Law and the Origins of the Arab–Israeli Conflict 1891–1949* (London: Pluto, 2009).

14 See the work of Matthieu Rey, especially his EHESS thesis (2013), 'Le parlementarisme en Irak et en Syrie entre 1946 et 1963: Un temps de pluralisme au Moyen-Orient'. One may quibble with Rey's beginning and end dates, but the general tenor of his argument is clear.

15 The popular movie *Charlie Wilson's War* (2007) is part parody, part useful reminder, of this mindset. See also, Steve Coll, *Ghost Wars: The Secret History of the CIA, Afghanistan, and Bin Laden, from the Soviet Invasion to September 10, 2001* (London: Penguin, 2004).

16 Steven Heydemann, 'Social Pacts and the Persistence of Authoritarianism in the Middle East', in Oliver Schlumberger (ed.), *Debating Arab Authoritarianism: Dynamics and Durability in Nondemocratic Regimes* (Stanford, CA: Stanford University Press, 2007), 21–38. For the state as the agent of public welfare, see p. 29.

17 See Laura Ruiz de Elvira and Tina Zintl, 'The end of the Ba'thist Social Contract in Bashar al-Asad's Syria: Reading Sociopolitical Transformations through Charities and Broader Benevolent Activism', *International Journal of Middle East Studies* 46,

no. 2, (2014): 329–49. The authors claim that subcontracting poor relief measures to private charities after 2000 eroded the political legitimacy of the regime, and was a major factor behind the 2011 uprising.

18 For Syria and Egypt, see Linda Matar, 'Twilight of "state capitalism" in formerly "socialist" Arab states', *Journal of North African Studies* 18 (2013): 416–30. For Iraq, 'The privatization of key sectors of the Iraqi economy left a large section of the salaried population ... vulnerable to malnutrition and black marketeering.' Dina Khoury, *Iraq in Wartime: Soldiering, Martyrdom and Remembrance* (Cambridge: Cambridge University Press, 2013), 148.

19 Peter Hessler, 'Letter from Cairo: the Shadow General', *New Yorker*, 2 January 2017, 44–55.

20 First proposed by Samuel Huntington, *Political Order in Changing Societies* (New Haven, CT: Yale University Press, 1968); summarized by Marina Ottaway and Michele Dunne in *Incumbent Regimes and the "King's Dilemma" in the Arab World: Promise and Threat of Managed Reform*, Carnegie Papers, Middle East Program, no. 88 (Washington, DC: Carnegie Endowment for International Peace, December 2007), 4: 'Limited reforms introduced from the top often increase rather than decrease bottom-up demand for more radical change.'

21 Sean L. Yom and Gregory Gause III, 'Resilient Royals: how Arab Monarchies hang on', *Journal of Democracy* 23, no. 4 (2012): 74–88.

22 Oil prices had been between $80 and $100 a barrel between 2010 and 2014, dropped first to a low of $26 and then flattened out to about $45–$48 in the summer and autumn of 2016. http://www.wsj.com/articles/are-low-oil-prices-good-for-the-economy-1479092581.

23 While this is probably true for the attacks in Paris (November 2015) and at Brussels airport (March 2016), where the perpetrators actually trained with Islamic State, it is rather less likely for those responsible for the attacks in San Bernardino (December 2015) and Orlando (June 2016).

24 According to the journalist John Pilger, 'More than 100,000 Islamic militants were trained in Pakistan between 1986 and 1992, in camps overseen by the CIA and MI6, with the SAS training future al-Qaeda and Taliban fighters in bomb-making and other black arts.' *Guardian*, 23 September 2003. I am not sure about the 100,000, but even if the figure was closer to 10,000, this training would play a crucial role in the future destabilization of the region.

25 See various articles by James Dorsey, especially 'Creating Frankensteins: the Saudi export of Wahhabism', 24 August 2016, mideastblogspot.com.

26 Personal observations in Damascus and Aleppo, 1987–8. It can also be argued that these were forms of silent protest against the Asad regime, to which the regime could scarcely object.

27 This is elaborated in much of Zoltan Pall's recent work. See Zoltan Pall, *Salafism in Lebanon: Local and Transnational Movements* (Cambridge: Cambridge University Press, 2018).
28 Charles Tripp, *The Power and the People: Paths of Resistance in the Middle East* (Cambridge: Cambridge University Press, 2013); John Chalcraft, *Popular Politics in the Making of the Modern Middle East* (Cambridge: Cambridge University Press, 2016). The 1977 uprising is described by Chalcraft, 412–21.
29 Given that some of the groups were formed in secret, or have gone through several changes in title, some of these dates may not stand up to detailed investigation, but they are at least approximately correct.
30 As well as taking extreme measures against religious minorities.
31 For more details, see Charles R. Lister, *The Syrian Jihad: Al-Qaeda, the Islamic State and the Evolution of an Insurgency* (New York: Oxford University Press, 2015), 39–42.
32 Jean-Pierre Filiu, *From Deep State to Islamic State: The Arab Counter-Revolution and its Jihadi Legacy* (Oxford: Oxford University Press, 2015). See also Joseph Sassoon, *Anatomy of Authoritarianism in the Arab Republics* (Cambridge: Cambridge University Press, 2016), and for a more general discussion, see Daron Acemoğlu and James A. Robinson, *Economic Origins of Dictatorships and Democracy* (New York: Cambridge University Press, 2006).
33 8 March has the Lebanese Forces (a former Maronite militia led by Samir Ja'ja') as well as the Jumayyils' fiefdom *al-Kata'ib*, while 14 March has 'Awn's *al-Tayyar al-Watani al-Hurr* (Free Patriotic Movement) side by side with Hezbollah.
34 It should be said that al-Qaeda/*Ansar al-Shari'a* is also anti-Saudi.

Chapter 1: The Muslim Brotherhood and Violence: Porous Boundaries and Context

1 Here and henceforth all quotes from original Arabic texts are the author's translation.
2 Author's notes from interviews with Tunisian Islamists, London, June–July 1993.
3 For example, only *porous boundaries* separate the intellectual and religious foundations of Wahhabism and extremist Salafi groups such as al-Qaeda and Daesh. On this, see Karen Armstrong, 'Wahhabism to ISIS: how Saudi Arabia exported the main source of global terrorism', *New Statesman*, 27 November 2014.
4 A telling series of six articles published by Zuhayr Salim, the spokesperson of the Syrian Brotherhood, in late 2014 remoulded the entire 'project' of the MB in the original *Ikhwani* motto with its five sub-declarations, published on the official website of the Syrian MB: http://www.asharqalarabi.org.uk/%D9%85%D8%B4%D8

%B1%D9%88%D8%B9%D9%86%D8%A7-%D8%A7%D9%84%D8%B3%D9%8A%D8%A7%D8%B3%D9%8A-%D9%802%D9%80--%D9%8A-%D9%85%D8%B6%D8%A7%D9%85%D9%8A%D9%86-%D8%A7%D9%84%D8%B4%D8%B9%D8%A7%D8%B1%D8%A7%D8%AA-%D8%A7%D9%84%D8%AE%D9%85%D8%B3%D8%A9--%D8%A7%D9%84%D9%84%D9%87-%D8%BA%D8%A7%D9%8A%D8%AA%D9%86%D8%A7-%E2%80%93-%D8%A7%D9%84%D8%B1%D8%B3%D9%88%D9%84-%D9%82%D8%AF%D9%88%D8%AA%D9%86%D8%A7_ad-id!274602.ks#.W1TMuthKhE4. See also an article by Mohammed Abdul Rahman Ramadan, member of the MB Shura Council, where the Egyptian uprising in 2011 against Hosni Mubarak is revisited from the perspective of that slogan, 12 February 2015: http://almorsy.com/%D8%AF%D8%B9%D9%88%D8%A9-%D8%A7%D9%84%D8%A5%D8%AE%D9%88%D8%A7%D9%86-%D8%AA%D8%AC%D9%85%D8%B9-%D8%A8%D9%8A%D9%86-%D8%A7%D9%84%D9%85%D9%86%D9%87%D8%AC-%D8%A7%D9%84%D8%A5%D8%B5%D9%84%D8%A7%D8%AD%D9%89/.

5 'Abdullah Yusuf 'Ali, *The Quran Translation*, 10th edn (Delhi: Kitab Bahvan, 2001), The Spoils, Sura 8, verse 60.
6 These conferences were named in sequence from the 'First' to the 'Sixth', and held in the years 1931, 1932, 1935, 1936, 1938 and 1941 respectively.
7 Hassan al-Banna, Risalat al-Mu'tamar al-Khamis ('Letter of the Fifth Conference') (1938); in Majmou'at Rasa'il al-Imam Hassan al-Banna [Collection of the Letters of Imam Hassan al-Banna], Cairo: Dar al-Da'wah, 1999.
8 Al-Banna, *Risalat al-Mu'tamar al-Khamis*.
9 An example of a 'praising' account written by an MB figure is the work of Mahmud al-Sabbagh, who was one of the founders of *al-Nizam al-Khass*, particularly his book *Haqiqat al-Nizam al-Khass wa Dawruhu fi Da'wat al-Ikhwan al-Muslimun* (The Truth About the Special Apparatus and Its Role in the Muslim Brotherhood) (Cairo: Dar al-I'tisam, 1986). An example of a 'critical' account written by an MB figure is the work of Salah Shadi, who took part in the MB military effort in Palestine, particularly the first volume of his book *Safahat min al-Ta'rikh: Hasad al-'Umr* (Pages of History: A Life's Harvest) (Cairo: Dar l-Nashr w-a'l-Tawzi al-Islamiyya, 1987).
10 On these incidents, see Mahmud al-Sabbagh, *Haqiqat al-Nizam al-Khass wa Dawruhu fi Da'wat al-Ikhwan al-Muslimun* (The Truth About the Special Apparatus and Its Role in the Muslim Brotherhood) (Cairo: Dar al-I'tisam, 1986).
11 It is repeatedly stated with pride in *Ikhwan* literature that Qutb indirectly referred to the group in the dedication to his book *Social Justice in Islam* (1948), before becoming a member of the *Ikhwan* himself: 'To those young men that I imagine coming around to restore this religion as it started ... to those young men that I have no doubt for a second that the great spirit of Islam will resurrect from the past to the present.' By the time a second edition of the book was published, in 1954, Qutb had

joined the organization and now had modified the dedication: 'To those young men that I used to envision in my imagination but now I see them in real life ... those young men had been in my imagination like hopes and dreams, but now they have become a reality that is greater than imagination ...'

12 Sayyid Qutb, *Amirica Allati Ra'ait* (The America That I Saw) (Cairo: n.p., 1950). A recent comparative account of Qutb's experience in America is offered in James L. Nolan Jr, *What They Saw in America: Alexis de Tocqueville, Max Weber, G. K. Chesterton, and Sayyid Qutb* (Cambridge: Cambridge University Press, 2016).

13 Sayyid Qutb, *Fi Dhilal al-Qur'an* (In the Shadow of the Qur'an) (Cairo: Dar al-Shuruq, 2003), vol. 4, 2122.

14 There is an unsettled controversy over the original authorship of this book, with two contending claims. The first is the MB's official view that the book was collectively authored by MB thinkers and writers (including Hudaybi himself), but carried the name of Hudaybi to give it greater impact. The second is the Egyptian security claim that the book was in fact their idea in order to counterbalance Qutb's radical views, and it was authored by religious scholars from al-Azhar and other moderate institutions. It was smuggled into the prison and Hudaybi was asked to approve it and put his name on it. For the first claim, see the introduction by the (MB) publisher to the second edition of Hasan Hudaybi's book, *Du'ah la Qudah* (Preachers, Not Judges) (Cairo: Dar al-Nashr w'al- Tawzi', 1987); for the second claim, see Fu'ad 'Allam (a former security officer), *al-Ikhwan wa Ana* (The Brotherhood and I) (Cairo: Akhbar al-Yawm, 1996).

15 *Hadith Sahih*, by Tarmathi. A verified saying by the Prophet Muhammad narrated by and in Tarmathi's hadith collection.

16 *Hadith Sahih*, 234.

17 'Our society is unlike Mecca *jahili* society', published on 8 July 2001, quoted from the official website of Qaradawi: https://www.al-qaradawi.net/node/2186.

18 Qaradawi: 'Qutb's ideas do not belong to the Muslim Brotherhood and they break away from *ahl al-Sunna*', 8 August 2009, http://archive.is/zy9ZY.

19 For more about this party, see: http://www.aljazeera.net/encyclopedia/movements andparties/2014/11/11/%D8%AD%D8%B2%D8%A8-%D8%A7%D9%84%D9%88%D8%B3%D8%B7-%D8%A7%D9%84%D8%AC%D8%AF%D9%8A%D8%AF.

20 This famous speech of Badi' was delivered on 5 July 2013, only two days after the Muslim Brotherhood president Mursi was forcibly removed from power by the army. The speech was given in Rabaa al-Adawiya Square where tens of thousands of the MB and their supporters sat in for forty-five days before the army crushed their protest by brute force, killing more than 800. On these events, see the Human Rights Watch report, *Egypt: Rab'a Killings Likely Crimes against Humanity*, 12 August 2014, https://www.hrw.org/news/2014/08/12/egypt-raba-killings-likely-crimes-against-humanity.

21 Numerous writers hold this view. See, for example, Graham Fuller, *The Future of Political Islam* (London: Palgrave Macmillan, 2003); Emile Nakhleh, *A Necessary Engagement: Reinventing America's Relations with the Muslim World* (Princeton, NJ: Princeton University Press, 2009); John Esposito and Karen Armstrong, *The Future of Islam* (Oxford: Oxford University Press, 2013). A more recent account of the aftermath of events and politics in three post-Arab Spring countries by Ibrahim Fraihat, *Unfinished Revolutions: Yemen, Libya and Tunisia after the Arab Spring* (New Haven, CT: Yale University Press, 2016), provides a compelling case for the engagement view. For the opposing view, see Shadi Hamid, *Temptations of Power: Islamist and Liberal Democracy in a New Middle East* (Oxford: Oxford University Press, 2014), where the author argues that the repression of Islamists makes them more moderate.

22 See the assessment of political and parliamentary engagement of Muslim Brotherhood parties in several Arab countries offered by Nathan J. Brown and Amr Hamzawi, *Between Religion and Politics* (New York: Carnegie Endowment for Peace, 2010).

Chapter 2: Understanding ISIS: The Interplay between Ideology and Context

1 The 'Second Arab Awakening' is a term used by various scholars and commentators. Adeed Dawisha reminds us that the history of what he describes as the Arabs' first awakening unfolded in the first two decades after the end of the Second World War, making the case that the first Arab awakening centred on anti-colonialism, and was less fundamentally concerned with democratic practices. The failure of the transformation of the post-colonial states into fully-fledged democracies after national liberation, and the defeat of imperialism, has become all too obvious, and in Dawisha's words, Arab societies are now awakening from authoritarianism. For an in-depth analysis of the term, see Adeed Dawisha, *The Second Arab Awakening: Revolution, Democracy, and the Islamist Challenge from Tunis to Damascus* (New York: Norton, 2013).

2 It seems obvious now that the concept of the 'Arab Spring' was something of a misnomer. The idea of rapid transformation from autocratic rule to democracy was and remains a far-fetched objective. Rather than taking the holding of elections as a straightforward benchmark, a political culture of tolerance and respect for minority rights, as well as institutions that provide for the rule of law, and the holding of regular elections in which the opposition can become the government, are the main requirements for the eventual introduction of representative democracy.

3 The first wave of jihadism emerged in Afghanistan during the 1980s as a response to the Soviet occupation of the country. It stretched over the 1990s and was clearly

evident in movements in Chechnya, Bosnia, Egypt and Algeria, whose purpose was to topple pro-Western and pro-Russian regimes. Their inability to mobilize the 'Muslim masses' under their banner secured their failure. A second generation of jihadists came to the fore with the purpose of attacking the 'far enemy', meaning the Western (or Russian) backers of opponents of jihad. After realizing that the resilience of the pro-Western regimes (the 'near enemy') was due to Western support, they decided to attack the West. It is in this context that al-Qaeda attacked the United States on 9/11.

4 Jean-Pierre Filiu, *From Deep State to Islamic State: The Arab Counter-Revolution and its Jihadi Legacy* (Oxford: Oxford University Press, 2015).

5 This impression is widespread in the Arab world. I have been asked this question many times by my students and colleagues. It is worth noting that such an impression exists especially in politicized societies where people are relatively powerless. Also, Arab publics do not want to believe that ISIS, although perhaps *facilitated* by the US, is essentially a home-grown product.

6 Hillary Rodham Clinton, *Hard Choices* (New York: Simon & Schuster, 2014).

7 For more details, see Naomi Klein, 'Baghdad Year Zero: Pillaging Iraq in Pursuit of Neocon Utopia', *Harper's Magazine*, September 2004, http://harpers.org/archive/2004/09/baghdad-year-zero/.

8 For more details, see Abu Mus'ab al-Zarqawi, 'Risala min Abi Mus'ab al-Zarqawi ila al-Shaykh Usama bin Ladin (hafidhahu Allah) (letter from Abu Mus'ab al-Zarqawi to Sheikh Osama bin Laden, may God protect him)', 15 February 2004, in *Majmu' Rasa'il al-Zarqawi* (A collection of al-Zarqawi's letters), 59 (no publication details).

9 For more details, see Mohammad Abu Rumman and Hassan Abu Hanieh, *The 'Islamic State' Organization: The Sunni Crisis and the Struggle of Global Jihadism* (Amman: Friedrich-Ebert-Stiftung, 2015), 71.

10 Johan Galtung, 'Violence, Peace, and Peace Research', *Journal of Peace Research* 6, no. 3 (1969): 167–91.

11 Aaron David Miller, 'Middle East Meltdown', *Foreign Policy*, 30 October 2014, http://foreignpolicy.com/2014/10/30/middle-east-meltdown/.

12 Miller, 'Middle East Meltdown'.

13 Abu Rumman and Abu Hanieh, *The 'Islamic State' Organization*, 311.

14 Omer Taspinar, 'Fighting Radicalism, not "Terrorism": Root Causes of an International Actor Redefined', *SAIS Review* 29, no. 2 (summer–fall 2009): 75–86. For a summary of a similar debate between two prominent French intellectuals working on contemporary Islam (Gilles Kepel and Olivier Roy), see https://www.nytimes.com/2016/07/13/world/europe/france-radical-islam.html.

15 Taspinar, 'Fighting Radicalism, not "Terrorism"', 77.

16 Taspinar, 'Fighting Radicalism, not "Terrorism"', 75. See also the Kepel–Roy debate.

17 For more details on Arab attitudes towards ISIS, see the opinion poll conducted and published by the Arab Center for Research and Policy Studies, http://english. dohainstitute.org/content/cb12264b-1eca-402b-926a-5d068ac60011.
18 See Pew Research Center, 'In nations with significant Muslim populations, much disdain for ISIS', http://www.pewresearch.org/fact-tank/2015/11/17/in-nations-with-significant-muslim-populations-much-disdain-for-isis/. It is worth pointing out that in Pakistan 28 per cent expressed an unfavourable view of ISIS whereas 62 per cent indicated no clear opinion.
19 For more details, see John Esposito and Dalia Mogahed, *Who Speaks for Muslims? What a Billion Muslims Really Think* (New York: Gallup Press, 2007).
20 Robert Satloff, 'Beyond the Oval Office: Filling in the Blanks of U.S. Strategy Against the Islamic State', Washington Institute For Near East Policy, http://www.washingtoninstitute.org/policy-analysis/view/beyond-the-oval-office-filling-in-the-blanks-of-u.s.-strategy-against-the-i.
21 Jeffery Goldberg, 'The Modern King in the Arab Spring', *The Atlantic*, April 2013, http://www.theatlantic.com/magazine/archive/2013/04/monarch-in-the-middle/309270/.
22 The original Mamluks ruled Egypt from 1250 to 1517 and Syria from 1260 to 1516. The original Mamluks gained legitimacy from a weak Caliph who remained under their control. By the same token, the modern Mamluks gained legitimacy from the popular 'votes' held under martial law. Filiu then links this categorization of the Mamluks to the concept of the *deep state* in contemporary Turkish history; Filiu, *From Deep State to Islamic State*, 115–18.
23 For more details on how the neo-Mamluks appeared in Syria in the 1960s, see Filiu, *From Deep State to Islamic State*, x. He sees the recent past as a 'historical process of power struggles that led to the consolidation of the modern Arab Mamluks, mainly in Algeria, Egypt, Syria and Yemen. Those four countries shared the same characteristics of a reframed nationalist narrative, a populist discourse, a ubiquitous repressive apparatus and a systematic plundering of national resources. More important, they extolled the virtues of the military as the dominant source of legitimacy, while the hegemonic ruling party organized regular plebiscites.'

Chapter 3: Between Religion, Warfare and Politics: The Case of Jabhat al-Nusra in Syria

1 Charles Lister, formerly of the Brookings Doha Center: http://www.spiegel.de/international/world/terror-expert-charles-lister-interview-on-is-and-syria-peace-a-1070626.html.
2 'Nusra Leader: no End to Conflict with ISIL in Syria', al-Jazeera, 4 June 2015.

3   Al-Nusra recaptured Idlib in January 2016.
4   We are not referring here to the jihadi organization, but to the ideal of an Islamic society ruled by one 'true' Islamic power.
5   'Syria's Nusra Front Leader urges wider attacks on Assad's Alawite areas to avenge Russian bombing', *Daily Telegraph*, 13 October 2015.
6   'Nusra Front issues bounties for Assad and Nasrallah', *al-Arabiyya*, 13 October 2015.
7   'Gulf Allies and "Army of Conquest"', *al-Ahram Weekly*, 28 May 2015.
8   'Turkey and Saudi Arabia alarm the West by backing Islamist extremists the Americans had bombed in Syria', *Independent*, 12 May 2015.
9   'US-trained Syria fighters gave equipment to Nusra Front', al-Jazeera, 28 November 2015.
10 'Nusra Leader: No End to Conflict with ISIL in Syria', al-Jazeera, 28 November 2015.
11 'Syria al-Qaeda Leader: Our mission is to defeat regime, not to attack West', al-Jazeera, 28 May 2015.
12 Syria Public Opinion – July 2015, ORB International, http://www.opinion.co.uk/perch/resources/syriadata.pdf.
13 'Otages italiennes en Syrie: polémique sur une rançon', Radio France Internationale, 16 January 2015.
14 'US Names Two Qatari Nationals as Financiers of Terrorism', *The National*, 6 August 2015.
15 'Qatar's Emir: We don't fund terrorists', CNN, 25 September 2014.
16 'Hamad Bin Jassim: We Supported Al-Qaeda in Syria', https://www.youtube.com/watch?v=9f33l30kQxg.
17 Among the non-Middle Eastern states involved today in the Syrian conflict, Al-Nusra has fought against Russia, especially in September and October 2015, when this country lanuched airstrikes against al-Nusra to help the regime. At that time, one of al-Nusra's members, Abu 'Ubayd al-Madani, released a video warning that the Front would kill any Russian soldier it could get its hands on: 'Al-Qaeda Affiliate Issues Bounty for Capture of Russian Soliders in Syria', *Newsweek*, 2 October 2015.
18 'Nusra Leader: no End to Conflict with ISIL in Syria', *Newsweek*, 2 October 2015.
19 Not to be confused with Islamic State.
20 'Turkey and Saudi Arabia alarm the West by backing Islamist extremists the Americans had bombed in Syria', *Newsweek*, 2 October 2015.
21 'Al-Nusra leader Jolani announces split from al-Qaeda', al-Jazeera, 29 July 2016.
22 'Syria's Jabhat al-Nusra splits from al-Qaeda and changes its name', *Washington Post*, 28 July 2016.
23 As an example, in October 2017, twelve al-Nusra commanders, including al-Jawlani, were severely injured or killed in an airstrike carried out by the Russian air force according to the Russian Defense Ministry. This information was quickly

contradicted. However, it illustrates the importance the Russians gave to the elimination of al-Nusra's leaders.

24 https://azelin.files.wordpress.com/2017/03/hay_at-tahcca3ricc84r-al-shacc84m-22clarifications-regarding-the-statement-by-michael-ratney-the-united-states-special-envoy-to-syria22-en.pdf.
25 http://www.all4syria.info/Archive/437312.
26 Charles Lister, *Terror Expert Charles Lister: 'Islamic State Is a Convenient Obsession'*, 2016, .

Chapter 4: The 2007 Hamas–Fatah Conflict in Gaza and the Israeli–American Demands

1 This Plan was first disclosed during the autonomy negotiations between Egypt and Israel in 1980, whereby Israel would place responsibility for the administration of Gaza's affairs in the hands of the Palestinians themselves before considering whether to withdraw from parts of the West Bank (Peres, 1995: 376–7; Waage, 2004: 67).
2 In April 1994, during negotiations for the Gaza–Jericho agreement, the military wing of Hamas launched its first suicide bomb attack in Israel in response to the shooting of twenty-nine Palestinians by a Jewish settler in Hebron (Youngs and Smith, 2007: 8).
3 In 2012 Arafat's body was exhumed and a team of Swiss scientists reported that it contained eighteen times the safe level of polonium, a highly radioactive and extremely dangerous chemical (Shlaim, 2014: 789).
4 The letter provoked widespread diplomatic protests from all quarters, including from former British and American diplomats who had served in the Middle East (*Guardian* online, 27 April 2004; Washington Report on Middle East Affairs online, 19 May 2004). Daniel Kurtzer, the United States Ambassador to Israel when the Bush–Sharon letters were exchanged, later explained in an article for the *Washington Post* that the letters were predicated on their being 'an agreed outcome' during negotiations. Moreover, 'the letter did not convey any US support for or understanding of Israeli settlements . . . in the run up to a peace agreement' (*Washington Post* online, 14 June 2009).
5 Mustafa's cousin, Marwan Barghouti, declared his candidacy from prison but then retired from the race.
6 Hamas' participation was part of a package of agreements reached at a meeting with the factions in Cairo in March 2005. Hamas had wanted the elections to have taken place earlier and as agreed with Fatah.
7 Shalit would be released five years later in exchange for 1,027 prisoners – mainly Palestinians and Arab-Israelis.

8 This was a reference to the war between Israel and Hezbollah in the summer of 2006.
9 In fact, the United Kingdom was in direct contact with Hamas through Michael Ancram, a Conservative politician and member of the House of Lords. The dialogue proved beneficial to the UK, especially when BBC journalist Alan Johnston was kidnapped by the Army of Islam, an armed gang in Gaza. Hamas secured his release. See Alan Johnston, 'My kidnap ordeal', BBC News online, 15 October 2007.
10 The other members were Abu Mazen, Ziad Abu Amr, Hani al-Qawasmah, Salam Fayyad, Sa'ib Erekat and Tawfiq Tirawi. No agreement had been reached regarding the National Security Forces Commander.
11 The American Consulate General in Jerusalem – like the British Consulate General in Jerusalem – is responsible for affairs with the Palestinians in East Jerusalem, the West Bank and Gaza Strip.
12 The Karni crossing was a cargo terminal on the Israel–Gaza Strip barrier. It was located at the north-eastern end of the Gaza Strip and was opened in 1994 after the signing of the Oslo Accords, in order to allow Palestinian merchants to export and import goods. The crossing was closed down by the Israeli authorities in March 2011.
13 Dahlan later told Rose that he had been in Germany convalescing from knee surgery.
14 Fayyad, a former World Bank economist, was respected in the West, but he was hardly known to Palestinians. As a candidate in the elections won by Hamas in 2006, Fayyad had received just 2.4 per cent of the vote (McGeough, 2009: 377–8).
15 The reference to previous Israel–PLO agreements was a reference to the Oslo agreements of the 1990s that do not bind Hamas. As a general rule, treaties cannot bind third parties without their consent.
16 'Egypt is reluctant to take a firm stand against Hamas publicly due to the strength and popularity of the Muslim Brotherhood, and thus Egypt is not inclined to act against these smuggling networks which are supported by Hamas,' Diskin confided to Ambassador Jones when they met in December 2007 (WikiLeaks, 28 December 2007).

Chapter 5: Hezbollah and the Lebanese State: Indispensable, Unpredictable – Destabilizing?

1 Michael Hudson, *The Precarious Republic: Political Modernization in Lebanon* (New York: Random House, 1969).
2 Which antedates the First World War. For an account of the structure of Lebanese politics, see Helena Cobban, *The Making of Modern Lebanon* (Boulder, CO: Westview, 1984). See also Kamal Salibi, *A House of Many Mansions: The History of*

Lebanon Reconsidered, Berkeley and Los Angeles: University of California Press, 1988). For a more complex analysis, see Fawaz Traboulsi, *A History of Modern Lebanon* (London: Pluto, 2007).

3   See Joel S. Migdal, *Strong Societies and Weak States: State–Society Relations and State Capabilities in the Third World* (Princeton, NJ: Princeton University Press, 1988). Lebanon is not unique in having both a weak state and a weak (civil) society.

4   I am most grateful to Dr Imad Mansour of Qatar University for this characterization of Lebanese politics, and for other helpful comments on this chapter.

5   Some were in existence before 1975.

6   See Peter Sluglett, 'Les milices chrétiennes au Liban', in Jean-François Dazugan and Stéphane Valter (eds), *Les Forces Armées Arabes et Moyen-Orientales* (Paris: ESKA, 2014), 154–86. Originally, one of the raisons d'être of the *Kata'ib* was its opposition to the Maronite political aristocracy, which it never fully succeeded in supplanting (or becoming part of).

7   See Lina Khatib and Dina Matar, 'Conclusion: Hizbullah at a Crossroads', in Lina Khatib, Dina Matar and Atef Alshaer, *The Hizbullah Phenomenon: Politics and Communication* (New York: Oxford University Press, 2014), 181–90, here 186.

8   Pierre Jumayyil (1905–84) sought the presidency twice, in 1964 and 1970. Frequently appointed to the Lebanese cabinet, he was a minister at the time of his death. The not always saintly Druze leader Kamal Jumblatt (father of Walid, killed by the Syrians in March 1977) fought unsuccessfully to make the necessary changes to the Lebanese constitution that would make it possible for him to stand for the position.

9   See Rania Maktabi, 'The Lebanese Census of 1932 Revisited. Who Are the Lebanese?', *British Journal of Middle Eastern Studies* 26, no. 2 (1999): 219–41.

10 Figures for 2011 are taken from the table, 'Officially Recognised Lebanese Sects in 2011', in William Harris, *Lebanon: A History, 600–2011* (Oxford: Oxford University Press, 2012), 14.

11 The beginnings, subtle nuances and complex dynamics of this process are captured in Michael Weiss, *In the Shadow of Sectarianism: Law, Shi'ism, and the Making of Modern Lebanon* (Cambridge, MA: Harvard University Press, 2010). See also Tamara Chalabi, *The Shi'is of Jabal 'Amil and the New Lebanon: Community and Nation State, 1918–1943* (London: Palgrave Macmillan, 2006).

12 See Weiss, *In the Shadow of Sectarianism*, Chapter 6, "Amili Shi'is into Shi'i Lebanese', 186–235.

13 See Augustus Richard Norton, *Hizbullah: A Short History* (Princeton, NJ: Princeton University Press, 2007), 1–46, and Ahmad N. Hamze, *In the Path of Hizbullah* (Syracuse, NY: Syracuse University Press, 2004).

14 Some 'Alawis objected to this 'act of amalgamation'; see Patrick Seale, *Asad of Syria: The Struggle for the Middle East* (London: I.B. Tauris, 1988), 173, 252, and Yvette

Talhamy, 'The *Fatwas* and the Nusayri/'Alawis of Syria', *Middle Eastern Studies* 46 (2010): 175–94.

15 Nadia von Maltzahn, *The Syria–Iran Axis: Cultural Diplomacy and International Relations in the Middle East* (London: I. B. Tauris, 2013), 17–40.

16 Norton, *Hizbullah*, 69–73.

17 Thomas Pierret, *Religion and State in Syria: The Sunni 'Ulama from Coup to Revolution* (Cambridge: Cambridge University Press, 2013), 1–23. In October 1980 an 'Islamic Front in Syria' (*al-Jabha al-Islamiyya fi Suriyya*), which brought ulama and lay Islamists together, was set up in Saudi Arabia: Pierret, *Religion and State in Syria*, 189.

18 See Raphaël Lefèvre, *Ashes of Hama: The Muslim Brethren in Syria* (London: Hurst, 2013), 77, 128.

19 See *Nass al-risala al-maftuha allati wajahaha Hizballah ila' l-mustad'afin fi Lubnan w'al-'Alam*, reproduced in http://www.cfr.org/terrorist-organizations-and-networks/open-letter-hizballah-program/p30967.

20 'As a mainstream political party, Hezbollah operates according to *Realpolitik* calculations of political expediency, benefit and *maslaha* (interest).' Joseph Alagha, 'Hezbollah's Conception of the Islamic State', in Sabrina Mervin (ed.), *The Shi'a Worlds and Iran* (London: Saqi, 2010), 111.

21 However, Hezbollah meetings and rallies showed (and continue to show) pictures of Ayatollahs Khomeni and Khamene'i alongside its secretary-general, Hasan Nasrullah (in office since 1992).

22 Which also removed the 'primary justification for Syria's military presence in Lebanon': Harris, *Lebanon*, 264.

23 Sune Haugbølle, *War and Memory in Lebanon* (Cambridge: Cambridge University Press, 2010), 69. See also Anja Peleikis, 'The Making and Unmaking of Memories: the Case of a Multi-Confessional Village in Lebanon', in Ussama Makdisi and Paul A. Silverstein (eds), *Memory and Violence in the Middle East and North Africa* (Bloomington and Indianapolis: Indiana University Press, 2006), 133–50; and Elizabeth Picard, 'The Political Economy of Civil War in Lebanon', in Steven Heydemann (ed.), *War, Institutions and Social Change in the Middle East* (Berkeley and Los Angeles: University of California Press, 2000), 292–322.

24 Greg Grandin, 'The Instruction of Great Catastrophe: Truth Commissions, National History and State Formation in Argentina, Chile and Guatemala', *American Historical Review* 110, no. 1 (February 2005): 46–67.

25 Such situations throw up unlikely bedfellows: thus in Angola, members of the MPLA elite sold weapons to UNITA, and the Bosnian Serb Army was often crucially dependent on Croatian petrol barons for fuel. See the editors' 'Introduction' in Mats Berdal and David Malone (eds.), *Greed and Grievance: Economic Agendas in Civil Wars* (Boulder, CO: Lynne Rienner, 2000), and R. T. Naylor, 'The insurgent

economy: black market operations of guerrilla organisations', *Crime, Law and Social Change* 20 (1993): 13–51.
26 See Elizabeth Picard, 'The Political Economy of Civil War in Lebanon'.
27 Norton, *Hizbullah*, 127.
28 Tareq Y. Ismael, *The Rise and Fall of the Communist Party of Iraq* (Cambridge: Cambridge University Press, 2008), and Johan Franzén, *Red Star Over Iraq: The Iraqi Communist Party and the Evolution of Ideological Politics in pre-Saddam Iraq* (London: Hurst, 2011).
29 Also it was and is generally the case that *identity-based conflict* does not seem to have functioned as a major factor: most civil wars derive from 'present day struggles for political power rather than [being] rooted in long-standing ethnic hatreds'. See Ann Hironaka, *Never-ending Wars: The International Community, Weak States and the Perpetuation of Civil War* (Cambridge, MA: Harvard University Press, 2005), 98.
30 Whose own relations with Israel have been quite 'ambiguous'; acceptance of this gift showed a fair degree of pragmatism on Hezbollah's part.
31 With the apparent encouragement of President Jacques Chirac, a personal friend.
32 '[In late 2004 and 2005] pro-Syrian political figures in Lebanon and their Syrian allies understood Hariri to be a serious threat to their political survival'. Norton, *Hizbullah*, 127.
33 A United Nations Special Tribunal for Lebanon was set up almost immediately to investigate the murder, and is now located in The Hague. It is something of an understatement to say that various political sensitivities have prevented it from coming to any clear conclusion.
34 Kassir and Tueni were well-known journalists; Hawi was Secretary-General of the Lebanese Communist Party, and Jumayyil was the son of the former president and a minister in Siniora's (14 March) government.
35 For the full text in English, see www.english.alahednews.com.lb/essaydetailsf.php?eid=4442&fid=25.
36 See Asher Kaufman, *Contested Frontiers in the Syria–Lebanon–Israel Region: Geography, Sovereignty and Conflict* (Washington, DC: Woodrow Wilson Center Press, 2014).
37 Norton, *Hizbullah*, 92.
38 Élizabeth Picard, *Liban–Syrie, intimes étrangers: Un siècle d'interactions politiques* (Paris: Sindbad, 2016), 312.
39 There was more fighting later that year: see Picard, *Liban–Syrie*, 318–20.
40 Eric Mohns and Francesco Cavatorta, '"Yes, He Can": A Reappraisal of Syrian Foreign Policy under Bashar al-Asad', *Mediterranean Politics* 15, no. 2 (2010): 289–98.
41 David Lesch, *The Fall of the House of Asad* (New Haven, CT: Yale University Press, 2012), 129.

42 http://www.jpost.com/Middle-East/Analysis-The-Syrian-war-has-exposed-Hezbollah-to-assassinations-454241.

43 See Lina Khatib and Dina Matar, 'Conclusion: Hizbullah at a Crossroads', in Khatib, Matar and Atef Alshaer, *The Hizbullah Phenomenon*, 187.

44 See two analyses published by the Lebanese Center for Policy Studies: http://www.lcps-lebanon.org/featuredArticle.php?id=48 (August 2015); http://www.lcps-lebanon.org/featuredArticle.php?id=50 (September 2015).

45 Olivier Roy, 'L'impact de la révolution iranienne au moyen orient', in Sabrina Mervin, *Les mondes chiiteset l'Iran* (Paris: Karthala,2007), 33.

46 Cf. 'In fact, the Saudi response to the Arab spring [in Bahrain] . . . was based on the fear that an opposition to the ruling family could emerge that would unite Sunni and Shia.' Toby Matthiesen, *Sectarian Gulf: Bahrain, Saudi Arabia and the Arab Spring that Wasn't* (Stanford CA: Stanford University Press, 2013), 19. *Divide et impera*, as they say.

Chapter 6: When the State Becomes a Non-State: Yemen between the Huthis, Hirak and Al-Qaeda

1 For a comprehensive history of the rise of the Huthis, see Brandt (2017). Hill (2017) and Lackner (2017) provide a concise history of the events leading up to the current conflict.

2 The dangers of this introduction of Salafism were pointed out by Abu Zayd (1991); see also Gause (1990) and Haykel (2002). For a study of Salafism in Yemen, see Bonnefoy (2011).

3 The writings of Husayn al-Huthi are readily available online: http://al-majalis.org/books/tag/%D9%85%D9%84%D8%A7%D8%B2%D9%85-%D8%A7%D9%84%D8%B3%D9%8A%D8%AF-%D8%AD%D8%B3%D9%8A%D9%86-%D8%A7%D9%84%D8%AD%D9%88%D8%AB%D9%8A/

4 The basic history of Yemen's tribe is by Dresch (1989). For a more recent assessment of the nature of tribalism in Yemen, see Adra (2016) as well as her earlier articles (Adra 1997, 1985).

5 The Saudi connection was noted by the US Embassy, as noted in a Wikileaks document from the time: https://wikileaks.org/plusd/cables/1977SANA04534_c.html.

6 Details of the destruction of Yemen's heritage are reported by the Arabian Rights Watch Association, http://arwarights.org/heritage.

7 Among the reports are Amnesty International (2015), Human Rights Council (2018), Human Rights Watch (2018) and Mwatana (2017).

Chapter 8: 'Being in Time': Kurdish Movement and Quests of Universal

1 Hamit Bozarslan, '"Being in Time": the Kurdish Movement and Quests of Universal', in Gareth Stanfield and Mohamed Shareef (eds), *The Kurdish Question Revisited* (London: Hurst, 2017), 65–71.
2 Gabriel Martinez-Gros, *Ibn Khaldûn et les sept vies de l'Islam* (Arles: Actes-Sud, 2006), 143–4.
3 Kenneth Thompson, *Beliefs and Ideology* (London: Open Press, 1986), 29.
4 For the documents, see Paul White, *Primitive Rebels or Revolutionary Modernizers? The Kurdish National Movement in Turkey* (London: Zed Press, 2000).
5 A. Vali (ed.), *Essays on the Origins of Kurdish Nationalism* (Costa Mesa, CA: Mazda, 2003).
6 Jean Leca, 'Nationalisme et universalisme', *Pouvoirs* 57 (1991): 31–42.
7 Talinn Ter Minassian, *Colporteurs du Komintern: l'Union soviétique et les minorités au Moyen-Orient* (Paris: Sciences-Po, 1997).
8 For the documents, see W. Jwadieh, *The Kurdish Nationalist Movement: Its Origins and Development* (Syracuse, NY: Syracuse University Press, 1960), 169.
9 Joost Jongerden and Jelle Velheij (eds), *Social Relations in Ottoman Diyarbékir, 1870–1915* (Leiden and Boston: Brill, 2012).
10 Quoted in Mehmet Bayrak, *Kürtler ve Ulusal Demokratik Mücadeleleri. Gizli Belgeler, Arastirmlar, Notlar* (Ankara: Özge Yayinlari, 1993), 110.
11 Hamit Bozarslan, *Entre le nationalisme et la 'umma: l'islam kurde au tournant du siècle* (Amsterdam: MERA Occasional Papers, 1992).
12 For the acts, see Khoybun, *Les massacres kurdes en Turquie* (Cairo: Khoybun, 1927), 35.
13 For Azadi, see Martin Van Bruinessen, *Agha, Cheikh and State: The Social and Political Structures of Kurdistan* (London: Zed, 1992), and Robert Olson, *The Emergence of Kurdish Nationalism and the Sheikh Said Rebellion (1880–1925)* (Austin: University of of Texas Press, 1989).
14 H. H. Serdî, *Görüş ve Anılarım, 1907–1985* (Istanbul: Med Yayınları, 1985).
15 Jordi Tejel Gorgas, 'La Ligue nationale kurde Khoybun: Mythes et réalités de la première organisation nationaliste kurde', *Etudes Kurdes*, special edition (2007).
16 Khoybun, *Les massacres des Kurdes en Turquie* (Cairo: n.p., 1928), 9.
17 Hamit Bozarslan, 'Correspondance entre le général Rondot et les frères Bederkhanî', *Etudes kurdes* 3 (2001): 73–4.
18 William Eagleton, *The Kurdish Republic of Mahabad* (Oxford: Oxford University Press, 1946), and Abbas Vali, *The Kurds and the State in Modern Iran: The Making of Kurdish Identity* (London: I.B. Tauris, 2011).
19 Abdurrahman Ghasemlou, *Kurdistan and the Kurds* (Prague: Czechoslovak Academy of Sciences, 1965).

20 For an interesting account of the left-wing movements in Iranian Kurdistan, see Selahettin Ali Arik, *Dr. Sivan. Sait Elçi-Süleyman Muini ve Kürt Trajedesi (1960–1975)* (Istanbul: Peri Yayınları, 2011), 336–56.
21 K. Cemil Paşa, *Doza Kurdistan. Kürt Milletinin 60 Yıllık Esaretten Kurtuluş Savaşı Hatıraları* (Ankara: öz-Ge, 1991), 181.
22 I. Ch. Vanly, *Le Kurdistan irakien entité nationale. Etude de la Révolution de 1961* (Neuchatel: Editions de la Baconnière, 1970).
23 Metin Yüksel, 'I Cry out so that you Wake up: Cegerxwin's Poetics and Politics of Awakening', *Middle Eastern Studies* 50, no. 4 (2013): 1–18.
24 Hamit Bozarslan, '49'ların Anıları Üzerine Tarihsel-Sosyolojik Okuma Notları ve Bazı Hipotezler', *Tarih ve Toplum* 16 (2013): 127–43.
25 Hamit Bozarslan, 'Türkiye'de Kürt Sol Hareketi', in *Modern Türkiye'de Siyasi Düşünce*, vol. 8 (Istanbul: Iletisim, 2007), 1167–207; Marlies Casier and Olivier Grojean, 'Between integration, autonomization and radicalization: Hamit Bozarslan on the Kurdish Movement and the Turkish Left', interview, *European Journal of Turkish Studies* (Internet edition) 14 (2013).
26 *Komal Yayınları, DDKO Dâvâ Dosyası*, vol. 1 (Ankara: Komal Yayınları, 1975), 489–630.
27 Ali Arık, *Dr. Sivan*, 98.
28 Frantz Fanon, *Pour la révolution africaine. Ecrits politiques* (Paris: La Découverte, 2006), 111.
29 For a selection of documents, see E. A. Türkmen and A. Özmen (eds), *Kürdistan Sosyalist Solu Kitabi. 60'lardan 2000'lere Seçme Metinler* (Ankara: Dipnot, 2014).
30 For this concept, see Clifford Geertz, 'Ideology as a Cultural System', in David Apter (ed.), *Ideology and Discontent* (New York: Free Press, 1964), 65, and Maxime Rodinson, *Marxisme et le monde musulman* (Paris: Seuil, 1972), 311.
31 KDP, *Irak Kürdistan Demokratik Partisi Yeni Stratejisi* (İstanbul: Üçüncü Dünya Yayınları, 1978); KDP, *The Road of the Kurdish Liberation Movement* (London: Calvert North Star Press, 1977).
32 Hamit Bozarslan, 'Revisiting the Middle East's 1979', *Economy and Society* 41, no. 4 (2012): 558–67.
33 Bernard Rougier, *Everyday Jihad: The Rise of Militant Islam among the Palestinians in Lebanon* (Cambridge, MA: Harvard University Press, 2009).
34 Hamit Bozarslan, 'The Kurds and the Middle Eastern "state of violence" in the 1980s and 2010s', *Kurdish Studies* 2 (2014): 4–13.
35 Nicole Watts, *Activists in Office: Kurdish Ethnic Politics, Political Resources, and Repression in Turkey* (Seattle: Washington University Press, 2009).
36 Anthony Giddens, *The Nation-State and Violence* (Berkeley and Los Angeles: University of California Press, 1987), 46–7.

Bibliography

Documents and speeches

An Action Plan for the Palestinian Presidency – 2 March 2007.
Dahlan, Mohammed – Bassil Jabar, interview transcript with David Rose, Tape 2, Giza Four Seasons Hotel, Cairo, December 2007.
De Soto, Alvaro, End of Mission Report, May 2007.
Hamas: A Document of General Principles and Policies, 1 May 2017.
Letter from President Bush to Prime Minister Sharon, 14 April 2004.
National Security Strategy of the United States of America, September 2002.
Revised Disengagement Plan, 6 June 2004.
'Security Cabinet declares Gaza hostile territory, communicated by the Prime Minister's media adviser', 19 September 2007.
Selected Speeches of George W. Bush 2001–8.
UN General Assembly Resolution 3237 (XXIX), 22 November 1974.

Palestine Papers

Notes from PA–US bilateral meetings, 22 September 2005 (Condoleezza Rice, David Welch and Salam Fayyad).
Meeting with Peres on border crossings, Rafah, and elections, 14 October 2005 (Ghassan Khatib, Sa'eb Erekat, Shimon Peres, Haim Ramon and Giora Eiland).
Meeting Minutes Erekat–Dayton, 10 May 2006 (attendance: Saeb Erekat, Zeinah Salahi, Rami Dajani and Keith Dayton, Jennifer Butte-Dahl and Dov Schwartz).
Quadripartite Meeting of Gaza Security Committee, Memorandum, 11 March 2007 (attendance: Mohamed Dahlan, Jamal Quaeid, Rashid Abu Shbek, Basil Jaber, name redacted, Gen Sharif, Nader, Amos Gilad, Yusaf Orlion, General Dayton, Mike Pierson, Paul Rupp, Neil Hopp, PJ Dermour).
Meeting Report – 2nd Quadrilateral Security Meeting, 3 April 2007.

WikiLeaks documents

Ambassador Jones' December 24 Meeting with ISA chief Diskin, 28 December 2007. Canonical ID: 07TELAVIV3629_a.
Ambassador and Shin Bet chief Diskin discuss Gaza, CT cooperation, mistreat of Amcits, 4 October 2006. Canonical ID: 06TELAVIV3910_a.

Dagan and Codel Lieberman discuss Hamas-led PA and Iran, 5 May 2006. Canonical ID: 06TELAVIV1754_a.

Erekat on the way forward, 4 April 2006. Canonical ID: 06JERUSALEM1348_a.

FM Livni seeks new mechanisms for delivering aid to Palestinians, 4 April 2006. Canonical ID: 06TELAVIV1318_a.

GI chief Al-Tirawi offers ideas on PASF control, predicts conflict with Hamas, 24 February 2006. Canonical ID: 06JERUSALEM799_a.

Gilad on Hamas' relations with Jordan, Egypt, and Iran, 4 April 2006. Canonical ID: 06TELAVIV1324_a.

Haniyeh's speech seeks to bolster Hamas legitimacy, blames outside actors for Palestine's problems, 27 June 2007 (speech given on 24 June 2007). Canonical ID: 07JERUSALEM1329_a.

Interior Ministry Security Plan: Long on Platitudes, Short on Security Specifics, and Already a Dead Letter, 3 May 2007. Canonical ID: 07JERUSALEM785_a.

ISA chief Diskin says Hamas to do well in PA elections, 13 January 2006. Canonical ID: 06TELAVIV204_a.

ISA chief Diskin: Hamas on the horizon, 16 February 2006. Canonical ID: 06TELAVIV696_a.

ISA Chief Diskin on Situation in the Gaza Strip and West Bank, 13 June 2007. Canonical ID: 07TELAVIV1732_a.

Israeli Defmin tells A/S Welch Israel will take no action against Hamas, will not talk with a Hamas Government, 4 April 2006. Canonical ID: 06TELAVIV1319_a.

Israeli NSC says clarity needed on Hamas in new Palestinian Government, 26 January, 2006. Canonical ID: 06TELAVIV366_a.

Military Intelligence Director Yadlin comments on Gaza, Syria and Lebanon, 13 June 2007. Canonical ID: 07TELAVIV1733_a.

Minister of Interior Proposes "100-day Security Plan", 6 April 2007. Canonical ID: 07JERUSALEM640_a.

Mofaz discusses Palestinian elections, northern border, crossings, and Iran with Welch and Abrams, 13 January 2006. Canonical ID: 06TELAVIV201_a.

MOI DG Salamah: Hamas will not collapse quickly, 14 February 2006. Canonical ID: 06JERUSALEM666_a.

National Unity Government Progress, 23 February 2007. Canonical ID: 07JERUSALEM378_a.

NEA Assistant Secretary David Welch and DNSA Abrams' July 11–12 Cairo Meetings, 16 July 2016. Canonical ID: 06CAIRO4382_a.

New Israeli MOD DG Buchris Shares His Priorities, 25 May 2007. Canonical ID: 07TELAVIV1558_a.

Olmert: Despite frustration, GOI will maintain Palestinian channel, 21 February 2007. Canonical ID: 07TELAVIV542_a.

Palestinian political figures on salaries, Hamas-Fatah Relations, and National Dialogue, 9 May 2006. Canonical ID: 06JERUSALEM1850_a.

UAE National Security Adviser Hazza Discusses Palestinian Assistance with USSC Dayton, 30 July 2007. Canonical ID: 07ABUDHABI1273_a

USSC Dayton raises Rafah, AMA and Badr Brigade with ISA Diskin, 12 October 2006. Canonical ID: 06TELAVIV4032_a.

Yemen's Big Brother: What Has Saudi Arabia Done for Yemen Lately? June 2008. https://wikileaks.org/plusd/cables/08SANAA1053_a.html.

Books and articles

Abbas, M. (1995). *Through Secret Channels*. London: Garnet.

Abrams, E. (2013). *Tested by Zion: The Bush Administration and the Israeli–Palestinian Conflict*. Cambridge: Cambridge University Press.

Abu Alouf, R. and Chu, H. (2007). 'Palestinian interior minister calls it quits'. *Los Angeles Times*, 15 May.

Abu Rumman, M. and Abu Hanieh, H. (2015). *The 'Islamic State' Organization: The Sunni Crisis and the Struggle of Global Jihadism* Amman: Friedrich-Ebert-Stiftung.

Abu Zayd, A. (1991). *al-Wahhabiyya wa-khataruha 'ala mustaqbal al-Yaman al-siyasi*. Beirut: Mu'assasat al-Basa'ir.

Adra, N. (1983). *The Impact of Emigration on Women's Roles in Agriculture in the Yemen Arab Republic*. Report prepared for FAO, Rome.

Adra, N. (1985). 'The Tribal Concept in the Central Highlands of the Yemen Arab Republic'. In N. S. Hopkins and S. E. Ibrahim (eds), *Arab Society: Social Science Perspectives*, 275–85. Cairo: American University of Cairo Press.

Adra, N. (1997). 'Dance and Glance: Visualizing Tribal Identity in Highland Yemen'. *Visual Anthropology* 11: 55–102.

Adra, N. (2011). *Tribal Mediation in Yemen and its Implications to Development*. AAS Working Papers in Social Anthropology, Volume 19. Austrian Academy of Sciences, 2011. http://www.najwaadra.net/Yemethn.html.

Adra, N. (2016). 'Tribal Mediation and Empowered Women: Potential Contributions of Heritage to National Development in Yemen'. *International Journal of Islamic Architecture* 5, no. 2: 301–37.

Affi, L., Elmi, A. A., Knight, W. A. and Mohamed, S. (2016). 'Countering piracy through private security in the Horn of Africa: prospects and pitfalls'. *Third World Quarterly*: 1–17.

Africa Economic Development Institute (AEDI). (2009). 'Pirates of Somalia'. AEDI Exclusives. Los Angeles. CA. Available at http://africaecon.org/index.php/exclusives/read_exclusive/1/1.

Agence France-Presse, A. (2015). *Al Qaeda's Syria Branch Seeks Image Makeover in West*. GlobalPost. http://www.globalpost.com/article/6563639/2015/05/28/al-qaedas-syria-branch-seeks-image-makeover-west.

Alagha, J. (2010). 'Hezbollah's Conception of the Islamic State'. In S. Mervin (ed.), *The Shi'a Worlds and Iran*. London: Saqi.

al-Banna, H. (1938). *Risalat al-Mu'tamar al-Khamis* (Letter of the Fifth Conference). Ikhwan. http://www.ikhwanwiki.com/index.php?title=%D8%B1%D8%B3%D8%A7%D9%84%D8%A9_%D8%A7%D9%84%D9%85%D8%A4%D8%AA%D9%85%D8%B1_%D8%A7%D9%84%D8%AE%D8%A7%D9%85%D8%B3.

Albrecht, P. and Haenlein, C. (2016). 'Fragmented Peacekeeping: The African Union in Somalia'. *Journal of the Royal United Services Institution* 161, no. 1: 50–61.

al-Dawsari, N. (2016). *'We Lived Days in Hell': Civilian Perspectives on the Conflict in Yemen*. Center for Civilians in Conflict. Washington, DC. http://civiliansinconflict.org/resources/pub/we-lived-days-in-hell-civilian-perspectives-of-the-conflict-in-yemen.

Ali, A. (2010), 'The anatomy of al-Shabaab'. http://www.trackingterrorism.org/sites/default/files/chatter/TheAnatomyOfAlShabaab_0.pdf

'Ali, A. Y. (2001). *The Quran Translation*, 10th edition Delhi: Kitab Bahvan.

Ali Arik, S. (2011). *Dr. Sivan. Sait Elçi-Süleyman Muini ve Kürt Trajedesi (1960–1975)*. Istanbul: Peri Yayınları.

Al Jazeera (2007). 'The US Campaign to Topple the Palestinian Government'. Interview with Alastair Crooke, 24 January.

'Allam, F. (1996). *al-Ikhwan wa Ana* (The Brotherhood and I). Cairo: Akhbar al-Yawm.

Allen, C. D. (2017). 'Pirates in West Africa and Somalia'. In C. Varin and D. Abubakar (eds), *Violent Non-State Actors in Africa*, 301–21. London: Palgrave Macmillan.

Al-Quds Al-Arabi (1998). 'Declaration of the World Islamic Front for Jihad against the Jews and Crusaders', 23 February.

al-Sabbagh, M. (1986). *Haqiqat al-Nizam al-Khass wa Dawruhu fi Da'wat al-Ikhwan al-Muslimun* (The Truth About the Special Apparatus and Its Role in the Muslim Brotherhood). Cairo: Dar al-I'tisam.

al-Shamahi, A. (2014). 'Yemen is More Nuanced than "Sunni" & "Shia"'. *Yemen Times*, 27 February. http://www.yementimes.com/en/1759/opinion/3540/Yemen-is-more-nuanced-than-%E2%80%98Sunni%E2%80%99-%C2%A0%E2%80%98Shia%E2%80%99.htm.

al-Sharif, K. (1984). *al-Muqawamah al-Sirriyya fi Qanat al-Suess* (Secret Resistance along the Suez Canal). Amman: Dar al-Wafa'.

Alsoswa, A. A. (2014). 'Challenges Facing Women in Yemen's Transition'. *Yemeni Journal*: 15–21.

Alwazir, A. Z. (2015). 'Yemen's enduring resistance: Youth between politics and informal mobilization'. *Mediterranean Politics*. http://dx.doi.org/10.1080/13629395.2015.1081446.

al-Zarqawi, A. M. (n.d.). *Majmu' Rasa'il al-Zarqawi* (A collection of al-Zarqawi's letters) (No publication details).

Amnesty International (2015). *'Bombs Fall from the Sky Day and Night': Civilians under Fire in Northern Yemen*. London: Amnesty International.

Arab Center for Research & Policy Studies (2015). 'The 2015 Arab Opinion Index: Results in Brief'. 21 December. http://english.dohainstitute.org/content/cb12264b-1eca-402b-926a-5d068ac60011.

Armstrong, K. (2014). 'Wahhabism to ISIS: How Saudi Arabia exported the main source of global terrorism'. *New Statesman*, 27 November.

Ayoob, M. (2008). *The Many Faces of Political Islam: Religion and Politics in the Muslim World*. Ann Arbor: University of Michigan Press.

Baabood, A. A. (2017). 'Omani–Yemeni Relations: Past, Present and Future'. In H. Lackner and D. M. Varisco (eds), *Yemen and the Gulf States: The Making of a Crisis*, 67–82. Berlin: Gerlach.

Bahadur, J. (2011). *The Pirates of Somalia: Inside Their Hidden World*. New York: Pantheon Books.

Baker, G. (2014). *Syrian Regime Accused of Chlorine Gas Attacks*. Aljazeera.com. http://www.aljazeera.com/news/middleeast/2014/04/syrian-regime-accused-chlorine-gas-attacks-201441703230338216.html.

Barrett, R. C. (2011). *Yemen: A Different Political Paradigm in Context*. Joint Special Operations University Report 11/3, MacDill AFB FL, May.

Bayrak, M. (1993). *Kürtler ve Ulusal Demokratik Mücadeleleri. Gizli Belgeler, Arastirmlar, Notlar*. Ankara: Özge Yayinlari.

BBC News (2013). 'Somali Islamic scholars denounce al-Shabaab in fatwa'. http://www.bbc.com/news/world-africa-24057725.

BBC News (2016). 'US air strike kills 150 Somali militants'. http://www.bbc.com/news/world-africa-35748986.

Beilin, Y. (1999). *Touching Peace: From the Oslo Accord to a Final Agreement*. London: Weidenfeld & Nicolson.

Berdal, M. and Malone, D. (eds) (2000). *Greed and Grievance: Economic Agendas in Civil Wars*. Boulder, CO: Lynne Rienner.

Bonnefoy, L. (2011). *Salafism in Yemen: Transnationalism and Religious Identity*. London: Hurst.

Bonnefoy, L. (2018). 'Reversals of Fortune: The Islah Party in Post-Salih Yemen'. In M.-C. Heinze (ed.), *Yemen and the Search for Stability: Power, Politics and Society after the Arab Spring*, 184–203. London: I.B. Tauris.

Boucek, C. (2009). *Yemen: Avoiding a Downward Spiral*. Washington, DC: Carnegie Endowment for International Peace. http://carnegieendowment.org/2009/09/10/yemen-avoiding-downward-spiral-pub-23827.

Bozarslan, H. (1992). *Entre le nationalisme et la 'umma: l'islam kurde au tournant du siècle*. Amsterdam: MERA Occasional Papers.

Bozarslan, H. (2001). 'Correspondance entre le général Rondot et les frères Bederkhani'. *Etudes kurdes* 3: 73–4.

Bozarslan, H. (2007). 'Türkiye'de Kürt Sol Hareketi'. In *Modern Türkiye'de Siyasi Düsünce*, vol. 8, 1167–207. Istanbul: Iletisim.

Bozarslan, H. (2012). 'Revisiting the Middle East's 1979'. *Economy and Society* 41, no. 4: 558–67.
Bozarslan, H. (2013). '49'ların Anıları Üzerine Tarihsel-Sosyolojik Okuma Notları ve Bazı Hipotezler'. *Tarih ve Toplum* 16: 127–43.
Bozarslan, H. (2014). 'The Kurds and the Middle Eastern "state of violence" in the 1980s and 2010s'. *Kurdish Studies* 2: 4–13.
Bozarslan, H. (2017). '"Being in Time": the Kurdish Movement and Quests of Universal'. In G. Stanfield and M. Shareef (eds), *The Kurdish Question Revisited*, 65–71. London: Hurst.
Bozek, J. D. (2009). *Sayyid Qutb: Analysis of Jihadist Philosophy*. Saarbrucken: VDM Verlag.
Brandt, M. (2013). 'Sufyan's "Hybrid" War: Tribal Politics during the Huthi Conflict'. *Journal of Arabian Studies* 3, no. 1: 120–38.
Brandt, M. (2014). 'The Irregulars of the Sa'ada War: "Colonel Sheikhs" and "Tribal Militias" in Yemen's Huthi Conflict (2004–2010)'. In H. Lackner (ed.), *Why Yemen Matters*, 105–22. London: Saqi Books.
Brandt, M. (2017). *Tribes and Politics in Yemen: A History of the Houthi Conflict*. London: Hurst.
Brandt, M. (2018). 'The Huthi Enigma: Ansar Allah and the Second Republic'. In M.-C. Heinze (ed.), *Yemen and the Search for Stability: Power, Politics and Society after the Arab Spring*, 160–83. London: I.B. Tauris.
Brown, N. J. and Hamzawi, A. (2010). *Between Religion and Politics*. New York: Carnegie Endowment for Peace.
Burke, J. (2015). *The New Threat from Islamic Militancy*. London: Bodley Head.
Burton, G. (2018). 'China, Jerusalem and the Israeli–Palestinian Conflict'. Middle East Institute, 20 February.
Byman, D. and Shapiro, J. (2014). 'Homeward Bound? Don't Hype the Threat of Returning Jihadists'. *Foreign Affairs*.
Byman, D. and Williams, J. (2015). *ISIS vs. Al Qaeda: Jihadism's Global Civil War*. Brookings Institution. http://www.brookings.edu/research/articles/2015/02/24-byman-williams-isis-war-with-al-qaeda.
Calvert, J. (2010). *Sayyid Qutb and the Origins of Radical Islamism*. London: Hurst.
Carapico, S. (1998). *Civil Society in Yemen*. Cambridge: Cambridge University Press.
Caroline, V. and Dauda, A. (eds) (2017). *Violent Non-State Actors in Africa*. London: Palgrave Macmillan.
Casier, M. and Grojean, O. (2013). 'Between integration, autonomization and radicalization: Hamit Bozarslan on the Kurdish Movement and the Turkish Left'. Interview, *European Journal of Turkish Studies* (Internet edition) 14.
Cemil Paşa, K. (1991). *Doza Kurdistan. Kürt Milletinin 60 Yıllık Esaretten Kurtuluş Savaşı Hatıraları*. Ankara: öz-Ge.
Chalabi, T. (2006). *The Shi'is of Jabal 'Amil and the New Lebanon: Community and Nation State, 1918–1943*. London: Palgrave Macmillan.

Chalcraft, J. (2016). *Popular Politics in the Making of the Modern Middle East*. Cambridge: Cambridge University Press.

Chalk, P. (2008). *The Maritime Dimension of International Security: Terrorism, Piracy, and Challenges for the United States*, Vol. 697. Santa Barbara, CA: RAND Corporation.

Chalk, P. (2010). 'Piracy off the Horn of Africa: scope, dimensions, causes and responses'. *Brown Journal of World Affairs* 16, no. 2: 89–108.

Chaudhry, R (2013). 'Violent non-state actors: contours, challenges and consequences'. http://www.claws.in/images/journals_doc/2140418965_RajeevChaudhry.pdf.

Chweya, E. (2016). 'KDF fought for 10 hours with Al Shabaab but lost due to organized ambush'. Tuko. https://tuko.co.ke/86561-how-al-shabaab-used-3-deadly-waves-of-attack-to-overrun-the-kdf-camp-in-somalia.html.

Clarke, The Moderate Face of Al-QaedC. P. (2017). 'a: How the Group Has Rebranded Itself'. *Foreign Affairs*. https://www.foreignaffairs.com/articles/syria/2017-10-24/moderate-face-al-qaeda.

Clinton, H. R. (2014). *Hard Choices*. New York: Simon & Schuster.

Cobban, H. (1984). *The Making of Modern Lebanon*. Boulder, CO: Westview.

Cobban, H., (1984). *The Palestinian Liberation Organization: People, Power, and Politics*. Cambridge: Cambridge University Press.

Cockburn, P. (2014). *The Rise of Islamic State: ISIS and the New Sunni Revolution*. London and New York: Verso.

Coll, S. (2004). *Ghost Wars: The Secret History of the CIA, Afghanistan, and Bin Laden, from the Soviet Invasion to September 10, 2001*. London: Penguin.

Comerford, M. (2015). *Jabhat al-Nusra: Moves Towards the Mainstream?* Tony Blair Faith Foundation. http://tonyblairfaithfoundation.org/religion-geopolitics/commentaries/opinion/jabhat-al-nusra-moves-towards-mainstream.

Commins, D. (2006). *The Wahhabi Mission in Saudi Arabia*. London: I.B. Tauris.

Conflicts Forum (2007). 'A Conflicts Forum Chronology: The Failure of the Palestinian National Unity Government and the Gaza Takeover'. Beirut–London–Washington, December 2005 to July 2007.

Conflicts Forum (2007). 'Elliot Abrams' Uncivil War'. 7 January.

Corbin, J. (1994). *Gaza First: The Secret Norway Channel to Peace between Israel and the PLO*. London: Bloomsbury.

Crooke, A. (2007). 'Our Second Biggest Mistake in the Middle East'. *London Review of Books* 29, no. 13 (5 July): 3–6.

Crooke, A. (2009). *Resistance: The Essence of the Islamist Revolution*. London: Pluto Press.

Dahlgren, S. (2018). 'Yemen: A Coup in the Making or a Return to Normalcy?' *Middle East Insights* 77 (February).

Dawisha, A. (2013). *The Second Arab Awakening: Revolution, Democracy, and the Islamist Challenge from Tunis to Damascus*. New York: Norton.

Dazugan, J.-F. and Valter, S. (eds). *Les Forces Armées Arabes et Moyen-Orientales*. Paris: ESKA.

Do, Q. T. (2013). *The Pirates of Somalia: Ending the Threat, Rebuilding a Nation*. Washington, DC: World Bank.

Dodge, T. (2003). *Inventing Iraq: The Failure of Nation Building and a History Denied*. New York: Columbia University Press.

Dresch, P. (1989). *Tribes, Government and History in Yemen*. Oxford: Clarendon Press.

Durac, V. (2015). 'The Role of Non-State Actors in Arab Countries after the Arab Uprisings'. *IEMed Mediterranean Yearbook 2015*, 35–41. Barcelona: Instituto Europeo del Mediterráno.

Eagleton, W. (1946). *The Kurdish Republic of Mahabad*. Oxford: Oxford University Press.

Economist (2013). 'Will the jihadists overreach?' *Economist*. http://www.economist.com/news/middle-east-and-africa/21587845-extremist-group-ruffling-feathers-including-those-its-islamist.

El-Affendi, A. (2014). *Turabi's Revolution: Islam and Power in Sudan*. London: Grey Seal.

Elmi, A. A. (2010). *Understanding the Somalia Conflagration: Identity, Political Islam and Peacebuilding*. London: Pluto Press.

Elmi, A. A. and Aynte, A. (2012), 'Somalia: The Case for Negotiating with Al-Shabaab'. *Al-Jazeera Centre for Studies* 16.

Elmi, A. A., Affi, L., Knight, W. A. and Mohamed, S. (2015). 'Piracy in the Horn of Africa Waters: Definitions, History, and Modern Causes'. *African Security* 8, no. 3: 147–65.

Entous, Adam (2007). 'Framers of Palestinian constitution challenge Abbas'. Reuters, 8 July.

Esposito, J. (2002). *Unholy War: Terror in the Name of Islam*. New York and Oxford: Oxford University Press.

Esposito, J. and Armstrong, K. (2013). *The Future of Islam*. Oxford: Oxford University Press.

Esposito, J. and Mogahed, D. (2007). *Who Speaks for Islam? What a Billion Muslims Really Think*. New York: Gallup Press.

Euben, R. L. and Muhammad, Q. Z. (2009). *Princeton Readings in Islamist Thought: Texts and Contexts from al-Banna to Bin Laden*. Princeton, NJ: Princeton University Press.

Fanon, F. (2006). *Pour la révolution africaine. Ecrits politiques*. Paris: La Découverte.

Filiu, J. P. (2015). *From Deep State to Islamic State: The Arab Counter-Revolution and its Jihadi Legacy*. Oxford: Oxford University Press.

Fraihat, I. (2016). *Unfinished Revolutions: Yemen, Libya and Tunisia after the Arab Spring*. New Haven, CT: Yale University Press.

Franzén, J. (2011). *Red Star over Iraq: The Iraqi Communist Party and the Evolution of Ideological Politics in pre-Saddam Iraq*. London: Hurst.

Fuller, G. E. (2003). *The Future of Political Islam*. New York: Palgrave Macmillan.

Galtung, J. (1969). 'Violence, Peace, and Peace Research'. *Journal of Peace Research* 6, no. 3: 167–91.

Gartenstein-Ross, D. and Jawad al-Tamimi, A. (2015). 'Druze Clues'. *Foreign Affairs*. https://www.foreignaffairs.com/articles/syria/2015-10-05/druze-clues.

Gause, G. F. (1990). *Saudi–Yemeni Relations: Domestic Struggles and Foreign Influence*. New York: Columbia University Press.

Geertz, C. (1964). 'Ideology as a Cultural System'. In D. Apter (ed.), *Ideology and Discontent*, 65. New York: Free Press.

Gelvin, J. (2016). *The Modern Middle East: A History*. New York: Oxford University Press.

Gerges, F. A. (2005). *The Far Enemy: Why Jihad Went Global*. New York: Cambridge University Press.

Gerges, F. A. (2006). *Journey of the Jihadist: Inside Muslim Militancy*. Orlando, FL: Harcourt.

Gerges, F. A. (2014). *The Rise and Fall of Al-Qaeda*. Oxford: Oxford University Press.

Gerson, A. (1991). *The Kirkpatrick Mission: Diplomacy without Apology, America at the United Nations 1981–1985*. New York: Free Press.

Gettleman, J. (2006). 'Islamists calm Somali capital with restraint'. *New York Times*, 24 September. http://www.nytimes.com/2006/09/24/world/africa/24somalia.html?pagewanted =2&n=Top/Reference/Times%20Topics/Subjects/R/Religion%20 and%20Belief&_r=1.

Gettleman, J. (2008). 'Somalia's Pirates Flourish in a Lawless Nation'. *New York Times*, 30 October. http://www.nytimes.com/2008/10/31/world/africa/31pirates.html?_r=0.

Gettleman, J. (2011). 'Misery follows as Somalis try to flee hunger'. *New York Times*, 15 July. http://www.nytimes.com/2011/07/16/world/africa/16somalia.html?_r=0.

Ghasemlou, A. (1965). *Kurdistan and the Kurds*. Prague: Czechoslovak Academy of Sciences.

Giambrone, J. (2015). *Why ISIS Exists: The Double Game*. International Policy Digest. http://www.internationalpolicydigest.org/2015/11/29/why-isis-exists-the-double-game/.

Giddens, A. (1987). *The Nation-State and Violence*. Berkeley and Los Angeles: University of California Press.

Glaser, E. (1993). *My Journey through Arḥab and Ḥāshid*. Translation of 'Meine Reise durch Arḥab und Ḥāschid' from *Petermanns Mitteilungen* 30: 170–83, 204–13 (1884). Sanaa: American Institute for Yemeni Studies.

Glaser, S., Roberts, P., Mazurek, R., Hurlburt, K. and Kane-Hartnett, L. (2015). 'Securing Somali fisheries report'. http://securefisheries.org/report/securing-somali-fisheries.

GlobalSecurity.org (2011). 'Vehicle borne IEDs (VBIEDs)'. http://www.globalsecurity.org/military/intro/ied-vehicle.htm.

Goldberg, J. (2013). 'The Modern King in the Arab Spring'. *The Atlantic*, April.

Goldberg, M. (2013). 'The Myth of the Gaza Withdrawal'. *The Times of Israel*, 7 February.

Goldenberg, S. (2000). 'Rioting as Sharon visits Islam holy site'. *Guardian*, 29 September.

Gorgas, J. T. (2007). 'La Ligue nationale kurde Khoybun: Mythes et réalités de la première organisation nationaliste kurde'. *Etudes Kurdes*, special edition.

Grandin, G. (2005). 'The Instruction of Great Catastrophe: Truth Commissions, National History and State Formation in Argentina, Chile and Guatemala'. *American Historical Review* 110, no. 1 (February): 46–67.

Greene, T. (2014). *Blair, Labour and Palestine: Conflicting Views on Middle East Peace After 9/11*. London: Bloomsbury.

Greenwald, G. (2016). 'Nobody knows the identities of the 150 people killed by U.S. in Somalia, but most are certain they deserved it'. *The Intercept.* https://theintercept.com/2016/03/08/nobody-knows-the-identity-of-the-150-people-killed-by-u-s-in-somalia-but-most-are-certain-they-deserved-it/.

Groll, E. (2015). *Jabhat al-Nusra Abandons Fight North of Aleppo as Turkey and U.S. Plot 'Safe Zone'.* Foreign Policy. http://foreignpolicy.com/2015/08/10/jabhat-al-nusra-abandons-fight-north-of-aleppo-as-turkey-and-u-s-plot-safe-zone/.

Halevy, E. (2006). *Man in the Shadows: Inside the Middle East Crisis with the Man Who Led the Mossad.* London: St Martin's Press.

Hamid, S. (2014). *Temptations of Power: Islamist and Liberal Democracy in a New Middle East.* Oxford: Oxford University Press.

Hamze, A. N. (2004). *In the Path of Hizbullah.* Syracuse, NY: Syracuse University Press.

Hansen, S. J. (2008). 'Private security and local politics in Somalia'. *Review of African Political Economy* 35, no. 118: 585–98.

Hansen, S. J. (2011). 'Debunking the Piracy Myth: How Illegal Fishing Really Interacts with Piracy in East Africa'. *RUSI Journal* 156, no. 6: 26–31.

Hansen, S. J. (2012). 'International interventions, state-building and democratization: justifying the role of the private security companies in Somalia?' *African Security* 5, nos 3–4: 255–66.

Hansen, S. J. (2013) *Al Shabab in Somalia: The History and Ideology of a Militant Islamist Group.* New York: Oxford University Press.

Harris, W. (2012). *Lebanon: A History, 600–2011.* Oxford: Oxford University Press.

Hassan, M. (2012). 'Understanding Drivers of Violent Extremism: The Case of al-Shabab and Somali Youth'. *CTC Sentinel* 5, no. 8: 18–20.

Hatina, M. (2001). *Islam and Salvation in Palestine: The Islamic Jihad Movement.* Tel Aviv: Tel Aviv University Press.

Haugbølle, S. (2010). *War and Memory in Lebanon.* Cambridge: Cambridge University Press.

Haykel, B. (2002). 'The Salafis in Yemen at a Crossroads: An Obituary of Shaykh Muqbil al-Wadi'i of Dammaj (d. 1422/2001)'. *Jemen Report* (October): 28–31.

Haykel, B. (2003). *Revival and Reform in Islam: The Legacy of Muhammad al-Shawkani.* Cambridge: Cambridge University Press.

Hegghammer, T. and Wagemakers, J. (2013). 'The Palestine Effect: The Role of Palestinians in the Transnational Jihad Movement'. *Die Welt des Islams* 53: 281–314.

Heikal, M. (1996). *Secret Channels: The Inside Story of Arab–Israeli Peace Negotiations.* London: HarperCollins.

Heinze, M. C. (2011). *Salafism in Yemen: Transnationalism and Religious Identity.* London: Hurst.

Heinze, M. C. (2017). *Tribes and Politics in Yemen: A History of the Houthi Conflict.* London: Hurst.

Heinze, M. C. (ed.) (2018). *Yemen and the Search for Stability: Power, Politics and Society after the Arab Spring.* London: I.B. Tauris.

Hersh, S. M. (2014). 'The Red Line and the Rat Line'. *London Review of Books* 36, no. 8: 21–4. http://www.lrb.co.uk/v36/n08/seymour-m-hersh/the-red-line-and-the-rat-line.

Hill, G. (2017). *Yemen Endures: Civil War, Saudi Adventurism and the Future of Arabia*. Oxford: Oxford University Press.

Hironaka, A. (2005). *Never-ending Wars: The International Community, Weak States and the Perpetuation of Civil War*. Cambridge, MA: Harvard University Press.

Hoehne, M. V. (2009). 'Counter-terrorism in Somalia: how external interference helped to produce militant Islamism'. *Social Science Research Council: Crisis in the Horn of Africa*. https://www.researchgate.net/profile/Markus_Hoehne/publication/ 267711489_Counter-terrorism_in_Somalia_How_External_Interference_Helped_ to_Produce_Militant_Islamism/links/5509e0ba0cf26198a639d03f/Counter-terrorism-in-Somalia-How-External-Interference-Helped-to-Produce-Militant-Islamism.pdf.

Holsti, K. J. and Holsti, K. J. (1996). *The State, War, and the State of War*. Cambridge: Cambridge University Press.

Homeland Security Research (n.d.). 'Standoff IED, Person-Borne and Vehicle-Borne Explosives and Weapon Detection: Technologies and Global Market – 2015–2020. (2015)'. http://homelandsecurityresearch.com/2015/06/Standoff-IED-Person-Borne-and-Vehicle-Borne-Explosives-and-Weapon-Detection-Technologies-and-Global-Market-2015-2020.

Hroub, K. (2002). *Hamas: Political Thought and Practice*. Washington, DC: Institute for Palestine Studies.

Hroub, K. (2010). *Political Islam: Context versus Ideology*. London: Hurst.

Hubbard, B. (2015). 'Nusra Front Announces Withdrawal From Front Line Against ISIS in Syria'. *New York Times*. http://www.nytimes.com/2015/08/11/world/middleeast/ nusra-front-announces-withdrawal-from-front-line-against-isis-in-syria. html?ref=world&_r=0.

Hudaybi, H. (1987). *Du'ah la Qudah* (Preachers Not Judges). Cairo: Dar al-Nashr w'al- Tawzi'.

Hudson, M. (1969). *The Precarious Republic; Political Modernization in Lebanon*. New York: Random House.

Human Rights Council (2018). *Situation of Human Rights in Yemen, including Violations and Abuses since September 2014*. United Nations High Commissioner for Human Rights, United Nations (August).

Human Rights Watch (2018). *Yemen: Houthi Hostage-Taking*. Human Rights Watch (25 September). https://www.hrw.org/news/2018/09/25/yemen-houthi-hostage-taking.

Huntington, S. (1968). *Political Order in Changing Societies*. New Haven, CT: Yale University Press.

Hussein, M., Schmitt, E. and Ibrahim, M. (2017). 'Mogadishu Truck Bombings Are Deadliest Attack in Decades'. *New York Times*, 15 October. https://www.nytimes. com/2017/10/15/world/africa/somalia-bombing-mogadishu.html

Ibrahim, M. (2010). 'Somalia and global terrorism: A growing connection?' *Journal of Contemporary African Studies* 28, no. 3: 283–95.

Ibrahim, Y. M. (1992). 'Official of P.L.O. is killed in Paris'. *New York Times*, 9 June.

'International Crisis Group, Palestinians, Israel and the Quartet: Pulling Back from the Brink' (2006). *Middle East Report* 54 (13 June).

IRIN. (2009) 'Attack on graduation ceremony the "last straw"'. http://www.irinnews.org/report/87387/somalia-attack-graduation-ceremony-.

Ismael, T. Y. (2008). *The Rise and Fall of the Communist Party of Iraq*. Cambridge: Cambridge University Press.

Jane's Terrorism and Security Monitor (2008). 'Unholy high seas alliance'. (31 October).

Jenkins, B. (2014). *The Dynamics of Syria's Civil War*. Perspective Expert insights on a timely policy issue. Santa Monica, CA: RAND Corporation.

Johnsen, G. D. (2012). *The Last Refuge: Yemen, Al-Qaeda, and America's War in Arabia*. New York: W. W. Norton.

Johnston, A. (2007). 'My kidnap ordeal'. BBC News online, 15 October.

Jongerden, J. and Velheij, J. (eds) (2012). *Social Relations in Ottoman Diyarbékir, 1870–1915*. Leiden and Boston: Brill.

Joscelyn, T. (2015). *Analysis: Al Nusrah Front 'committed' to Ayman al Zawahiri's 'orders'*. The Long War Journal. http://www.longwarjournal.org/archives/2015/05/analysis-al-nusrah-front-committed-to-ayman-al-zawahiris-orders.php.

Juneau, T. (2016). 'Iran's Policy towards the Houthis in Yemen: A Limited Return on a Modest Investment'. *International Affairs* 92, no. 3: 647–63.

Jwadieh, W. (1960). *The Kurdish Nationalist Movement: Its Origins and Development*. Syracuse, NY: Syracuse University Press.

Kampfner, J. (2003). *Blair's Wars*. London: Free Press.

Kamrava, M. (2011). 'Mediation and Qatari Foreign Policy'. *Middle East Journal* 65, no. 4): 539–56.

Kattan, V. (2009). *From Coexistence to Conquest: International Law and the Origins of the Arab–Israeli Conflict 1891–1949*. London: Pluto Press.

KDP (1977). *The Road of the Kurdish Liberation Movement*. London: Calvert North Star Press.

KDP (1978). *Irak Kürdistan Demokratik Partisi Yeni Stratejisi*. İstanbul: Üçüncü Dünya Yayınları.

Khatab, S. (2009). *The Power of Sovereignty: The Political and Ideological Philosophy of Sayyid Qutb*. London: Routledge.

Khatib, L., Matar, D. and Alshaer, A. (2014). *The Hizbullah Phenomenon: Politics and Communication*. New York: Oxford University Press.

Khoybun (1927). *Les massacres kurdes en Turquie*. Cairo: Khoybun.

Kirkpatrick, J. J. (1981). 'US Security & Latin America'. *Commentary* 72 (1 January): 29.

Klein, N. (2004). 'Baghdad Year Zero: Pillaging Iraq in Pursuit of Neocon Utopia'. *Harper's Magazine*, September.

Koehler-Derrick, G. (2011). *A False Foundation: AQAP, Tribes, and Ungoverned Spaces in Yemen*. West Point, NY: Combating Terrorism Center.

Komal Yayınları, *DDKO Dâvâ Dosyası* (1975). Vol. 1. Ankara: Komal Yayınları.

Lackner, H. (2017). *Yemen in Crisis: Autocracy, Neo-liberalism and the Disintegration of a State*. London: Saqi Books.

Lackner, H. (ed.) (2014). *Why Yemen Matters*. London: Saqi Books.

Lackner, H. and Varisco, D. M. (eds) (2017). *Yemen and the Gulf States: The Making of a Crisis*. Berlin: Gerlach.

Lacroix, S. (2012). 'Osama bin Laden and the Saudi Muslim Brotherhood'. Foreign Policy, 3 October. http://foreignpolicy.com/2012/10/03/osama-bin-laden-and-the-saudi-muslim-brotherhood/.

Lebanese Center for Policy Studies (2015). http://www.lcps-lebanon.org/featured Article.php?id=48 (August); http://www.lcps-lebanon.org/featuredArticle.php?id=50 (September).

Leca, J. (1991). 'Nationalisme et universalisme'. *Pouvoirs* 57: 31–42.

Lefèvre, R. (2013). *Ashes of Hamah: The Muslim Brotherhood in Syria*. Oxford: Oxford University Press.

Lesch, D. (2012). *The Fall of the House of Assad*. New Haven, CT: Yale University Press.

Li, D. (2006). 'The Gaza Strip as a Laboratory: Notes in the Wake of Disengagement'. *Journal of Palestine Studies* 35, no. 2 (Winter): 38–55.

Linke, A. and Raleigh, C. (2011). 'State and stateless violence in Somalia'. *African Geographical Review* 30, no. 1: 47–66.

Linke, A. M. (2008). 'The localized political geographies of Somalia's landscapes of violence'. MA thesis, University of Colorado at Boulder.

Lister, C. (2014a). 'Profiling the Islamic State'. *Brookings Doha Center Analysis Paper* 13: 17.

Lister, C. (2014b). *The Anti-Jihadist Revolt in Syria*. Brookings Institution. http://www.brookings.edu/research/opinions/2014/01/19-anti-jihadist-revolt-syria-lister.

Lister, C. (2014c). *The 'Real' Jabhat al-Nusra Appears to Be Emerging*. Huffington Post. http://www.huffingtonpost.com/charles-lister/the-real-jabhat-al-nusra_b_5658039.html.

Lister, C. (2014d). *An Internal Struggle: Al Qaeda's Syrian Affiliate Is Grappling With Its Identity*. Huffington Post. http://www.huffingtonpost.com/charles-lister/an-internal-struggle-al-q_b_7479730.html.

Lister, C. (2015). 'Profiling Jabhat al-Nusra'. *Brookings Doha Center Analysis Paper* 24: 6.

Lister, C. (2016). *The Syrian Jihad: Al-Qaeda, the Islamic State and the Evolution of an Insurgency*. New York: Oxford University Press.

Lister, C. (2017). *Al-Qaeda's Turning Against its Syrian Affiliate*. Middle East Institute. http://www.mei.edu/content/article/al-qaeda-s-turning-against-its-syrian-affiliate.

Liwang, H., Ringsberg, J. W. and Norsell, M. (2013). 'Quantitative risk analysis–ship security analysis for effective risk control options'. *Safety Science* 58: 98–112.

Longley Alley, A. (2010). 'The Rules of the Game: Unpacking Patronage Politics in Yemen'. *Middle East Journal* 64, no. 3: 385–409.

Lynch, M. (2016). 'Is the Muslim Brotherhood a Terrorist Organization or a Firewall against Violent Extremism?' *Washington Post*, 7 March.

Maktabi, R. (1999). 'The Lebanese Census of 1932 Revisited. Who Are the Lebanese?' *British Journal of Middle Eastern Studies* 26, no. 2: 219–41.

Maltzahn, N. (2013). *The Syria–Iran Axis: Cultural Diplomacy and International Relations in the Middle East*. London: I.B. Tauris.

Margariti, R. (2008). *Aden and the Indian Ocean Trade: 150 Years in the Life of a Medieval Arabian Port*. Durham: University of North Carolina Press.

Martinez-Gros, G. (2006). *Ibn Khaldûn et les sept vies de l'Islam*. Arles: Actes-Sud.

Masoud, T. (2014). *Counting Islam: Religion, Class, and Elections in Egypt*. Cambridge: Cambridge University Press.

Matthiesen, T. (2013). *Sectarian Gulf: Bahrain, Saudi Arabia and the Arab Spring that Wasn't*. Stanford, CA: Stanford University Press.

Mbekeani, K. K. and Ncube, M. (2011). 'Economic Impact of Maritime Piracy'. *Africa Economic Brief* 2, no. 10: 1–8.

McGeough, P. (2009). *Kill Khalid: The Failed Mossad Assassination of Khalid Mishal and the Rise of Hamas*. New York: New Press.

McKnight, T. and Hirsh, M. (2012). *Pirate Alley: Commanding Task Force 151 off Somalia*. Annapolis, MD: Naval Institute Press.

Mearsheimer, J. and Walt, S. (2008). *The Israel Lobby and US Foreign Policy*. London: Penguin.

MEMO (2015). *Former US Ambassador to Syria: Syrian Regime in a Defensive Position*. Middle East Monitor – The Latest from the Middle East. https://www.middleeastmonitor.com/news/americas/18456-former-us-ambassador-to-syria-syrian-regime-in-a-defensive-position.

MEMO (2015). *HRW Accuses Syrian Opposition of Recruiting Children Under Guise of Education*. Middle East Monitor – The Latest from the Middle East. https://www.middleeastmonitor.com/blogs/lifestyle/12315-hrw-accuses-syrian-opposition-of-recruiting-children-under-guise-of-education.

MEMO (2015). *UN chief Accuses Syrian Regime and Six Armed Groups of Sexual Violence*. Middle East Monitor – The Latest from the Middle East. https://www.middleeastmonitor.com/news/americas/18085-un-chief-accuses-syrian-regime-and-six-armed-groups-of-sexual-violence.

Menkhaus, K. (2003). 'State collapse in Somalia: Second thoughts'. *Review of African Political Economy* 30, no. 97: 405–22.

Menkhaus, K. (2007). 'Governance without government in Somalia: spoilers, state building, and the politics of coping'. *International Security* 31, no. 3: 74–106.

Menkhaus, K. (2010). 'Non-state actors and the role of violence in stateless Somalia'. In K. Mulaj (ed.), *Violent Non-State Actors in World Politics*, 343–80. New York: Columbia University Press.

Menkhaus, K. (2014). 'Calm between the storms? Patterns of political violence in Somalia, 1950–1980'. *Journal of Eastern African Studies* 8, no. 4: 558–72.

Méouchy, N. and Sluglett, P. (eds) (2004). *The British and French Mandates in Comparative Perspectives/Les mandats français et anglais dans une perspective comparative.* Leiden: Brill.

Mervin, S. (ed.). *The Shi'a Worlds and Iran.* London: Saqi Books.

Middleton, R. (2008). *Piracy in Somalia: Threatening Global Trade, Feeding Local Wars.* London: Chatham House (Royal Institute of International Affairs).

Migdal, J. S. (1988). *Strong Societies and Weak States: State–Society Relations and State Capabilities in the Third World.* Princeton, NJ: Princeton University Press.

Miller, A. D. (2014). 'Middle East Meltdown'. *Foreign Policy*, 30 October. http://foreignpolicy.com/2014/10/30/middle-east-meltdown/.

Milton-Edwards, B. and Farrell, S. (2010). *Hamas: The Islamic Resistance Movement.* Cambridge: Polity Press.

Minassian, T. T. (1997). *Colporteurs du Komintern: l'Union soviétique et les minorités au Moyen-Orient.* Paris: Sciences-Po.

Mishal, S. and Sela, A. (2006). *The Palestinian Hamas: Violence, Vision, and Coexistence.* New York: Columbia University Press.

Mitchell, R. P. (1969). *The Society of the Muslim Brothers.* London: Oxford University Press.

Mohamed, A. (2008). *The Many Faces of Political Islam: Religion and Politics in the Muslim World.* Ann Arbor: University of Michigan Press.

Moynihan, D. P. (1981). 'Joining the Jackals: The US at the UN 1977–1980'. *Commentary* 72 (1 February): 23.

Mugisha, N. (2011), 'The way forward in Somalia'. *Journal of the Royal United Services Institution* 156, no. 3: 26–33.

Mulaj, K. (2010), 'Violent non-state actors: exploring their state relations, legitimation, and operationality'. In K. Mulaj (ed.), *Violent Non-State Actors in World Politics*, 1–26. New York: Columbia University Press.

Mulaj, K. (ed.) (2010). *Violent Non-State Actors in World Politics.* London: Hurst.

Murphy, M. N. (2010). 'Dire straits: taking on Somali pirates'. *World Affairs* (July–August): 90–7.

Mwangura, A. (n.d.). 'African sea pirates'. European Community on Protection (ECOP).

Mwatana (2017). *The Woes of Arabia Felix: The Human Rights Situation in Yemen in 2017.* Mwatana for Human Rights, Yemen. http://mwatana.org/en/woes-of-arabia-felix-report/.

Nakhleh, E. (2009). *A Necessary Engagement: Reinventing America's Relations with the Muslim World.* Princeton, NJ: Princeton University Press.

Nass al-risala al-maftuha allati wajahaha Hizballah ila' l-mustad'afin fi Lubnan w'al-'Alam (n.d.).

Naylor, R. T. (1993). 'The insurgent economy: black market operations of guerrilla organisations'. *Crime, Law and Social Change* 20: 13–51.

Neep, D. (2012). *Occupying Syria under the French Mandate: Insurgency, Space and State Formation.* Cambridge: Cambridge University Press.

Netanyahu, B. (ed.) (1986). *Terrorism: How the West Can Win*. New York: Farrar, Straus, & Giroux and the Jonathan Institute.

Nolan, J. L. Jr (2016). *What They Saw in America: Alexis de Tocqueville, Max Weber, G. K. Chesterton, and Sayyid Qutb*. Cambridge: Cambridge University Press.

Norton, A. R. (2007). *Hizbullah: A Short History*. Princeton, NJ: Princeton University Press.

Nossiter, A. (2016). '"That Ignoramus": 2 French Scholars of Radical Islam Turn Bitter Rivals'. *New York Times*, 12 July. https://www.nytimes.com/2016/07/13/world/europe/france-radical-islam.html.

Ohikere, O. (2016). 'Kenya attack al-Shabaab from the air, high-level terrorist reported dead'. World: Real Matters. https://world.wng.org/2016/02/kenya_attacks_al_shabaab_from_the_air_high_level_terrorist_reported_dead.

Olson, R. (1989). *The Emergence of Kurdish Nationalism and the Sheikh Said Rebellion (1880–1925)*. Austin: University of Texas Press.

Onuoha, F. (2009). 'Sea piracy and maritime security in the Horn of Africa: the Somali coast and Gulf of Aden in perspective'. *African Security Studies* 18, no. 3: 31–44.

Owen, R. (2010). *State, Power and Politics in the Making of the Modern Middle East*. London and New York: Routledge.

Pall, Z. (2018). *Salafism in Lebanon: Local and Transnational Movements*. Cambridge: Cambridge University Press.

Pargeter, A. (2010). *The Muslim Brotherhood: From Opposition to Power*. London: Saqi Books.

Pearlman, W. and Cunningham, K. G. (2012). 'Nonstate Actors, Fragmentation, and Conflict Processes'. *Journal of Conflict Resolution* 56, no. 1: 3–15.

Peleikis, A. (2006). 'The Making and Unmaking of Memories: the Case of a Multi-Confessional Village in Lebanon'. in U. Makdisi and P. A. Silverstein (eds), *Memory and Violence in the Middle East and North Africa*, 133–50. Bloomington and Indianapolis: Indiana University Press.

Peres, S. (1995). *Battling for Peace: Memoirs*. Edited by David Landau. London: Orion Books.

Pew Research Center (2015). 'In nations with significant Muslim populations, much disdain for ISIS'. 17 November. http://www.pewresearch.org/fact-tank/2015/11/17/in-nations-with-significant-muslim-populations-much-disdain-for-isis/.

Pham, P. (2008) 'The challenge of Somali piracy'. Foundation for the Defense of Democracies. http://www.defenddemocracy.org/media-hit/the-challenge-of-somali-piracy/.

Picard, E. (2000). 'The Political Economy of Civil War in Lebanon'. In S. Heydemann (ed.), *War, Institutions and Social Change in the Middle East*, 292–322. Berkeley and Los Angeles: University of California Press.

Picard, E. (2016). *Liban Syrie, intimes étrangers: Un siècle d'interactions politiques*. Paris: Sindbad.

Pierret, T. (2013). *Religion and State in Syria: The Sunni 'Ulama from Coup to Revolution*. Cambridge: Cambridge University Press.

Potgieter, T. and Schofield, C. (2010). 'Poverty, poaching and pirates: geopolitical instability and maritime insecurity off the Horn of Africa'. *Journal of the Indian Ocean Region* 6, no. 1: 86–112.

Provence, M. (2017). *The Last Ottoman Generation and the Making of the Modern Middle East*. Oxford: Oxford University Press.

Qaradawi, Y. (2001). 'Our society is unlike Mecca *jahili* society'. Qaradawi website, 8 July. http://www.qaradawi.net/new/Articles-2564.

Qaradawi, Y. (2009). 'Qutb's ideas do not belong to the Muslim Brotherhood and they break away from ahla al-Sunna'. archive.today, 8 August. http://archive.is/zy9ZY.

Qutb, S. (1948). *al-'Adala al-Ijtima'iyya fi'l-Islam* (Social Justice in Islam). Cairo: n.p.

Qutb, S. (1950). *Amirica Allati Ra'ait* (America That I Saw). Cairo: n.p.

Qutb, S. (1979). *Ma'alim fi'l-Tariq* (Milestones). Cairo: Dar al-Shuruq.

Qutb, S. (2003). *Fi Dhilal al-Quran* (In the Shades of the Quran), vol. 4. Cairo: Dar al-Shuruq.

Reno, W. S. (2010). *Persistent Insurgencies and Warlords: Who Is Nasty, Who Is Nice, and Why*. Stanford University Press: 57-94. Stanford, CA.

Reuters (2015). 'Sri Lanka plans South Africa-style commission to confront war crimes'. 14 September. http://uk.reuters.com/article/2015/09/14/uk-sri-lanka-warcrimes-un-idUKKCN0RE0RV20150914.

Reuters (2015). *Syria's Al Qaeda Branch Kills Druze Villagers*. Huffington Post. http://www.huffingtonpost.com/2015/06/11/nusra-front-kill-druze_n_7560272.html.

Reuters (2015). 'Syria's Nusra Front leader urges wider attacks on Assad's Alawite areas to avenge Russian bombing'. *Daily Telegraph*. http://www.telegraph.co.uk/news/worldnews/islamic-state/11927760/Syrias-Nusra-Front-leader-urges-wider-attacks-on-Assads-Alawite-areas-to-avenge-Russian-bombing.html.

Rice, C. (2011). *No Higher Honor: A Memoir of My Years in Washington*. New York: Crown Publishers.

Riedel, B. (2013). *Al Nusra: Al Qaeda's Syria Offensive*. Daily Beast. http://www.thedailybeast.com/articles/2013/02/23/al-nusra-al-qaeda-s-syria-offensive.html.

Rodinson, M. (1972). *Marxisme et le monde musulman*. Paris: Seuil.

Rose, D. (2008). 'The Gaza Bombshell'. *Vanity Fair* online, 31 March.

Ross, S. and Ben-David, J. (2009). 'Somali piracy: an escalating security dilemma'. *Harvard Africa Policy* 5: 55–70.

Rougier, B. (2009). *Everyday Jihad: The Rise of Militant Islam among the Palestinians in Lebanon*. Cambridge, MA: Harvard University Press.

Roy, O. (2007). 'L'impact de la révolution iranienne au moyen orient'. In S. Mervin, *Les mondes chiites et l'Iran*. Paris, Karthala.

Salad, O. (2008). 'Somalia: balance sheet of one-year Ethiopian occupation – mass genocide, destruction, displacement, and starvation'. http://somalitalk.com/2008/feb/ethipia_occupation.pdf.

Salibi, K. (1998). *A House of Many Mansions: The History of Lebanon Reconsidered*. London: I.B. Tauris.

Salisbury, P. (2016). *Yemen: Stemming the Rise of a Chaos State*. London: Chatham House.
Samatar, A. I. (2007). 'Ethiopian invasion of Somalia, US warlordism and AU shame'. *Review of African Political Economy* 34, no. 111: 155–65.
Salmoni, B. A., Loidolt, B. and Wells, M. (2010). *Regime and Periphery in Northern Yemen: The Huthi Phenomenon*. Santa Monica, CA: RAND Corporation.
Sassoon, J. (2016). *Anatomy of Authoritarianism in the Arab Republics*. Cambridge: Cambridge University Press.
Satloff, R. (2015). 'Beyond the Oval Office: Filling in the Blanks of U.S. Strategy Against the Islamic State'. *Washington Institute for Near East Policy*, 11 December.
Schlumberger, O. (ed.) (2007). *Debating Arab Authoritarianism: Dynamics and Durability in Nondemocratic Regimes*. Stanford, CA: Stanford University Press.
Schmid, A. P. (2014). *Violent and Non-violent Extremism: Two Sides of the Same Coin*. The Hague: International Center for Counterterrorism (ICCT) Research Paper.
Seale, P. (1988). *Assad of Syria: The Struggle for the Middle East*. London: I.B. Tauris.
Sengupta, K. (2015). 'Turkey and Saudi Arabia shock Western countries by supporting anti-Assad jihadists in Syria'. *Independent*. http://www.independent.co.uk/news/world/middle-east/syria-crisis-turkey-and-saudi-arabia-shock-western-countries-by-supporting-anti-assad-jihadists-10242747.html.
Serdî, H. H. (1985). *Görüş ve Anılarım, 1907–1985*. Istanbul: Med Yayınları.
Sergi, B. S. and Morabito, G. (2016). 'The Pirates' Curse: Economic Impacts of Maritime Piracy'. *Studies in Conflict and Terrorism* 39, no. 10: 1–18.
Shadi, S. (1987). *Safahat min al-Ta'rikh: Hasad al-'Umr* (Pages of History: A Life's Harvest). Cairo: Dar al-Nashr w'al-Tawzi' al-Islamiyya.
Sharp, J. (2015). *Yemen: Background and U.S. Relations*. Washington, DC: Congressional Research Service (February).
Sheikh, A. and Ahmed, M. (2011). 'Al Shabaab kill 70 in Mogadishu bomb'. Reuters. http://mobile.reuters.com/article/idUSTRE79317Y20111004.
Sherlock, R. (2012). 'Inside Jabhat al Nusra – the most extreme wing of Syria's struggle'. *Daily Telegraph*. http://www.telegraph.co.uk/news/worldnews/middleeast/syria/9716545/Inside-Jabhat-al-Nusra-the-most-extreme-wing-of-Syrias-struggle.html.
Shlaim, A. (2014). *The Iron Wall: Israel and the Arab World*. London: W.W. Norton & Company.
Silverstein, R. (2016). *The Enemy of my Friend is my Friend: Israel Accepts Billions from the US, but Maintains Ties with al-Nusra*. MintPress News. http://www.mintpressnews.com/israel-accepts-billions-from-the-us-but-maintains-ties-with-al-nusra/219124/.
Sluglett, P. (2014). 'Les milices chrétiennes au Liban'. In J.-F. Dazugan and S. Valter (eds), *Les Forces Armées Arabes et Moyen-Orientales*, 154–86. Paris: ESKA.
Sly, L. and DeYoung, K. (2016). 'Syria's Jabhat al-Nusra splits from al-Qaeda and changes its name'. *Washington Post*. https://www.washingtonpost.com/world/middle_east/syrias-jabhat-al-nusra-splits-from-al-qaeda-and-changes-its-name/

2016/07/28/5b89ad22-54e6-11e6-b652-315ae5d4d4dd_story.html?utm_term=.29ac3f95b7a1.

Somalia Report (2011). 'Government Calls for Clan Ceasefire'. 2 July. http://www.somaliareport.com/index.php/post/1090/Government_Calls_for_Clan_Ceasefire.

Stevenson, J. (2010). 'Jihad and piracy in Somalia'. *Survival* 52, no. 1: 27–38.

Strzelecka, E. K. (2018). 'A Political Culture of Feminist Resistance: Exploring Women's Agency and Gender Dynamics in Yemen's Uprising (2011–2015)'. In M.-C. Heinze (ed.), *Yemen and the Search for Stability: Power, Politics and Society after the Arab Spring*, 47–40. London: I.B. Tauris.

Stuster, J. (2015). *U.S.-Supported Syrian Rebels Captured by Jabhat al-Nusra*. Foreign Policy. http://foreignpolicy.com/2015/07/30/u-s-trained-syrian-rebels-captured-by-jabhat-al-nusra/.

Stuster, J. (2015). *U.S.-Trained Rebels in Syria Surrender Weapons to Terrorist Group*. Foreign Policy. http://foreignpolicy.com/2015/09/23/u-s-trained-rebels-in-syria-surrender-weapons-to-terrorist-group/.

Talhamy, Y. (2010). 'The *Fatwas* and the Nusayri/'Alawis of Syria'. *Middle Eastern Studies* 46: 175–94.

Tamimi, A. (2007). *Hamas: Unwritten Chapters*. London: Hurst.

Taspinar, O. (2009). 'Fighting Radicalism, not "Terrorism": Root Causes of an International Actor Redefined'. *SAIS Review* 29, no. 2 (summer–fall): 75–86.

Tawil, Camille (2010). 'Al-Qaeda in the Middle East, North Africa and Asia: Jihadists and Franchises'. In K. Hroub (ed.), *Political Islam: Context versus Ideology*. London: Hurst and SOAS London Middle East Institute.

Thiel, T. (2018). 'Governance in Transition: The Dynamics of Yemen's Negotiated Reform Process'. In M.-C. Heinze (ed.), *Yemen and the Search for Stability: Power, Politics and Society after the Arab Spring*, 117–33. London: I.B. Tauris.

Thomas, T. S. and Casebeer, W. D. (2004). 'Violent non-state actors: countering dynamic systems'. *Strategic Insights* 3, no. 3 (March).

Thomas, T. S. and Casebeer, W. D. (2004). 'Violent systems: defeating terrorists, insurgents, and other non-state adversaries'. Institute for National Security Studies, US Air Force Academy. CO. https://www.google.com/url?sa=t&rct=j&q=&esrc=s&source=web&cd=1&ved=0ahUKEwj0zvqYiqDcAhWoHTQIHVjhCXMQFggqMAA&url=http%3A%2F%2Fwww.au.af.mil%2Fau%2Fawc%2Fawcgate%2Fusafa%2Focp52.pdf&usg=AOvVaw1wBbfYeuQw4pt8YJkDGaV3.

Thompson, K. (1986). *Beliefs and Ideology*. London: Open Press.

Toth, J. (2013). *Sayyid Qutb: The Life and Legacy of a Radical Islamic Intellectual*. Oxford: Oxford University Press.

Traboulsi, F. (2007). *A History of Modern Lebanon*. London: Pluto Press.

Tripp, C. (2013). *The Power and the People: Paths of Resistance in the Middle East*. Cambridge: Cambridge University Press.

Türkmen, E. A. and Özmen, A. (eds) (2014). *Kürdistan Sosyalist Solu Kitabi. 60'lardan 2000'lere Seçme Metinler*. Ankara: Dipnot.

United Nations. (1988). *Convention for the Suppression of Unlawful Acts against the Safety of Maritime Navigation*. Rome: International Maritime Organization, http://www.un.org/en/sc/ctc/docs/conventions/Conv8.pdf

United Nations Security Council. (2015). *Report of the Monitoring Group on Somalia and Eritrea pursuant to Security Council resolution 2244 (2015): S/2015/801.* New York.

United Nations Security Council (2015). *Report of the Secretary-General on the Situation with Respect to Piracy and Armed Robbery at Sea off the Coast of Somalia.* https://reliefweb.int/sites/reliefweb.int/files/resources/N1630358.pdf.

United Nations Security Council (2015). Letter dated 9 October 2015 from the Chair of the Security Council Committee pursuant to resolutions 751 (1992) and 1907 (2009) concerning Somalia and Eritrea addressed to the President of the Security Council.

UNOCHA (2018). *Global Humanitarian Overview 2018*. New York: United Nations Office for the Coordination of Humanitarian Aid. https://www.unocha.org/story/global-humanitarian-overview-2018-six-months.

Urgo, M. (2009). 'Current patterns of IED use in Somalia'. https://info.publicintelligence.net/JIEDDO-SomaliaIEDs.pdf.

Vali, A. (2011). *The Kurds and the State in Modern Iran: The Making of Kurdish Identity*. London: I.B. Tauris.

Vali, A. (ed.) (2003). *Essays on the Origins of Kurdish Nationalism*, Costa Mesa, CA: Mazda.

Van Bruinessen, M. (1992). *Agha, Cheikh and State: The Social and Political Structures of Kurdistan*. London: Zed Books.

Vanity Fair online (2008). 'The proof is in the paper trail'. Michael Hogan interviews David Rose, 31 March.

Vanly, I. Ch. (1970). *Le Kurdistan irakien entité nationale. Etude de la Révolution de 1961.* Neuchatel: Editions de la Baconnière.

Varin, C. and Abubakar, D. (eds) (2017). *Violent Non-State Actors in Africa*. London: Palgrave Macmillan.

Varisco, D. M. (2015). *Drone Strikes in the War on Terror: The Case of Post-Arab-Spring Yemen*. Monograph #1 (November). Gulf Studies Center, Qatar University. http://www.qu.edu.qa/artssciences/gulfstudies-center/gulf_series.php.

Waage, H. H. (2004). *'Peacemaking is a Risky Business': Norway's Role in the Peace Process in the Middle East, 1993–96*. Oslo: International Peace Research Institute.

Waldo, M. A. (2009). 'The two piracies in Somalia: why the world ignores the other'. Wardheernews. http://www.wardheernews.com.

Watson, G. (2000). *The Oslo Accords: International Law and the Israeli–Palestinian Peace Agreements*. Oxford: Oxford University Press.

Watts, C. (2015). *Al Qaeda Loses Touch*. Foreign Affairs. https://www.foreignaffairs.com/articles/middle-east/2015-02-04/al-qaeda-loses-touch.

Watts, N. (2009). *Activists in Office: Kurdish Ethnic Politics, Political Resources, and Repression in Turkey*. Seattle: Washington University Press.

Weiss, M. (2010). *In the Shadow of Sectarianism: Law, Shi'ism, and the Making of Modern Lebanon*. Cambridge, MA: Harvard University Press.

Weldemichael, A. T. (2018). *Piracy in Somalia: Violence and Development in the Horn of Africa*. Cambridge: Cambridge University Press.

Whitaker, B. (2001). 'Sharon likens Arafat to Bin Laden'. *Guardian*, 14 September.

White, P. (2000). *Primitive Rebels or Revolutionary Modernizers? The Kurdish National Movement in Turkey*. London: Zed Press.

Wickham, C. R. (2013). *Muslim Brotherhood: Evolution of an Islamist Movement*. Princeton, NJ: Princeton University Press.

Williams, P. (2008) 'Violent non-state actors and national and international security'. International Relations and Security Network. http://www.isn.ethz.ch/Digital-Library/Publications/Detail/?id=93880.

Wilson, S. (2007). 'Fatah troops enter Gaza with Israeli assent'. *Washington Post*, 18 May.

World Bank (2006). *Republic of Yemen Country Social Analysis*. Report No. 34008-YE. Water, Environment and Rural Development Department, Middle East and North Africa Region (11 January).

Youngs, T. and Smith, B. (2007). 'Hamas and the seizure of Gaza'. House of Commons Library Research Paper 07/60, 6 July.

Yüksel, M. (2013). 'I Cry out so that you Wake up: Cegerxwin's Poetics and Politics of Awakening'. *Middle Eastern Studies* 50, no. 4: 1–18.

Zollner, B. (2009). *The Muslim Brotherhood: Hasan al-Hudaybi and Ideology*. London: Routledge.

Index

9/11 attack 101

Abbas, Mahmud 17, 102, 104, 110, 116
Abrams, Elliot 94, 102, 103, 107–8, 109
Abubakar, D. 163
Action Plan for the Palestinian Presidency (2007) 109–11, 113–14
Adra, Najwa 146, 147, 154
Affi, L. 170
Afghanistan 57
Africa 187, 190
Afweyne, Mohamed Hassan 168
Ahrar al-Sham 69, 86
al-Ali, Hamid Hamad Hamid 77
al-Anfal 32
al-Assad, Bashar 7, 52, 73–4, 126
al-Assad, Hafiz 68
al-Assad regime 68, 70, 177
'Alawis 124
al-Baghdadi, Abu Bakr 72
al-Banna, Hasan 25, 30, 33–4, 35, 36, 38
al-Dawsari, N. 142
al-Fadli, Mushin 77
Algeria 5
al-Hadawi, 'Umar 76
al-Hamawi, Saleh 77, 90
al-Huthi, Husayn 138, 140–1
al-Ittihad al-Islami (AIAI) 164–5
al-Jawlani, Abu Muhammad 68, 69, 70, 77–8, 86–7
   al-Assad 74
   al-Qaeda 72, 85–6, 90
   Hayat Tahrir al-Sham (HTS) 89
al-Juburi, Maysar Ali 77
Al-Kata'ib 122
al-Maliki, Nuri 13–14, 54
al-Nizam al-Khass. *See* Special Apparatus (SP)
al-Nusra 14–16, 66–92
   foundation 10
   Hayat Tahrir al-Sham (HTS) 88–91
   international support 74, 81–4

   leadership and hierarchy 76–8
   military tactics 73–4
   origins 67–70
   political strategy 70–3, 74–6
   relations with other groups 72–3, 84–6
   split from al-Qaeda 86–8
   territorial control 78–81
   weaponry 74, 75
al-Qaeda 57, 91–2
   and al-Nusra 71, 86–8, 89–90
   and ISIS 52, 53, 54
   Yemen 146–7, 152
al-Qaeda in the Arabian Peninsula (AQAP) 138, 152
al-Qatani, Abu Maria. *See* al-Juburi, Maysar Ali
al-Qawasmi, Hani 113
al-Shabab 22, 23, 164–7
   foundation 10
   international fight against 173–5
   and piracy 170–1
   reasons for resilience 171–3
al-Shami, Abu Muhammad. *See* al-'Uraydi, Sami
al-Sharif, K. 35
al-Sharikh, 'Abd al-Muhsin 'Abdullah Ibrahim 78
al-Shiqaqi, Fathi 97
al-'Uraydi, Sami 71, 78
al-Wadi'i, Muqbil bin Hadi 140
Alwazir, A.Z. 155
al-Zarqawi, Abu Mus'ab 51–3, 54
al-Zawahiri, Ayman 71, 72, 85, 88, 89
Amal 123–4, 124–5, 126
anarchy 56
Arab nationalism 4
Arab Spring 7–8
   ISIS 48, 49, 53, 55, 60
   Muslim Brotherhood 45
   Saudi Arabia 149
   Yemen 141, 145, 152, 155
Arafat, Yasser 16, 97, 101, 102–93

armed forces 4
Armenian movement 182
Assad regime. *See* al-Assad regime
'Awn, Michel 130–1, 134

Baabood, A.A. 150
Badi, Muhammad 46
Bahadur, J. 168, 169
Barrett, R.C. 143
Barzandji, Mahmud 183
Barzani rebellion 185–6, 188
Beilin, Yossi 98
Bin Jassim, Hamad 82
Bin Laden, Osama 101
Bonnefoy, L. 152
Boucek, C. 159
Boyah, Abshir 168
Brandt, M. 142, 145
Buchris, Pinchas 115
Burton, G. 99
Bush, George W. 51, 102, 103, 112

Calvert, J. 37
Camp David Accords 100
Casebeer, W.D. 163
Chalk, P. 170, 171, 174
Chweya, E. 167
Clinton, Hillary 51
Cobban, H. 96
colonialism 2–4
Comerford, M. 67, 72, 74
Commins, D. 145
context. *See* porous boundaries vs context perspective of violence
coopetition 84
Corbin, J. 98, 99
Country Social Assessment of Yemen (World Bank) 155
Crooke, Alastair 94
cultural violence 55
Cunningham, K.G. 137, 148–9

Dahlan, Muhammad 94, 103–4, 105, 109, 110, 111, 114, 118
Dahlgren, S. 152
da'wa 182
    Wahabi *da'wa* 9, 19
DDKO (Revolutionary Cultural Hearts of the East) 186

de Soto, Alvaro 105–6, 108
decolonialization 3, 190
deep states 48, 60–1, 93
defensive developmentalism 2
Dib, Roger 128
direct violence 55
Diskin, Yuval 105, 108–9, 115
Doha Agreement 132
Durac, Vincent 157

Egypt
    as deep state 61
    as failed state 56
    Hamas 17
    interwar period 3
    Muslim Brotherhood (MB) 26, 34–6, 44–6
    national independence 4
    nationalist movements 5
    Palestine Liberation Front (PLO) 96
    Quadrilateral Security Forum 111–13, 118
    revolution 7, 8, 10, 45–6
    security rent 60
    social contract 7
Eid, Farah Ismail 173
Elmi, A.A. 164, 165, 166, 167, 168, 169, 170
El-Sherif, Ashraf 7
Esposito, J. 28, 59
Ethiopia 161, 167, 172, 173
Eyl pirates 168

failed states 55, 56
Fanon, Franz 187, 190
Farrell, S. 111
Fatah 16, 17, 93–5
    differences with Hamas 97–9
    Hamas' takeover of Gaza 107–20
    parliamentary elections 2006 104–6
    in a post-9/11 world 99–102
    relations with Amal 123
    relationship with Hamas 95–6
Filiu, Jean-Pierre 13, 48, 60
firewall perspective 28, 29, 43
fishing 168, 172
food aid 169
foreign fighters
    al-Nusra 72, 75
    ISIS 48

Free Patriotic Movement (FPM), Lebanon 130–1
Free Syrian Army (FSA) 70, 75, 84–5, 133
From Deep States to Islamic State (Filiu) 13, 60
Fuccaro, Nelida 3

Galtung, Johan 55
Gartenstein-Ross, D. 75
Gaza 93–5, 103, 104, 107–16, 117–20
Gaza-Jericho agreement 98
Gelvin, James 2
gender 154–5
Gerges, F.A. 44, 92
Gettleman, J. 167, 173
Glaser, Eduard 146
globalization 127–8
Greenwald, G. 174

Ha'aretz 114
Hadi, 'Abd Rabbuh Mansur 142, 144, 152
Halevy, Ephraim 103
Hamas 16–17, 93–5
    differences with Fatah 97–9
    foundation 10
    Gaza takeover 107–20
    parliamentary elections 2006 104–7
    in a post-9/11 world 99–102
    relationship with Fatah 95–6
Hamid, S. 45
Hansen, S.J. 164, 166, 168, 171
Haradere pirates 168
Hariri, Rafiq 129–30
Hatina, M. 96, 97
Haugbølle, Sune 127
Hayat Tahrir al-Sham (HTS) 88–91
Haykel, B. 153
Heikal, M. 98
Heydemann, Steven 7
Hezbollah 18–19, 122, 124–5
    and al-Nusra 86
    foundation 10
    and the Free Patriotic Movement (FPM) 130–1
    Hüda-Par 191
    Israel's incursion into Lebanon 132
    Lebanese Civil War 126, 127
    Rafiq Hariri 129
    in Syria 133–4

Hirak 137, 138
Hirsh, M. 168, 169
Holsti, K.J. 163
Hroub, K. 43, 97, 98, 99, 100
Hudaybi, Hasan 37, 40–1
Hudson, Michael 121
Hussein, Saddam 149
Huthis 20–2, 137, 140–2
    al-Qaeda 147, 149, 157
    foundation 10
    Iranian support 150
    Zaydi heritage 151

identity 53, 179
ideology 48
illegal fishing 168, 172
improvised explosive devices (IEDs) 166
incubator perspective 28, 29, 43
independence movements 4–5
Iran
    Hamas 117
    Iraq 52, 56
    Kurdish movement 177, 188–9
    revolution 7, 125
    US support 187
    Yemen 149–51
Iraq
    armed forces 4, 50
    as failed state 55, 56
    Kurdish movement 183, 185–6, 192, 193, 194
    left-wing ideas 187
    national independence 4
    nationalist movements 5
    sectarianism 50, 52, 53, 54, 57
    US invasion 13, 18, 51
    US policy 52, 53–4, 62
ISIS 12–14, 47–62
    and al-Nusra 72, 85–6
    deep states 60–1
    defeat 177
    foreign fighters 48
    historical context 50–4
    public opinion of 59
    radicalism vs terrorism 58–60
    structural and cultural violence 55–8
    Yemen 147, 152
Islamic Courts Union (ICU) 22, 165
Islamic Jihad 95–6, 97, 101

Israel 17
  Action Plan for the Palestinian Presidency (2007) 110
  deep state 93
  disengagement from Gaza 103
  Fatah 98, 108, 114, 115
  Hamas 98, 119–20
  Lebanon 98, 124, 126, 129, 131–3
  Palestine Liberation Front (PLO) 99, 101
  Palestinian elections 2006 104–5, 106, 107
  Quadrilateral Security Forum 111–13
  US support 97, 100, 101

Jabhat al-Nusra. *See* al-Nusra
Jabhat Fath al-Sham 87, 88
Jawad al-Tamimi, A. 75
Jaysh al-Fath 86
jihad 26, 30, 31
  Sayyid Qutb 39
  Sura of War/Jihad 32
jihadism 67–8, 204n3
Jones, Richard 115
Jumblatt, Walid 131
Juneau, Thomas 150

Kampfner, J. 102
Kenya 170, 172, 173, 174
Kenyan forces (KDF) 166–7
Khazindar, Ahmad 35
Khoybun Committee 184
Khurasan group 69
Kirkpatrick, J. 99
Koehler-Derrick, G. 146
Kurdish movement 23–4, 177–94
  Islamism, 1980s-2010s 190–1
  left-wing radicalization, 1970s 188–90
  minority nationalism 180–2
  post-World War II 185–8
  pre-World War II 182–4
  vacuum of 2000s-2010s 192–4
Kurdish national identity 179
Kurdish Republic 185
Kurdistan Democratic Party (KDP) 185–6
Kurdistan Workers' Party (PKK) 189–90

Lackner, Helen 158
Lacroix, S. 44

Law of the Sea 167
Lebanon 18–19, 121–35
  Al-Kata'ib 122
  armed forces 4
  Civil War 122, 123, 126–9
  Hezbollah 122
  Israeli invasion 98, 124, 131–3
  Michel 'Awn 130–1
  national independence 4
  Rafiq Hariri 129–30
  Shias' political influence 122–6
  Syrian invasion 123–4
  Syrian occupation 129–30
leftist opposition 6
left-wing ideas
  hegemony of 185–8
  radicalization 188–90
Lesch, David 133
"Letter pf the Fifth Conference" (al-Banna) 33–4
Libya 49
Linke, A. 161–2
Lister, C. 68, 71, 75, 85, 87, 88, 89, 90, 91
Liwang, H. 169
Longley, A. 157
Lynch, M. 28

Makdisi, Ussuma 3, 197n4
Margariti, R. 138
Martelli, Greta 80
Martinez-Gros, Gabriel 180
Marxism-Leninism 187, 189–90
Marzullo, Vanessa 80
Masoud, T. 28
Mbekeani, K.K. 169
McGeough, P. 103, 106, 107, 108, 115
McKnight, T. 168, 169
Mearsheimer, J. 102
Mecca agreement 109
media activism 75–6
Menkhaus, Ken 163–4
Middleton, R. 169
Milestones (Qutb) 39
Miller, Aaron David 55–6
Milton-Edwards, B. 111
Minassian, T.T. 182
minority nationalism 180–2
Mitchell, R.P. 35
Mogadishu 165, 167

Muhammad, Qadi 185
Mulaj, K. 163
Murphy, M.N. 168
Mursi, Muhammad 29
Muslim Brotherhood (MB) 10–12, 25–46, 96, 100
   Fatah 95
   foundational ambiguities 30–4
   Hasan Hudaybi 37, 40–1
   porous boundaries vs context perspective of violence 27–30, 32, 37, 42–6
   Sayyid Qutb 11–12, 36–40, 41, 42, 44
   Special Apparatus (SP) 27, 34–6
   Syria 26, 125
   use of force/jihad 26
   Yusuf Qaradawi 37, 41–2
Mwangura, A. 168

Nasrullah, Hasan 73–4, 130, 131
Nasser, Gamal Abdel 35–6
nationalism 180–1
nationalist movements 4–5
national-populist special pact 7
Ncube, M. 169
neo-Mamluks (security services) 48, 60
Netanyahu, Benjamin 102, 103
non-state actors 137
Nuqrashi, Mahmud Fahmi 35
Nusra Front. *See* al-Nusra

Obama, Barack 50, 53–4
Öcalan, Abdullah 24, 181, 190
Ohikere, O. 174
oil 54, 80–1, 85, 138–9, 145
oil tankers 169
Olmert, Ehud 102
Oman 150
Oslo peace process 97–8
Ottoman Empire 2, 4, 182–3

Palestine. *See also* Fatah; Hamas
   First Palestinian Intifada 98
   Islamism 191
   parliamentary elections 2006 104, 104–7
   Second Palestinian Intifada 101

Palestine Liberation Front (PLO) 10, 16–17, 96, 98–9
   relations with Amal 123–4
Palestinian Authority (PA) 94, 107, 112, 113, 114, 117, 118
Pargeter, A. 44
particularism 181, 182, 184
Patriotic Union of Kurdistan (PUK) 177
Pearlman, W. 137, 148–9
Pham, P. 170
pirates 22–3, 163, 167–70
   and al-Shabab 170–1
   international fight against 173–5
   reasons for resilience 171–3
PKK (Kurdistan Workers' Party) 189–90
political opposition 6–8
politics of identity 53
population growth 154
porous boundaries vs context perspective of violence 27–30, 32, 37, 42–6
post-colonialism 4–5
Precarious Republic, The (Hudson) 121
privatization 7

qabyala (tribal honour code) 146
Qaradawi, Yusuf 37, 41–2
Qatar
   al-Nusra 74, 81–2, 83
   Hamas 117
   Hezbollah 129
Qur'an 32
Qutb, Sayyid 11–12, 36–40, 41, 42, 44

Rabin, Yitzhak 16, 101
radicalism vs terrorism 58–60
Raleigh, C. 161
Reagan, Ronald 99
Reno, William 162
Republic of Mahabad 185
Rice, Condoleezza 94, 104, 105, 109
Riedel, B. 74
Ringsberg, J.W. 169
Rose, David 110, 111, 114
Ross, S. 170
Russia 177

Sadr, Musa 123–4
Salafis 68
Salafism 9

Salih, 'Ali 'Abdullah 20, 137, 138, 140, 141, 143–5, 147, 148, 156
Salisbury, P. 144, 156
Salmoni, B.A. 141
Satloff, Robert 60
Saudi Arabia
　al-Nusra 74
　gender 154
　security rent 60
　tribalism 145
　Yemen 21, 147–53
Schmid, A.P. 28
sectarianism 50, 52, 53, 54, 57
secular state opposition 6
security rent 60
security services (neo-Mamluks) 48, 60
Sharon, Ariel 102, 103
Sharp, J. 150
Sheikh Said rebellion 183–4
Sherlock, R. 69, 73, 75
Silverstein, R. 83
Smith, B. 105
smuggling 118
social compact 7
socialism 187
Somali National Movement (SNM) 161
Somali Salvation Democratic Front (SSDF) 161, 164
Somalia 22–3, 161–75
　al-Shabab 10, 20, 23, 164–7, 170–1, 172–5
　Civil War 161
　pirates 22–3, 163, 167–71, 172, 173–5
　violent non-state actors 161–2, 163–4
Soviet Union 126, 128, 185, 187
Special Apparatus (SP) 27, 34–6
strategy of oblivion 127
structural violence 55–8, 59
Strzelecka, E.K. 155
Sudan Islamists 26
suicide bombs 73, 166
Sura of War/Jihad 32
Syria. *See also* al-Nusra
　armed forces 4
　as deep state 61
　as failed state 55, 56, 65–6
　Hezbollah 132–4
　Iraq 52
　Kurdish movement 177–8, 186, 192, 193, 194

Lebanon 123–4, 126, 128–9, 129–30
left-wing ideas 187
modernization 7
Muslim Brotherhood (MB) 26, 125
national independence 4
nationalist movements 5
neo-Mamluks (security services) 60
Turkish bombardment 178
Wahabi *da'wa* 9
Syrian National Coalition 70

Taliban 57
Tamimi, A. 96, 98
Taspinar, Omar 58
terrorism 82–3
　vs radicalism 58–60
Thiel, Tobias 142
Thomas, T.S. 163
Toth, J. 37
tribalism 145–6, 147, 157
Troupes Spéciales du Levant 4
Tunesia
　Islamists 26
　revolution 7, 8
Turkey 177
　al-Nusra 74
　Hüda-Par 191
　Kurdish movement 183–4, 186, 192, 193, 194
　Syria bombardment 178
　US support 187

United Arab Emirates (UAE) 152
United States
　9/11 attack 101
　Afghanistan 57
　al-Nusra 69, 84
　al-Shabab 166, 174
　Hamas 17
　invasion of Iraq 13, 18, 51
　Iraq policies 52, 53–4, 62
　ISIS 50, 51
　Israel-Palestine conflict 94, 99–100, 103, 108
　　Action Plan for the Palestinian Presidency (2007) 109–11, 113–14
　　National Security Strategy 2002 102

Palestinian elections 2006 104, 106–7
 Quadrilateral Security Forum 111–13
 radicalism debate 58
 Syria 177
 Yemen 152
universalism 181–2
Urgo, M. 166

Varin, C. 163
Varisco, D.M. 143, 152
Violence and the City in the Modern Middle East (Fuccaro) 3
violent non-state actors 8–10. *See also individual actors*
 goals and motivation 162–3

Wahabi *da'wa* 9, 10
wa'iddu 32–3
Waldo, M.A. 172
Walt, S. 102
weapon smuggling 118

West Bank 103, 104, 119–20
Wickham, C.R. 28
Williams, P. 162, 163
women 154–5
World Bank 169, 170
World Food Programme 169

Yadlin, Amos 119
Yemen 20, 21
 'Ali 'Abdullah Salih 20, 137, 138, 140, 141, 143–5, 147, 148
 future outlook 153–60
 ISIS 147
 non-state actors 137–8
 political history 138–9
 proxy war 147–53
 rise of the Huthis 140–2
 tribes 145–6, 147, 157
Youngs, T. 105

Zollner, B. 36